Object Relations
Brief Therapy

Object Relations Brief Therapy

THE THERAPEUTIC RELATIONSHIP IN SHORT-TERM WORK

Michael Stadter, Ph.D.

JASON ARONSON INC.
Northvale, New Jersey
London

The author gratefully acknowledges permission to reprint material from the following sources:

Excerpts from the Brief Therapy with Personality Disorders Seminar by Michael Stadter for the American Healthcare Institute. Copyright © 1993 American Healthcare Institute.

Quotations from *Theory and Practice of Brief Therapy* by Simon H. Budman and Alan S. Gurman. Copyright © 1988 The Guilford Press.

This book was set in 10 pt. New Baskerville by Alpha Graphics of Pittsfield, New Hampshire and printed and bound by Book-mart of North Bergen, New Jersey.

Library of Congress Cataloging-in-Publication Data

Stadter, Michael.
    Object relations brief therapy : the therapeutic relationship in
short-term work / Michael Stadter.
        p. cm.
    Includes bibliographical references and index.
    ISBN 1-56821-660-2 (alk. paper)
    1. Brief psychotherapy.   2. Object relations (Psychoanalysis)
3. Psychotherapist and patient.   I. Title.
RC480.55.S7   1996
616.89'14—dc20   95-20678

Manufactured in the United States of America. Jason Aronson Inc. offers books and cassettes. For information and catalog write to Jason Aronson Inc., 230 Livingston Street, Northvale, New Jersey 07647.

For Chris, Greg, and Nancy—

Thanks for your inspiration and patience.

THE LIBRARY OF OBJECT RELATIONS

A SERIES OF BOOKS EDITED BY
DAVID E. SCHARFF AND JILL SAVEGE SCHARFF

Object relations theories of human interaction and development provide an expanding, increasingly useful body of theory for
the understanding of individual development and pathology, for
generating theories of human interaction, and for offering new
avenues of treatment. They apply across the realms of human experience from the internal world of the individual to the human
community, and from the clinical situation to everyday life. They
inform clinical technique in every format from individual psychoanalysis and psychotherapy, through group therapy, to couple and
family therapy.

The Library of Object Relations aims to introduce works that
approach psychodynamic theory and therapy from an object relations point of view. It includes works from established and new
writers who employ diverse aspects of British, American, and international object relations theory in helping individuals, families,
couples, and groups. It features books that stress integration of
psychoanalytic approaches with marital, family, and group therapy,
as well as those centered on individual psychotherapy and psychoanalysis.

Refinding the Object and
  Reclaiming the Self
    David E. Scharff

The Primer of Object Relations
  Therapy
    Jill Savege Scharff and
    David E. Scharff

Object Relations Couple Therapy
    David E. Scharff and
    Jill Savege Scharff

From Inner Sources: New Directions
  in Object Relations Psychotherapy
    N. Gregory Hamilton, Editor

Object Relations Family Therapy
    David E. Scharff and
    Jill Savege Scharff

Projective and Introjective
  Identification and the Use
  of the Therapist's Self
    Jill Savege Scharff

Foundations of Object
  Relations Family Therapy
    Jill Savege Scharff, Editor

The Practice of Psychoanalytic
  Therapy
    Karl König

Repairing Intimacy: An Object
Relations Approach to
Couples Therapy
Judith Siegel

Family and Couple Therapy
John Zinner

Close Encounters: A Relational View
of the Therapeutic Process
Robert Winer

The Autonomous Self: The Work of
John D. Sutherland
Jill Savege Scharff, Editor

Crisis at Adolescence: Object
Relations Therapy with the
Family
*Sally Box, Beta Copley,
Jeanne Magagna, and
Errica Moustaki
Smilansky, Editors*

Personal Relations Therapy:
The Collected Papers of
H. J. S. Guntrip
Jeremy Hazell, Editor

Psychoanalytic Group Therapy
*Karl König and
Wulf-Volker Lindner*

Countertransference Analysis
Karl König

Intricate Engagements:
The Collaborative Basis
of Therapeutic Change
Steven A. Frankel

Object Relations Theory and
Practice
David E. Scharff, Editor

From Instinct to Self: Selected
Papers of W. R. D. Fairbairn
vol. I: Clinical and Theoretical
Contributions
*David E. Scharff and
Ellinor Fairbairn Birtles,
Editors*

From Instinct to Self: Selected
Papers of W. R. D. Fairbairn,
vol. II: Applications and Early
Contributions
*Ellinor Fairbairn Birtles and
David E. Scharff, Editors*

Object Relations Therapy of
Physical and Sexual Trauma
*Jill Savege Scharff and
David E. Scharff*

Object Relations Individual Therapy
*David E. Scharff and
Jill Savege Scharff*

How to Survive as a Psychotherapist
Nina Coltart

A Prophetic Analyst: Erich Fromm's
Contribution to Psychoanalysis
*Mauricio Cortina and
Michael Maccoby, Editors*

A Primer of Kleinian Therapy
Irving Solomon

Containing Rage, Terror, and
Despair: An Object
Relations Approach to
Psychotherapy
Jeffrey Seinfeld

Object Relations Brief Therapy
Michael Stadter

Love and Hate in the Analytic Setting
Glen O. Gabbard

Contents

therapy /Cautionary tales / The therapeutic relationship in the age of industrialization

Foreword

by David E. Scharff, M.D.

Object relations theory and its application to therapy has been chiefly seen as offering a reorientation of long-term psychotherapy and psychoanalysis. In the view of some, it has been further limited by the view that it deals chiefly with the vicissitudes of the earliest or preoedipal years of development because of its emphasis on the centrality of two-person relationships, while other branches of psychodynamic theory have emphasized three-person or oedipal dynamics.

Michael Stadter's book takes a welcome place in a less-recognized tradition in object relations: the practical application of object relations theory to forms of therapy beyond psychoanalysis. The originators of object relations, Fairbairn, Klein, Winnicott, Balint, and Bion were all interested in applications of their ideas to wider arenas such as the psychology of art, social policy, education, and medicine. But particularly, those interested in object relations have applied it to a wide variety of issues and modalities of psychotherapy—Bion to group therapy; Fairbairn to sexual abuse, sex of-fenders, and war trauma; Winnicott to brief pediatric consultation, education, and cultural issues; Klein's colleagues, Elliott Jaques and Isabel Menzies Lyth, to institutions and organizational consultation; Bowlby to child development; Enid Balint and Henry Dicks to marital dynamics and therapy; and Michael Balint to the practice of medicine, specifically to brief psychotherapy.

Out of this tradition of "applied psychoanalysis" the study of brief psychotherapy became a focus in the hands of Michael Balint and later David Malan, both at the Tavistock Clinic. Their work flourished long before the current pressure on psychotherapists to abbreviate therapy. It grew out of the problem posed by Winnicott, from whom I paraphrase: The question is often not one of "How much can be done?" but "How little need be done?" This question faced psychotherapists as they consulted to doctors, social workers, probation officers, marriage and guidance counselors, and educators. As consultants, they had only a short time with patients and were in all likelihood consulting to those on the front lines who also had limited time. So the question of how best to apply object relations understanding in the many settings with limited resources and time has faced our field for a long time.

One center of object relations thinking that has developed several forms of brief intervention is the Tavistock Clinic in London. Besides Balint and Malan's work on brief therapy, the Tavistock's Adolescent Department has long had a program of brief intervention, offering up to four sessions of counseling to adolescents who seek help directly, often without the knowledge of their parents.

Michael Stadter's work is a timely extension of this tradition. An advocate of thoughtful and responsible brief psychotherapy, he has drawn on object relations to build a coherent, sensible theory and a reliable clinical guide for his work. He is equally knowledgeable about the field of brief therapy itself, both those parts that have grown out of the psychodynamic tradition and those that stem from other schools of psychotherapy. In this book, he reviews the literature of the major contributors, picking and choosing the most useful aspects of diverse contributions. He emerges with a remarkably coherent, practical tool: object relations brief therapy. His way of working is focused, yet responsive to the patient's needs, and he describes cases ranging in duration from a single session to fifty sessions. The method is rooted equally in a careful assessment of the critical issues facing the patient and in the transference as guide to the unconscious roots of those issues. It is centered on the therapist's use of the structure of the therapy to frame the rapidly emerging issues and forces, which can then be understood by both patient and therapist to constitute the current dilemma. This shared experience provides an increment of knowledge previously unavailable to the patient and offers new tools for the patient's next steps.

Dr. Stadter also examines the issues raised by managed care and provides guidelines on the limits of brief therapy. It is a branch of psychotherapy with many uses and wide application but it is not a cure-all! In the current climate in which economic and social factors relentlessly press medicine and mental health to provide quick fixes, there is substantial danger that mental health professionals will be asked to do more in less time than is possible. This pressure threatens to discredit legitimate therapies and none more so than brief psychotherapy. Stadter's exploration of the uses and limitations of brief psychotherapy are, therefore, a particularly important part of the book.

This book has much to offer: a comprehensive and erudite view of theory, extensive and clear clinical examples, and, perhaps most of all, the creative application of solid common sense. As we join our patients with their increasingly difficult life problems in an atmosphere less and less hospitable to our attempts to help them, this is the kind of guide to which we will turn with confidence and gratitude.

Acknowledgments

Perhaps it goes without saying because it is so obvious, but it must be said that I owe the greatest debt of gratitude to my patients, past and present. This book is fundamentally a manifestation of only some of what I have learned and internalized from them. I expect that I am more grateful than they know.

I am also very appreciative of my teachers, supervisors, students, and supervisees throughout my career. I would like to particularly thank Gerald Perman, who, as both teacher and supervisor, introduced me in 1977 to object relations theory when I was a student in the Advanced Psychotherapy Training Program of the Washington School of Psychiatry. My work has not been the same since.

There are five organizations and staffs that I would like to acknowledge. First, I want to thank the Washington School of Psychiatry, which has been my professional home for the past twenty years. I have had the honor of being a student, alumnus, therapist, program chair, and faculty member there and it has provided a fine holding environment for me and for the process of questioning and discovery. Thanks to the WSP faculty and students I have worked with and learned from. Second, thanks to Steven Winter and the staff of the American Healthcare Institute. Many of my thoughts about brief therapy with personality disorders (Chapters 11 and 12) were developed as part of my teaching throughout the United States for AHI. I appreciate their help and being able to use some of that material in the present volume. Third, I am grateful to Suzanne Reynolds and her staff at the Sheppard-Pratt Employee Assistance Program, Washington, DC office. I have had the pleasure of consulting with them on their very brief therapy cases and have benefited from their skills and struggles on how to offer meaningful psychological interventions in a very short period of time. Fourth, thanks to Terry DiNuzzo and her excellent staff at the Center for Psychological and Learning Services at American University. They have assisted the development of my brief therapy work and writing in ways too varied and numerous to list. Fifth, it has been a wonderful and supportive experience to work with the staff of my publisher, Jason Aronson. I would like to particularly thank senior production editor, Judy Cohen, for her precise and thoughtful assistance.

I am very grateful to the following individuals for their insightful comments on sections of the manuscript and/or for their permission to use some of their clinical work in the book: Lawrence Carroll, Martha Chescheir, Macario Giraldo, Carolyn Johnson, Enid McKitrick, William Menzin, Suzanne Reynolds, and Victoria Wilson. Two special notes of thanks go to the following: to Dana Blackmer, for his wise and detailed comments on Chapters 4 and 5; and to Lauren Hill, my graduate assistant, for all of her help, especially for her thorough and speedy literature searches.

Finally, I want to especially underscore my gratitude to my editor, David Scharff. For years I have had the pleasure of working with him as a teaching colleague, which has deepened immeasurably my knowledge of object relations theory. Throughout the writing of this book he has steadfastly encouraged, supported, and challenged me. The care he has taken with the writing has enhanced this book in ways both large and small. In addition to his profound and incisive comments on theoretical and clinical issues throughout the book, he persistently challenged me to keep it clear and interesting. The book is much more readable because of David's input.

Notes to the Reader

In presenting the case material, I have indicated in the text when I was the therapist, which was almost always. In the few instances in which I was not the therapist, I refer simply to "the therapist." I am indebted to my colleagues and students for their permission to use their clinical work. Of course, I have disguised the identities of all of the patients discussed but have retained the accuracy of the clinically relevant material.

A word on writing style. I have tried to empathize (projectively identify) with the reader. As a reader myself, I feel I have had to struggle too often with a writer who has something important to say but who says it in a turgid, needlessly complex manner. So, as a writer, I have tried to make my points clearly and without needless complexity. I hope I have at least partially succeeded. In the service of this goal, I have dealt with the issue of gender in the writing by alternating female and male references whenever I wrote about a hypothetical patient or therapist. I chose that approach because I have found the use of he/she or plurals to be more awkward and clumsy, at least in my hands.

Introduction

IS THERE A TYPICAL BRIEF THERAPY PATIENT?

Susan

Susan is still furious at the man she encountered in the parking lot yesterday. A 23-year-old divorced mother, she was driving out of her company's lot and got into an altercation with another driver. She got out of her car and pounded on his window with her fist, shouting, "I'm going to punch your goddamn face in!" Interestingly, she works as a customer service representative for a financial institution. She has been referred by her supervisor to me as part of the company's employee assistance program (EAP) services. In the past she has had some difficulty with her temper on the job and elsewhere. I see her for three sessions, the maximum allowed in the EAP.

Alan

Alan is an 18-year-old college freshman, intelligent, awkward. He makes little eye contact. He is suicidal following a rejection by a classmate and has actually practiced his suicide plan. Alan has never been in psychotherapy before but he makes it clear in this session that he wishes for therapy to be brief, as brief as possible. Fears of dependency and intimacy are intense issues for him. He is seen for twenty sessions.

Bea

Bea comes to see me in my private practice and describes her life as having fallen apart since her divorce four years ago. A 43-year-old woman with two children, Bea is moderately depressed and profoundly pessimistic about her abilities to handle her life on her own. Despite years of therapy she has been unable to actively look for and find a job. She was referred to me specifically for brief therapy and hopes it can get her going. She is seen for fourteen sessions.

Diane

When 32-year-old Diane begins the first session, she says that she'd have killed herself were it not for the fact that she couldn't do such a terrible thing to her four children. She has been acutely suicidal for the past two weeks, since she was arrested for embezzling thousands of dollars from her employer. This is particularly ironic since she is married to a "nail 'em and jail 'em" prosecuting attorney. She describes generally being responsible but at times she has had outbursts of very impulsive self-destructive behavior. Money is understandably tight and her insurance does not cover seeing me (their insurance is through an HMO). We meet for twenty-five sessions.

Philip

Sour, critical, and condescending are my early impressions of this 23-year-old recent college graduate. He is angry that he cannot find a job in the field of finance. He is paralyzed in his job search and has not done anything on it for several weeks. Philip says he doesn't think he needs much help, he just wants to get back to finding a job. He spends the first few sessions persistently criticizing me. We meet for ten sessions.

Linda

Linda rushes into my office, 25 minutes late. She had made two previous appointments but did not keep them. A lawyer on her first job, this 30-year-old divorced woman is plagued by a chronic procrastination pattern that has become a serious problem at work. Linda sighs, "How can I respect myself if I can't even get in to work on time?" Yet, she presents the material in a breezy, rather flirtatious manner. She has been in therapy before and she says that she and the therapist identified the problem as "I'm too optimistic about getting things done." Linda thinks this is accurate but it hasn't helped. Her employer is transferring her to another city in a few months and she wants to "get on top of this" by then. We meet for eleven sessions.

THE DEMAND FOR BRIEF THERAPY

There is no such thing as a "typical" brief therapy patient. There is, however, a diverse range of people with symptoms and character structures who begin and benefit from brief therapy. Similarly, an array of disparate factors causes therapy to be limited in terms of time:

1. Limited patient motivation
2. Patient fear of intimate relationships

3. Therapist orientation
4. Agency or institutional policies and constraints
5. Patient or therapist moving to another geographical area
6. Limited therapeutic goals on the part of either patient or therapist (e.g., work through an uncomplicated bereavement)
7. Patient resistance to discovery and exploration of painful material
8. Limited financial resources.

It is probably the last point that has most fueled the strong current interest in brief therapy. The practice of psychotherapy in the United States in the 1990s is characterized by insurance carriers using managed care strategies to limit treatment; by the widespread presence of HMOs, which usually tightly limit access to mental health services; and by the watchword of cost containment in deliberations on government regulation of the provision of health care. Certainly for these reasons alone, brief therapy is a timely and important topic. However, the managed care/cost containment issues can eclipse the other factors in considerations of brief therapy. We need also to be aware of these other factors when we look at what brief therapy is and what it involves.

THE PREVALENCE

Most of the psychotherapy performed in the United States is, in fact, brief. Pardes and Pincus (1981) found that the median number of therapy sessions in mental health clinics and agencies was 3.7 sessions. They reported that most private practice therapies did not exceed twenty-six sessions. Schacht and Strupp (1989) have noted that most psychotherapy is of twenty-five sessions or shorter duration. Stern (1993) summarized studies on duration of psychotherapy and stated that consistently the median length of treatment in all settings is six to ten sessions and that 75 to 90 percent of patients terminate before twenty-five sessions. He concluded, "A tremendous proportion of the psychotherapy conducted in this country is what might be called *naturally occurring brief therapy*" (Stern 1993, p. 169).

Is this due to managed care/cost containment initiatives? Probably not, because earlier reports also show similar trends. Garfield (1978) investigated treatment length from 1948 to 1970 and found that most patients' therapy lasted fewer than twenty sessions. Rubenstein and Lorr (1956) found that the typical outpatient psychotherapy contract was for a duration of fewer than ten sessions.

In sum, brief psychotherapy is and has been the rule rather than the exception, although many of the therapies were not expected by the therapist to be brief.

DEFINITION

Definitions abound, but I like the simple definition offered by Budman and Gurman (1988), "What is, in fact, being examined in any discussion of brief treatment is therapy in which the time allotted to treatment is rationed" (pp. 5–6). They note that brief therapy cannot be adequately defined by simply looking at the numbers of sessions held. In Chapter 4 I will review some of the models of psychodynamic brief therapy, and these range from one to forty sessions. Budman and Gurman describe their own way of looking at brief therapy as "'time-sensitive,' 'time-effective,' or 'cost-effective' therapy." They also make the point that it is important to distinguish between therapy that is brief "by design" and therapy that is brief "by default." Therapy by default is unplanned, with the therapist not attending to the issue of the limits of time (such therapies are often evaluated, sometimes inaccurately, by the therapist as having "premature terminations").

Brief therapy, then, is more about patient and therapist attitudes than it is about numbers. The therapist considers what can we do here—how much and how little—given the unique limitations of the therapist, the patient, and the exigencies of the moment. The psychodynamically oriented therapist might also approach the case from the following perspective: "I'll think dynamically, address some underlying issues, and do what I can." This attitude toward therapy was exemplified by Winnicott (1962): "In analysis one asks how much can one be allowed to do? By contrast, in my clinic the motto is: how little need be done?" (p. 166).

EFFECTIVENESS

Does brief therapy work? This is such a broad question that it is very difficult to answer it meaningfully. One needs to know what particular type of brief therapy, what do we mean by "work," and with which patients? With these qualifications in mind we can, however, confidently conclude that *most patients who have been through an episode of brief therapy have received significant benefit.* Crits-Christoph (1992) performed a careful meta-analysis on eleven very well controlled studies of dynamic brief therapy and found it to be very effective when compared with no-treatment waiting lists in (1) reducing specific target symptoms, (2) reducing the general level of psychiatric symptoms, and (3) improving social functioning.

Smith and colleagues (1980) reviewed 375 studies on the effectiveness of psychotherapy. The vast majority of the studies found the therapy to be effective. Interestingly, the mean number of sessions was seventeen! There is a great body of research that indicates the effectiveness of psychotherapy and most of it is on relatively brief treatment. Most of the research on psychotherapy outcomes is actually on the outcomes of *brief* psychotherapy. It is, of course, much easier to design and carry out research involving, say, fifteen sessions, than it is to study twice weekly psychotherapy that lasts for two years.

Moreover, in research that compares brief therapy with long-term treatment, brief treatments tend to do as well. Bloom (1992) lists nine studies and states:

> Virtually without exception, these empirical studies of short-term outpatient psychotherapy, or short-term inpatient psychiatric care . . . have found that planned short-term psychotherapies are essentially equally effective and are, in general, as effective as time-unlimited psychotherapy, virtually regardless of diagnosis or duration of treatment (Koss and Butcher 1986).

Indeed, perhaps no other finding has been reported with greater regularity in the mental health literature than the equivalence of effect of time-limited and time-unlimited psychotherapy. [p. 9]

The above statement, however, needs qualification. My own opinion is that much of the unique benefit of long-term therapy is not discerned in most of these research studies and that long-term therapy does provide help that goes beyond what can generally be done in brief therapy.

What does one mean by therapeutic effectiveness? Howard and his colleagues (1986) examined the relationship between therapy effectiveness and amount of therapy received (the "dose" of therapy) by comparing the results of a large number of studies of eclectic therapy. They found that 75 percent of patients attained symptom relief within twenty-six sessions. On the other hand, Kopta and colleagues (1994) conducted an excellent study that involved 685 patients and 141 therapists at five different sites. They found that, overall, 75 percent of the patients showed symptomatic recovery after fifty-eight sessions of weekly psychotherapy. They interpreted the difference in the findings of the two studies (twenty-six versus fifty-eight sessions) as a difference in improvement versus recovery. Howard and colleagues (1986) were looking at general symptomatic improvement while Kopta and colleagues (1994) were studying patterns of symptomatic recovery to normal functioning. This is a good example of how psychotherapy is viewed depends on which effects are sought and measured. As Kopta and colleagues (1994) concluded, "It makes sense that fewer sessions are needed to simply improve rather than to recover" (p. 1016).

So, there is quite impressive evidence of the benefits of brief treatment. Of course, symptom relief is only one of the measures of effectiveness of psychodynamic models of psychotherapy. As Crits-Christoph (1992) has noted, many outcome measures do not gauge the particular areas where psychodynamic therapies might be most successful. He listed dynamic conflicts, transference themes, and relationship patterns. Change in such areas that psychodynamic therapists emphasize may not occur until some time after brief therapy has ended and there has been time for a more extended working-through process. Most studies of psychotherapeutic efficacy do not include measures of such phenomena nor do they include follow-up assessment.

To conclude this very quick look at the effectiveness of brief therapy, I will note Schacht and Strupp's (1989) conclusions from research on brief psychodynamic therapy:

1. The basic principles of psychoanalytic treatment can be applied to brief interventions.
2. Neurotic and character problems can be treated effectively and in a shorter time than previously believed.
3. Brief psychodynamic therapy can lead to enduring changes in character structure.

THE PERSPECTIVE OF THIS BOOK

To Emphasize the Relationship in Brief Therapy

Interestingly (and unfortunately), this issue has received very little attention in the brief therapy literature. At the same time, the long-term intensive psychotherapy literature has been giving it more consideration, largely through the increasing acceptance of object relations and self-psychology theories. The emphasis in most of the writing on brief therapy, however, is on technique. Kupers (1986) has expressed concern that the very nature of brief therapy makes the therapist more a technician than an explorer and much less likely to attend to countertransference.

Many brief therapy writers have attempted to document their approach through research and specific, detailed treatment protocols (e.g., Davanloo 1980, Mann 1973, Mann and Goldman 1994, Sifneos 1987, Strupp and Binder 1984). This has been a wonderful contribution to brief therapy in particular and to psychotherapy in general. One could not do much better in learning psychodynamic technique than to read Malan (1976) or Davanloo (1980).

However, I believe that with this emphasis on technique the importance of the relationship between patient and therapist has not been given adequate regard in brief therapy writing. During a recent series of symposia, one of the leading practitioners of brief therapy was asked by a member of the audience how important did he feel the relationship between patient and therapist was in affecting the positive outcome. His answer was, "Not at all." He said that success in his brief therapy approach depended almost totally on careful patient selection and the technical skill of the therapist.

I found this to be a rather incredible statement. I would argue that how effective a particular technique or intervention will be is critically determined by the context of the relationship—the intersubjective space that develops between the patient and therapist, the way the patient feels psychologically held by the therapist, and the way the therapist (consciously and unconsciously) contains the dynamic material of the therapy. It can be inspiring and very educational to see a videotape or to read a transcript of a master clinician at work. However, to try to then just "do" what he "did" is impossible. Two therapists could work with the same patient and perform the same technique and yet get radically different results— because of the difference in the context of the relationship.

Moreover, each therapeutic relationship is unique—a one-of-a-kind matrix of therapist and patient intersubjectivities at a particular point in time and at a particular point in the psychological development of each. Therefore, experience and training are crucial contributions that the therapist makes, but she must also be open to what is new and not seen before in the therapeutic encounter.

To Use the Conceptual Framework of Object Relations Theory

No other psychological theory places as much emphasis on the therapeutic relationship as does object relations theory. The therapist's attention to the "real" relationship, transference and counter-transference projections and introjections, projective identification, and the therapist as object as well as the therapist as "background" are all crucial therapeutic concepts that have applicability to brief therapy. As discussed in Chapter 11, an object relations approach is particularly helpful in working with personality-disordered patients. I will draw on the work of early British object relations writers (Klein, Fairbairn, Guntrip, Winnicott) as well as on contemporary authors (Bollas, Ogden, and D. and J. Scharff).

To Approach the Therapy with a Flexible and Eclectic Technical and Theoretical Style

The approach outlined in Chapter 5 does not develop a new model for brief therapy. Rather, it describes a perspective that emphasizes the therapeutic relationship and draws on some of the work of previous and current models. I have found the work of Budman and Gurman (1988), Malan (1976), and especially Strupp and Binder (1984) to be particularly helpful. There is an attempt to borrow selected elements from these psychodynamic models to enhance the therapy. Also, selected nonpsychodynamic techniques are sometimes utilized. My intent is to look at brief therapy from the applied perspective of a practicing clinician. As such, I see a wide array of personalities and symptoms and develop quite different relationships with different patients. For various reasons, I may see someone only once or three times or twenty-five times or for several years. As noted earlier, my guiding approach is to think dynamically, address some dynamic issues when possible, and do what I can.

Why Is There So Much Resistance to Brief Therapy?

> It needs to be stated categorically that in the early part of this century Freud unwittingly took a wrong turning which led to disastrous consequences for the future of psychotherapy. . . . The most obvious effect has been an enormous increase in the duration of treatment.
>
> David Malan, 1980

> The only reason I'm here is that managed care is killing my practice and I've got to do this short stuff.
>
> Therapist at a brief therapy seminar (1992)

At seminars and conferences one frequently hears much negativity from therapists about brief therapy. The reactions can range from mild skepticism to outright hostility and can prevent a thoughtful examination of the power and promise of brief therapy. These responses are often especially from therapists with psychodynamic training and backgrounds. This is particularly unfortunate since psychoanalysis began as a brief approach and some of Freud's most famous cases were quite brief (see Chapter 4). Moreover, brief therapy has been intimately linked in some therapists' minds with the restrictions of managed care, and they wonder "How can I conduct brief therapy with integrity?"

Malan (1963) provides us with a useful introduction to this topic. He notes that brief therapy runs counter to the "lengthening factors" in therapy and identifies therapist passivity as the most important factor in causing therapies to become longer and longer. He also lists the following factors, which I briefly describe:

Resistance: the powerful defenses that patients maintain to defend against the pain that comes from self-knowledge and change

Overdetermination: patient problems and symptoms being caused by multiple factors

Need to work through: the need for repeated interventions and persistent internal processing of material for change to be lasting

Negative transference: working with the patient through difficult negative reactions (e.g., hatred, anger) toward the therapist based on feelings transferred from significant others

Sense of timelessness: a perception (often unconscious) that the patient and therapist have unlimited amounts of time within which to work

Therapeutic perfectionism: the therapist's desire (unconscious need?) to *completely* address the symptomatic and characterological problems of the patient

Preoccupation with deeper and earlier issues: dealing with pre-oedipal, characterological issues

Financial considerations: it is usually in the financial interest of the therapist (especially in private practice) to see patients for extended periods of time.

FACTORS CAUSING THERAPIST RESISTANCE

The Belief that Brief Therapy Equals Managed Care

Unfortunately, many therapists do not give brief therapy a fair hearing because they equate brief therapy with the emotionally charged issue of the managed care model for mental health services.

Certainly some of the criticisms and problems with managed care models are valid, and these models put a premium on brief therapy, sometimes very brief therapy. However, as presented in Chapter 1, short-term interventions have been the predominant therapy offered in the United States for decades. Even many therapists who describe themselves as long-term, intensive psychotherapists, if truth be told, have a sizable percentage of their practices made up of short-term cases (often unplanned).

Brief therapy and managed care are two separate entities. *Brief therapy* is a term for a diverse group of often highly effective therapies that are used much more frequently than long-term approaches. Brief therapy needs to be carefully evaluated on its own. *Managed care* is a system whereby the initiation and continuation of a given patient's psychotherapy is monitored and influenced by a third-party payer or representative to contain costs and promote quality of service. Clearly, managed care does affect some brief therapy contracts adversely, and this is discussed in Chapter 13. However, a therapist need not feel that she is a proponent of the managed care model of mental health care because she values and offers brief therapy.

Splitting: The Belief that Long-Term Treatment Is Good, Short-Term Treatment Is Bad

There is a belief system among some therapists that goes something like this:

> "The only way to truly get to the basic, change-producing issues for a patient is through long-term open-ended psychotherapy. This approach allows the patient to go at his own rate, to feel fully heard in an unhurried way, to thoughtfully and patiently examine one's experience of 'being.' If treatment reaches an impasse, the way to break it is often to provide more therapy—more frequent sessions and/or extend the duration of the therapy. Brief therapy, on the other hand, is about 'doing,' it causes the patient to hurriedly address his/her issues and promotes 'false self' experience. It is simply supportive and oriented toward symptom relief. Brief treatment is superficial and offers temporary relief. It does not teach him how to live more fully and effectively."

I would suggest that this belief system exemplifies the psychological mechanism of splitting, wherein psychotherapy is seen as coming in two forms: a good, long-term form and a bad, short-term form. I would in fact agree with some of the points listed in that belief system, and it does speak to some of the cautions we need to have in conducting brief therapy (discussed below). However, splitting does oversimplify the world by distorting it. All "good" dynamic psychotherapies have much in common whether the approach is long-term, brief, or just a single session. Brief therapy often does produce lasting change beyond simple symptom relief and, in some cases, character change is evidenced (Schacht and Strupp 1989).

Long-term, intensive psychotherapy is not invariably benign and it can cause harm (Frances and Clarkin 1981). Most of us know of patients with profound infantile dependency issues who unconsciously approach therapy in a manner that denies personal responsibility for the treatment and who can continue for years and years with no real therapy going on. In such cases the comfort of the therapy and the delusion (patient's *and* therapist's?) that it is helping to address their issues may actually impair personal progress. As Mann (1973) notes, "There comes a point in the treatment of patients, whether in psychoanalysis or in psychotherapy, where time is no longer on the therapist's side insofar as the possibility of helping the patient to make further changes is involved, and where time serves far more the search by the patient for infantile gratification" (p. xi).

Therapist's Narcissism

With a belief system like the one described above, it is small wonder that a therapist would not want to think of herself as a brief therapist. Malan (1963) touches on the issue of therapist narcissism with his lengthening factor of therapist perfectionism. Many of our patients have a great deal of difficulty accepting and dealing with personal limits. Therapy often involves the dynamic tension between a hard-nosed acknowledgment of what is and a vision of what potentially can be. This issue of limits can be a difficult one for therapists, too. When faced at times with profoundly disturbing, intense human suffering and dysfunction, a rather common reaction on a hopeful therapist's part may be, "This is awful but we have time and with enough time, we'll be able to address it."

That may, in fact, be delusional. The model of therapy continuing indefinitely may cause the therapist to avoid the painful acknowledgment that time is limited for all of us and that, often, as time moves on and a patient does not make certain changes, reality forecloses some options (even though therapy is continuing). If therapy is unlimited we can think that, like Scarlett O'Hara, unresolved issues can be dealt with tomorrow: "Okay, so the patient has a lot more work to do, this is still a work in progress—therapy continues!" The difficulty of accepting the reality and limits of time is one of the most vexing existential issues human beings have to deal with (Mann 1981) and it is vexing for both therapists and patients.

While long-term therapy can obscure the limits of therapy outcome and time, brief therapy painfully confronts both patient and therapist with it. In Chapter 4, I discuss Mann's (1973) concept of child time—infinite, the future is forever: "The greater the ambiguity as to the duration of treatment, the greater the influence of child time on unconscious wishes and expectations. The greater the specificity of duration of treatment, the more rapidly and appropriately is child time confronted with reality and the work to be done" (p. 11). Mann is emphasizing here the effect on patients, but a similar effect can be expected on the therapist as well.

In sum, as brief therapy confronts the therapist with the limits of both time and outcome of therapy, it challenges the therapist on her own limits and professional self-image.

Long-Term Treatment Is More in the Financial Interests of Therapists

Many therapists see their incomes decreasing as their treatment becomes more brief. For example, if you have thirty patients and you see them for an average of two years' duration, you only need fifteen new patients each year to maintain your practice. However, if you see your thirty patients for an average of six months, you would need sixty new patients each year. Even if your income did not diminish, you would likely have to invest more time in practice development to assure this greater flow of new patients. Most therapists are highly ethical and do not and would not keep patients in treatment longer than needed—consciously. Nor would they subscribe to a particular treatment philosophy only because it earns them more money—consciously. However, as students of the unconscious, we know that unconscious forces inevitably affect us all and need to be acknowledged and dealt with.

Some of the resistance to a careful consideration of brief therapy comes about because brief therapy can be bad for business. On the other hand, there is an unrealistically negative reaction to long-term therapy among groups such as clinics and managed care organizations because long-term treatment seems to be "bad for business"—it costs more than briefer approaches, or at least *appears* that way in the short run.

The Belief that Significant Change Occurs Only If Therapy Is Continuous

Some therapists are genuinely convinced that real, lasting therapeutic change always requires continuous long-term therapy and does not occur with brief therapy. This belief is not in touch with reality. As discussed elsewhere in this book, there is a large body of research that clearly indicates the significant and lasting effects of brief episodes of therapy. Also, the clinical experience of even predominantly long-term therapists usually includes sometimes dramatic and lasting change begun by brief treatment (e.g., Oremland 1991). It is too glib to write off such cases as transference cures (although some probably are). Certainly, some patients do require the holding and containing functions of continuous long-term treatment to make use of therapy. But many do not and continue the therapeutic process on their own, outside of and after therapy. Budman and Gurman (1988) state that a crucial part of the belief system of the effective brief therapist is that change does occur after therapy and that the therapist need not be there for it to occur.

The Desire to Be with the Patient for the Changes

One of the gifts of long-term treatment for the therapist is the opportunity for him to actually see the progress of patients as their lives are enriched by the change and growth catalyzed by therapy (of course, this is one of the stresses when therapy is not going well).

To do a piece of work with a patient and not know whether she was able to really use it or grow with it is frustrating.

> I saw Paula and Neil who wanted help in coming to a decision about marriage. Both consciously wanted to but could not bring themselves to make that commitment. During seven sessions we examined together Neil's fears of intimacy—he would withdraw emotionally and physically following Paula's positive expression of affection for him. We looked at her underlying hurt and fears beneath her very angry exterior—Paula had started off the first session by saying, "I know exactly what the problem is, Neil is a goddamn asshole!" We also looked at how they seemed to be reenacting some patterns from their respective parents' marriages. They had entered therapy asking for a brief intervention citing finances and skepticism about therapy and I indicated that the shortest amount of time I would recommend was seven sessions. At the end of the seven sessions, they were still undecided as to whether they would marry or not (no surprise to me about that) and reported feeling that the therapy was vaguely helpful but were disappointed that things were not clearer to them. I felt disappointed, too. I had recommended an additional ten sessions to them and felt, with their refusal, that I had been unsuccessful in sufficiently challenging their skepticism about therapy. Moreover, the therapy was not characterized by much experiential work and I was skeptical (note the skepticism and disappointment in both me and the couple) that the work had gotten through to them in a meaningful way. I was pleasantly surprised, then, when a year later the referral source told me that they had gotten married and felt that the therapy was instrumental in that coming about. From what she additionally reported, it also sounded like they had made more use of the therapy than I would have predicted.

I usually do not get such follow-up information on my patients and with brief contracts like this one it is often frustrating to know so little about the impact of the therapy.

Brief Therapy Is Harder

Many long-term therapists might disagree with this statement and certainly each approach has its own unique challenges and hardships. My own experience, though, is that the brief work I do is, on balance, much more taxing than the longer-term work.

> As I write this, I am thinking about a very troubled female patient who has been struggling with a fragmented personality structure over the course of her five decades of life and over the course of the more than eight years of treatment with me. Yesterday, she was describing in detail how profoundly depressed and hopeless she was feeling and how useless and cut off from other people she felt. She reported that she had gotten literature from the Hemlock Society (an organization that provides information on how to carry out suicide) and was reviewing suicide plan options.
>
> I was aware of the following reactions: I was puzzled as to why she should be feeling this particularly strongly at this moment and my thoughts drifted to various losses that she has suffered over her life and I wondered if any of them had been activated by some recent experiences. I found myself saddened by this state of profound emptiness and isolation that she recurrently returned to. I was also irritated by her return to this state since she had recently had several experiences that I thought might start a more positive interpersonal cycle for her. I felt mildly self-critical for expecting, as I now realized, more progress than was realistic and wondered (for the thousandth time) am I really of any help to her. I was aware of anxiety as she talked of reviewing the suicide literature but thought that, based on the experience of working with her over the past several years, she is not likely to act upon it. I returned to my irritation and thought that her raising of the suicide literature with me at this point may have been an attempt to connect more intensely with me at a time when she is feeling very disconnected from other people.

I remembered several situations from her past when a crisis reconnected her with life and with significant others. And my reactions went on and on.

In working with patients like this I am frequently required to contain primitive experiences of emptiness, despair, and anxiety and sometimes required to intervene in self-defeating and self-destructive situations. The context of long-term treatment provides three elements that make it more bearable to contain these difficult experiences. First, the long-term perspective allows for the space to reflect upon the material and to better appreciate the existential meaning of it. Second, it gives the therapist more data to use to put the material into a context. In the example just presented, I not only was assisted by a wealth of knowledge about the patient's history and recurring maladaptive interaction patterns, but I also had had some of those experiences directly with her within the therapeutic relationship itself. Third, the therapeutic relationship can become over an extended period of time a more sturdy holding environment for painful experience for both the therapist and the patient as they look at issues of mutual trust and limitations.

Consider the much greater difficulty in dealing with the above material if it had come up in, say, the tenth session of a contract of only fifteen sessions. In the context of a brief therapy, I would have to rapidly develop a working alliance and work as intimately as possible on the clinical material, including this suicidal material. It would be a much more formidable task to understand its meaning and I would struggle with how to assess the risk of suicide and how to subsequently intervene. While it would be useful for me to contemplate the meaning of my own countertransference reactions (anxiety, disappointment, irritation, self-reproach, etc.) the time constraints of having only five more sessions would make that much more difficult. I also would have much less information from the patient to grasp the intersubjective significance of her and my reactions. Then, I would strive for a termination that would permit the patient to leave treatment feeling that something meaningful had been accomplished without going away with intense longings for more (see the description below and in the following chapter on exciting object experience). Quite a strain on the therapist as well as on the patient! It is this type of strain that causes many therapists to defensively retreat to approaching brief therapy simply as a body of technical interventions rather than as a complex, real, human encounter.

These are some of the ways that I believe brief therapy puts additional demands on therapists. Moreover, if a therapist sees patients for shorter periods of time, he will be seeing a larger number of patients and will experience the strain not only of keeping straight the personal narratives of many different patients but also of authentically, openly, and intimately relating to a larger number of people. What are the therapist's limits?

The Belief that the Trend Toward Brief Therapy Is a Symptom of Our Society's Frantic Search for Quick Gratification and Avoidance of Intimacy

Unfortunately, there is some truth in this belief. We live in a society that prizes fast food, photo development and prescription eye glasses within an hour, and television shows where everything gets resolved within each hour. Small wonder that people are looking for fast therapy, too. Also, I think there are some signs of increasingly paranoid and schizoid processes (this mode of experience is described in Chapter 3) in the general culture that work against intimate relatedness. However, the current trend and interest in brief therapy is caused by many other factors as well—for example, offering effective psychotherapy to a large number of people in an economical manner.

If American culture is fixated on quick gratification and avoidance of true intimacy, then I think it is all the more compelling to conduct psychotherapy, brief or otherwise, in a manner that attends to, respects, and even emphasizes the quality of the relationship between therapist and patient.

CAUTIONS AND LIMITATIONS

Having discussed the various factors and attitudes that cause resistance to brief therapy, we still need to be mindful of its limitations and unique characteristics.

Limited Space for the Receptive Capacity

Bollas (1987) describes the importance of the receptive capacity of the therapist, a state in which the therapist attends to "news from within." This is a state of rather quiet reflection that permits subtle, preconscious internal data to emerge that might otherwise be lost amid the other more dominant stimuli and topics of the therapeutic session.

For this capacity to be present, the therapist and patient must create some space (and this requires some time) to permit this channel of subtle internal experience to be discerned. It is difficult for this space to occur in the midst of crisis management or when the therapist and patient are focusing in a directed manner on a particular issue. Due to the press of limited time, the need to accomplish goals quickly, and the concentration on a focus, the brief therapist (and patient) may not allow for much or any space to be created and protected for the receptive capacity. A frequent countertransference reaction to brief therapy is impatience. This can cause the therapy to be hurried and superficial rather than efficient and practical. Certainly, many patients contribute to this countertransference of impatience as both an understandable reaction to the time limitations of brief therapy and as a defense against the painful experiences that can emerge when the receptive capacity is activated.

While time *is* at a premium in brief therapy, some opportunity for the evocation of the receptive capacity in both the therapist and patient is usually crucial if therapy is to be more than superficial. Moreover, if the therapist does direct the therapy in a too narrow, focused manner, it can be yet another reenactment of previous unempathic relationships. This issue of the therapist's receptive capacity is but one of many points discussed in the present volume that argue for the brief therapist to be especially highly skilled and educated.

Therapy as an Exciting Object Experience

In his theory of personality, Fairbairn (1952) describes the concept of the exciting object (see Chapter 3). This is a part of the personality that is formed from experiences with others (initially the mother) when the other excites needs but ultimately disappoints the person. Hopes and expectations are raised but the follow-through is lacking and the experience is ultimately frustrating. It is tantalizing—it stimulates needs but leaves them unsatisfied.

Because time and goals in brief therapy are so limited, it is very easy for patients to expect more from the experience than is possible. Some of the "marketing" of brief approaches, especially nondynamic ones, even promotes the idea that as much can be done in brief therapy as in long-term therapy.

This exciting object potential is particularly present when the patient has very strong primitive dependency needs. It also nota-bly comes up when the therapy gets off to an unusually promising start. For instance, the patient comes in crisis and fairly quickly begins to feel better. She may also feel truly understood in a way she never has before. Depending on the patient's past experience and character structure, she may idealize the therapy and the thera-pist and expect that much more can be accomplished than is pos-sible within the limits of the therapeutic contract. As termination comes, the patient may come to feel bitterly misled and tantalized but largely disappointed by the process.

To some extent, this process of excessive expectations followed by disappointment is a normal progression in therapy and fre-quently is the object of important therapeutic work. However, the tighter limits in brief therapy can intensify the problematic experi-ence of exciting object phenomena. A motto in customer service programs in business and government is "Under-promise but over-deliver." This also would be a useful guideline for the brief thera-pist. The major way this is done is by repeated and persistent attention to the agreed upon therapeutic focus or foci. This con-fronts the patient (and therapist, too) with what can and what *cannot* be done in therapy. This issue of brief therapy becoming a counterproductive exciting object experience is often a particularly important issue for patients with borderline and dependent char-acter structures (see Chapter 11).

Inadequate Containment of Regression

The more limited time and structure of brief therapy provides more constricted containing and holding for the patient. Therefore, if, in the course of therapy, the patient regresses to primitive affective states or to less appropriate and effective functioning, it may be very difficult to deal with it within the limitations of the resources of brief therapy. Many of the brief therapy contraindications described in the literature are to exclude patients who would have a tendency toward profound or malignant regression (Balint 1968). For instance, Malan (1976) lists serious suicide attempts, previous long-term hospitalizations, and incapacitating chronic obsessive-compulsive disorders and phobic symptoms among his exclusionary criteria for his model of brief therapy. Davanloo (1980) identifies major affective disorders, psychotic breakdown, and certain life-threatening psychosomatic symptoms as contraindications for his model. However, as noted in the previous chapter, the time limits and focused approach of brief therapy do frequently have the counteracting effect of reducing the regressive pull of the therapeutic process.

Key Dynamic Material Emerges Near Termination

This issue is similar to the problem of limited containment for regression. As the patient works in brief therapy he benefits from the safety of the space created by the therapist and himself and also from the exploratory work along the way. Newer, deeper material may then come into awareness and become part of the therapeutic relationship. It may have taken almost all of the brief therapy contract to accomplish that. What happens then? An obvious answer would be to set up another episode of brief therapy or to begin longer-term work. However, it is not always that simple since limited financial resources (personal and insurance) is one of the reasons brief therapy may have been chosen.

> A therapist was referred a single female patient in her twenties. The patient was referred by her employer's EAP because she was having uncontrollable outbursts of anger at work directed toward co-workers and toward her supervisors. The patient had managed health insurance and she was allotted ten sessions. She and the therapist made considerable progress through some practical behavioral interventions (e.g., increased awareness of the anger build-

ing and strategies to either remove herself from the situation or to delay her response) and through the awareness of her previously unconscious identification with her abusive father. In the eighth session, she came in and was very distraught, crying about having just recovered memories of sexual abuse at the hands of her father. The health insurance plan would not authorize additional treatment since the treatment of the sexual abuse that occurred decades ago did not fit with their definition of short-term problem-focused treatment.

The therapist offered to work out a reduced fee for continued treatment but the patient said that she could not afford even that. The therapist made a referral to a private low-fee clinic to a specific therapist that she knew there. The patient terminated, as planned, in the tenth session and it did appear that her ability to control her anger had improved. However, she did not follow through on the referral.

This is not an isolated example. In teaching over the past four years in various U.S. cities, I have used this example. In many of those audiences, therapists have volunteered their own similar experiences. It raises an ethical issue for therapists. Having begun a treatment that then unexpectedly uncovers disturbing material near the end of the therapeutic contract, what is the therapist's responsibility to the patient? I believe that this therapist did act ethically and responsibly by her willingness to reduce her fee and through her careful referral for more affordable treatment.

Yet, the patient did not follow through on the referral and the therapist was left with considerable guilt about uncovering intensely painful material without being able to work on it with the patient. She had some feeling that this was a harmful, exciting object experience for her—the patient had trusted her, let herself become increasingly vulnerable, and then she had "abandoned" her. The therapist never got any direct confirmation of this from the patient, although the patient did express strong anger toward the insurance company about not being able to continue in therapy (at least, under the previous arrangements). The therapist wondered whether this was experienced at some level by the patient as a transference reenactment of the abuse. We should certainly be concerned here that a good relationship that caused this patient to feel safe enough to recover traumatic memories may have, at termination, also caused her to feel angry, abandoned, and less likely to trust or to seek help in the future.

While what I have just described is a serious problem for brief therapists (and patients) to confront, other dynamics in such situations are probably at play as well. It is likely that the abuse material did not emerge earlier because it took the therapeutic process that amount of time for it to appear and to be shared with the therapist. After all, eight sessions is a short time for repressed traumatic material to be uncovered—it sometimes takes years, if it emerges at all. However, it may be that it also came to light when it did *because* there was little time to deal with it and the patient was not yet ready to really address it. This may have been a factor in why she did not agree to the reduced fee arrangement with the therapist and did not follow through on the referral. It is possible that she felt safe in telling it only *as she was leaving* but took some real comfort in having shared it with the therapist. It was now left to the therapist, too, to painfully process what she had experienced, and this is part of what makes doing brief therapy even harder work.

Therapy May Be Superficial

The process of personal change occurs at varying speeds. It also takes people differing amounts of time to develop an adequate sense of safety and trust. In the time limits of a particular brief therapy, the truly change-producing material may not yet have emerged and/ or the therapy may not have yet provided adequate time for the safety and trust to occur. In such situations the therapy may end having been exclusively a supportive therapy experience. This is not to be discounted—the rapid alleviation of human suffering is a worthy goal in itself and this is all that many patients want. However, in many instances, if therapy had continued for a longer duration, more substantial changes could have occurred that would lead to more lasting improvement. Subsequent episodes of brief therapy—serial brief therapy (see Chapters 5 and 9)—can touch on more in-depth parts of the psyche even though the first episode was initially supportive.

Limited Opportunity for Working through or for Support of New Changes

Therapeutic changes often occur toward the end of brief treatment—it takes that long to get there. New growth can also be rather fragile and require some care and protection as it becomes more a part of the patient's personality and behavioral repertoire. Ongoing therapy can provide both an opportunity for the working through necessary to make the modifications in the patient's internal world more durable and to support the external behavioral changes. The time and holding environment of brief therapy may not offer much of that.

> Jane, a married woman in her fifties, began therapy to deal with the loss of meaning in her life due to her children all having grown and left home. She had lived her life defining herself rather exclusively in terms of how helpful she had been to others and had tended to defer to husband, children, and friends concerning activities and decisions. As she worked in therapy over a period of three months, Jane became more aware and respectful of her own needs and desires and began to take some independent steps (looking for a job, taking a college course). There was evidence that she was beginning to see herself differently and to live her life with more assertion and autonomy.
>
> On the intrapsychic level, this new image of herself was not yet firmly in place. Under the pressure of stress and frustration her new self-image was vulnerable to regression back to a state where self-worth was almost exclusively tied to meeting others' needs. On the interpersonal level, Jane was experiencing some resistance to her new independence from significant others who had become accustomed to her compliant style. Continued therapy could assist in working through the internal object and self dialogue of "You're nothing unless you're

taking care of others," "You're being selfish," and so on. It could also support her in dealing with the irritation and criticism from others. In short, the continuing internal and external forces that run counter to the new, not-yet-sturdy change could be dealt with in continuing therapy. However, the fact that brief therapy would be stopping in a few weeks removed this assistance at a crucial time.

This is, I think, a significant limitation of brief therapy. One way to address it is to openly talk during the termination process about the potential for relapse. Another strategy is to have follow-up sessions set at some later time to cope with these countertherapeutic forces.

While the above example illustrates a limitation of brief therapy, it also has embedded in it some of brief therapy's strengths. Jane was in a developmental crisis—a frequently fertile time for personal change. This developmental crisis coupled with her rather positive life history and skills made her a good candidate for brief therapy. There was a positive element to her not being able to depend on the therapist indefinitely. She had to deal with not having me for years and years and had to find new relationships and contacts. This paralleled her needing to let go of her grown children and finding a new life for herself. Similarly, *I* had to bear the anxiety of letting *her* go despite the limits of the progress, the newness and potential fragility of the changes, and the awareness of more that could be done.

Object Relations Concepts and Brief Therapy

> The technique helps us to investigate the problems which the therapeutic relationship, when it is therapeutic, enables the patient to reveal. It is the relationship with the therapist that creates the situation in which the problems can be solved.
>
> Harry Guntrip, 1969

This chapter is an overview of the object relations perspective and presents some key concepts that will be used in subsequent chapters. The discussion is directed toward therapists who are not very familiar with object relations theory. Readers interested in further examination of these ideas are referred to Scharff and Scharff (1992) for a detailed primer of object relations concepts and to Greenberg and Mitchell (1983) for an in-depth exposition and comparison of object relations and other psychoanalytic theories.

It is difficult to give an overview of object relations theory because there are actually several theories. My overview is selective rather than comprehensive and emphasizes concepts with applied utility for clinical practice.

Pine (1990) has argued that the myriad theories of psychoanalytic thought can be divided into four psychologies of psychoanalysis, object relations theory being one of the four, with each one emphasizing a particular aspect of human experience. *Drive theory* emphasizes biological drives (sex and aggression) that have profound psychological manifestations. *Ego psychology* centers on the way the person manages the demands of these internal drives and the demands of external reality. *Self psychology* focuses on the person's ongoing subjective experience of self. The core of *object relations theory* is the human relationship—both the internalized relationships that make up the psyche and the external ones in the real world. No other approach to human experience or to psychotherapy so centers on the human need for relationship and its role in psychopathology and therapeutic change. Therapists new to object relations thinking often find it puzzling that a theory that emphasizes relationships is named *object relations theory*. The term comes from the shift away from the Freudian emphasis on *drives* to the *object of the drives*, most significantly, other people.

The starting point of object relations thinking is the person's need for relationships. Humans are born in such an undeveloped, dependent state that we require another person for both physical and psychological survival. A fundamental fact, then, of human existence is our dependence on one another, initially for both physical and psychological survival and later for psychological health. This basic fact forms human personality and the way the person deals with his dependency needs is a key issue in psychological health and illness. Some theorists, such as Fairbairn (1952), place dependency as *the* key psychological issue.

An object relations approach is not simply a theory but it is a way of doing psychotherapeutic work. It concentrates on *understanding relating as the way of relating* (Scharff and Scharff 1991). Consequently, the approach emphasizes the therapeutic relationship including transference and countertransference. Moreover, the therapeutic relationship and the understanding of it are principal factors in promoting growth and change.

Klein is most often cited as the first object relations writer, although object relations concepts clearly go back to Freud—see, for example, *Mourning and Melancholia* (1917) and *The Ego and the Id* (1923). Other important contributors to the body of object relations theory include Fairbairn, Guntrip, Winnicott, Bion, and Balint. Contemporary object relations writers who are continuing to add to our knowledge base are Ogden, Bollas, D. and J. Scharff, Kernberg, and Masterson.

It is no overstatement to say that Klein's work (1964, 1975) fundamentally changed our view of the topography of the human psyche. Freud saw personality from the standpoint of the dynamic interactions among and between the id, ego, and superego (1923) in response to instinctual tension and adaptation to reality. Klein changed the intrapsychic emphasis to the dynamic interaction between *self* (she used the term *ego*) and *object*. This shift was crucial: "She places object relations at the center of her theoretical and clinical formulations. The organization and content of object relations, particularly relations with the fluid and complex world of internal objects, are the central determinants of experience and behavior" (Greenberg and Mitchell 1983, p. 145). However, she continued to examine this inner world from the perspective of Freudian drive theory: the internal objects are connected by unconscious fantasy resulting from the force of the life and death instincts. It remained for Fairbairn (1952), described later in this chapter, to move to a fully relational model that emphasized different varieties and levels of relationship between self and object.

INTERNAL SELF AND OBJECT REPRESENTATIONS

Within each person there are multiple pairings of self and object representations that make up both a sense of the person's experience of self and serve as a template for the experience of subsequent relationships. (In the interests of clarity, I will use the term *representations*, favored by American writers, rather than the generic *internal objects,* used by British writers like Klein and Fairbairn.) These internal representations come about through experience with significant others (notably the mother or primary caregiver) from the earliest days of life and into the present. Most object relations perspectives especially emphasize the contributions of development during the first few years of life, but a number of contributors (Bowlby 1969, Mitchell 1988) have emphasized the continuing role of relationships in shaping personality throughout the life span. The object relations perspective sees therapy as providing a change experience based on the therapeutic relationship. In Chapters 5 and 9, I discuss the role of brief therapy throughout one's life (serial brief therapy).

Internal self and object representations have the following characteristics: First, they are made up of the experience of aspects of a significant person in the individual's life (object representation) or the experience of self (self representation) during the interactions with that other person. Second, the representations can be conscious or unconscious. The therapist frequently tries to help the patient become more conscious of these internal representations. Third, these internal representations are not simply thoughts but they are cognitive-affective complexes that evoke particular ways of thinking, feeling, and acting. The personality includes multiple self and object pairings. These representations can be modified over time by therapy or by other experience. In psychopathology, however, they can be so rigidly organized as to be a "closed system" (Fairbairn 1958) preventing experience from affecting the internal world and resisting the attempts of therapy to promote growth and change.

Clinical Example: Paul

Consider a clinical example that is simplified for purposes of illustrating one self and object pairing.

> Paul was a successful, married lawyer in his late-thirties. His father had been frequently harsh and critical, seemingly never satisfied with what he did. If, as a boy, he cleaned his room today, it should have been done yesterday. If he received an A in school, it should have been an

A+. Over time, Paul internalized these interactions, this object relationship, with his father.

What is internalized? Three elements became part of his internal world: First, Paul internalized his father's way of being toward him—critical, disappointed, judgmental. Second, he internalized his own experience of himself during these interactions—being inadequate, never good enough, anxious about his performance, depressed. Third, the complex, at times subtle, dynamic relationship and interplay between these self and object representations were internalized along with the feelings that characterized the painful interactions.

Therefore, this self and object pairing became part of Paul's personality, unconsciously affecting the way he viewed himself and his world. In relating to others, this internal object relationship could affect him in three ways.

Projection of the Internal World onto the External World

Paul went to a dinner party where he met new people. He unconsciously projected the object representation of his father onto some of the others at this party and experienced them similarly to how he had experienced his father. He expected that they would be critical and that they would find him to be lacking in significant ways. Correspondingly, his own self experience at the party was like it was *in relation* to his father. He felt inadequate, had performance anxiety, and was convinced that he would disappoint the others. So, sometimes the person projects his internal object representations onto the external world.

Alternatively, he could have projected his self representations onto others. Remember, all of this is typically unconscious. In that case, he would have experienced the others at the dinner party much as his father seemed to experience him. Shortly after he walked into the party he would begin to feel like he had wasted his time, that these people would be disappointing and he would find fault with various aspects of each person.

Even without the effects of these internal objects, Paul might have found the people to be disappointing or they may have found him so. The point here is that Paul's internal object world *predisposed* him to experience it in particular ways and to distort it. Therefore, Paul was not really experiencing these human interactions at dinner as they were in the present but, rather, he was continuing to repeat his past experience and live it in the present. In addition, he may have been unconsciously searching for particular aspects of the dinner party interactions that would confirm his unconscious expectations that the interactions would be like those between him and his father.

As may be apparent by this point, what I am describing is transference, the distortion of present relationships by projecting past relationships onto them. In object relations terms, transference is understood as the projection of self and object representations onto others. It is the externalization of the inner world (Ogden 1986).

Choice of Others in the External World

In addition to distorting the experience of the external world, the internal world can cause the person to unconsciously select significant others who are, in fact, similar to the important others from the past. This frequently occurs in spite of the person's *conscious* attempts to be involved with people who are very different from those in past relationships. Even though the past relationships may have been troubled and unsatisfying, the person unconsciously gravitates toward the same type of individual because this is the relationship that the person is familiar with and/or he attempts to master a failed relationship. This is similar to Freud's (1920) conception of repetition compulsion and accounts for why people can hold on so tenaciously to painful experience and self-defeating relationships. Also, as Fairbairn (1952, 1958) notes, people stay in bad relationships or hold onto bad internal objects because it seems better than no relationship at all.

In selecting his wife, Paul married a woman who had very low self-esteem and who seemed to frequently experience herself as lacking, much as Paul had felt about himself in his interaction with his father. Not surprisingly, Paul was often disappointed with her and would persistently criticize her in person and to others, much as his father had done to him. Alternatively, Paul could have unconsciously repeated the old pattern by choosing a wife who was harsh and critical, like his father and then he would be in the role of the disappointing son, his inadequate self.

Influence on Others to Act like the Internal Representation

In addition to the distortion of the external world or in choice of significant others who are similar to the old objects, the power of the internal world is felt in another way. Sometimes through a process of unconscious cueing, the person exerts unconscious interpersonal pressure on the other to act out the role of the old object.

For example, Paul had a junior attorney working with him. Right from the beginning of his relationship with her, he seemed to view her as being inadequate (he viewed her as his father had viewed him). He reported that while he was convinced that she would not be an effective associate, he had to admit that she seemed to do excellent work for other partners and was highly regarded by them. However, with him she seemed to be bumbling and made frequent errors that were very inconsistent with the general quality of her work, especially with the other partners. She eventually took a job at another law firm, and in her exit interview she described how intimidated she had felt in working with Paul and felt uncharacteristically inept in projects with him.

How can we understand this from an object relations perspective? Paul's inner world distorted his view of this associate so that he saw her as inadequate before he had any real evidence to that effect. His perception of her and his reactions were repetitions of his old object relationship with his father. Paul had projected his self representation onto the associate. But more occurred than that. The associate's behavior and affect were actually *influenced* by the interactions with Paul (she unconsciously identified with what he had projected into her) so that she was uncharacteristically ineffective when she worked with him. In other words, she actually came to act in the way that was expected, based on his internal world—disappointing, inept, not good enough. This is an example of the powerful process of projective identification discussed later in this chapter.

Summary

The patient's personality and problems are seen in terms of an internal drama that has its origins in the past but is reenacted in the present. Pathology is viewed as the degree to which present experience is determined by these internal self and object pairings as opposed to being determined by the actual situation or relationship. The nature and the degree of pathology is also determined by the particular internal drama being replayed. For instance, a severe abuse drama is more disturbed than a dynamic of transient feelings of inadequacy. Psychotherapy is fundamentally a relationship in which these internal dramas are played out with the person of the therapist, whether in brief or long-term therapy. The therapist and patient affect one another reciprocally through the processes of projection and introjection.

It is useful for therapists to figure out which part in the drama falls to them at different times. One way of getting in touch with this is to ask ourselves two simple questions that Paula Heimann suggested to her supervisees (quoted by Bollas 1987): *"Who is speaking?"*—what part of the patient's inner world is being given expression at that particular moment?; and *"To whom is the person speaking?"*—what part of the patient's inner world is being represented by the therapist at that moment?

For the object relations therapist, as Scharff and Scharff (1991) point out, understanding relating is the way of relating to the patient. Thus, ideally the patient and therapist work frequently and collaboratively using the various elements of the relationship—transference, countertransference, working alliance, and real relationship. How much can be explicitly dealt with in brief therapy very much depends on the particular situation. However, even when the therapist does not directly discuss these issues with the patient, her therapeutic effectiveness is enhanced by her own attention to this dimension of the clinical encounter.

MODES OF EXPERIENCE

To understand our relationships with our patients we need to understand how individuals create and organize psychological experience. Klein (1964, 1975) presented two psychological positions—the paranoid-schizoid and the depressive. Incorporating her work as well as some more recent material, Ogden (1989, 1994) has added a third form of human experiencing: the autistic-contiguous mode. I will discuss them in order from the most basic, less developed mode of experiencing (autistic-contiguous) to the most developed (depressive).

These modes come about through early developmental processes in the infant and continue as ways of experiencing the world in adult life. As Ogden (1994) emphasizes,

> None of the three modes exists in isolation from the others: each creates, preserves, and negates the others dialectically. Each mode generates an experiential state characterized by its own distinctive form of anxiety, types of defense, degree of subjectivity, form of object relatedness, type of internalization process, and so on. [pp. 139–140]

While each person shows evidence of functioning in any of the three modes of experience, it is useful to note which mode may emerge at a particular time, which mode may be generally predominant in the person's experiencing of the world, and what are the interrelationships among them. Each type of experiencing may at times be either pathological or healthy or both.

Aspects of these three dimensions are outlined in Table 3–1. The paranoid-schizoid and depressive modes are based on Klein's (1948, 1958) concept of developmental positions. Ogden's autistic-contiguous mode is an extension of the contributions of Bick (1986), Meltzer (1975), and Tustin (1986).

Table 3–1. Ogden's Three Modes of Experience

	Autistic-Contiguous	Paranoid-Schizoid	Depressive
Experience	Sensory floor	Fragmenting and evacuative	Linkages and subjectivity, ambivalence
Anxiety	Disintegration, leaking, dissolving	Fragmenting attacks, annihilation	Harmed or driven objects away
Objects	Autistic shapes and objects	Split and part objects	Whole objects
Transference	Bodily sensation; contextual response	Re-creation of experience	Recapture of experience
Subjectivity	Self through skin surface and rhythmicity	Self as object	Self as subject

Note: No mode exists in isolation; they create, negate, and preserve one another. From Ogden 1989, 1994. Table used by permission of Thomas Ogden.

Autistic-Contiguous Mode

This is Ogden's most important theoretical contribution to date. The autistic-contiguous mode is the most primitive mode of experiencing. Self and world are experienced in a fundamental, presymbolic manner—through the basic organization of sensory experience. There are two major dimensions to this organization, the skin surface and rhythmicity. Through the sense of touch at the skin surface, the person experiences the boundary of her existence and this serves as the basis for a cohesive self. Rhythmic activity like rocking or humming serves a similar function in giving the person the experience of "staying together." These activities may be intensified or be particularly obvious at times of high anxiety and distress.

The predominant anxiety in the autistic-contiguous mode is of disintegrating or dissolving. For example, one patient has described the terrifying fear of falling into a black hole of senseless, thoughtless numbness. She keeps a "second skin" (Bick 1986) of sound around her by ensuring that the television or music is always playing at home, and that the radio is always on in her car. Any silence in our sessions is difficult for her to tolerate. Other clinical examples of autistic-contiguous behaviors include the following:

Emphasizing the sensory impressions of the therapist's office in statements like these: "It feels so warm and safe in here." "The sunlight on your carpet makes me feel calm." "I just can't get comfortable in your chair today."

Stroking self, playing with hair

Rubbing or pushing hand on chair or table

Cutting the skin and other self-mutilation

Engaging in compulsive rituals of touch, for example, hand washing or repetitive touching of a door frame when entering

Repeating some obsessive thoughts such as "Why me? Why me? Why me?" "I'm OK. I'm OK. I'm OK."

All of these behaviors are an attempt in the autistic-contiguous mode to keep a sense of boundedness and cohesion. Internal objects are not experienced in the manner described in the previous section because there is little or no internal space for the capacity to symbolize in the autistic-contiguous mode. Instead, they consist of tactile sensations of things. There are two types of experience that make up the autistic-contiguous inner world—"autistic shapes" and "autistic objects." Autistic shapes are sensations of soft objects such as a padded chair, a blanket, a bed, that the person can make an impression on when they are touched. Connection with autistic shapes tend to give the person a sense of security, connectedness, and comfort. Autistic objects are sensations of things that are hard and have an edge such as a wall, a desk, a crib railing. Connection with autistic objects provides a sense of a protective armor, of separateness and rigidity. Remember, these internal "objects" of the autistic-contiguous mode are not what we typically think of as constituting the inner world, but they are an important part of it. It is not the autistic shape or object that is taken in but the experience of the tactile sensation of the shape or object and the experience of the *self* being defined by coming up against it.

Psychological change can occur in the autistic-contiguous mode but it does not occur through identification or introjection. These processes would require a better developed and structured internal world. Instead, the person simply imitates another person and changes in that way. "In imitation, the qualities of the external object are felt to alter one's surface, thus allowing one to be 'shaped by' or 'to carry' attributes of the object" (Ogden 1994, p. 141). For example, the patient may begin to dress like his therapist.

> One of my patients, Barry, a teacher who had seen me present a lecture, described relating to his own students "like you do." He also would frequently talk about the sensory experience of being in my office (the feel of the chair, the warmth of the sun, etc.). His ability to move from imitation to self-reflection so he could then verbalize the event in his class indicates another mode of experience, in this case, the depressive mode, which will be discussed later in this chapter. Imitation is a very simple but significant way that therapy, including brief therapy, can help to shape the patient's sense of self. Especially when there is a strong positive transference, as with Barry, imitation may play an important change-promoting role in brief therapy.

Paranoid-Schizoid Mode

This is a more developed mode than the autistic-contiguous, although Klein saw it as her beginning position. There is more internal space than in the autistic-contiguous mode, it is organized, and internal objects as described in the section on self and object representations are part of the internal world. However, experience is organized into rather narrow, concrete categories. There are no shades of gray; splitting is the predominant mechanism in the paranoid-schizoid position. Object and self are experienced as all or nothing—either good or bad, either satisfying or unsatisfying, either accepting or rejecting, not mixtures of these states. There is a vital intensity, states of exhilaration or terror, in this mode.

The world, others, and self are seen as battlegrounds of dichotomous forces—love and hate, life and death, creation and destruction. As one patient said to me, "I feel like I'm either hot shit or just plain shit!" Splitting is a process whereby these warring forces are kept separate and provides some order to the chaos of existence beyond the order provided by the sensory floor of the autistic-contiguous mode. The prime anxiety in the paranoid-schizoid mode is the fear of fragmenting into split off and split up bits and being annihilated.

There is no real empathy for the other; paranoid-schizoid experiencing does not include appreciation of the *experience* of the other. There is no concern or guilt over hurting the other. Distress over hurting the other comes from fear of either retaliation on the part of the harmed person or loss of what the other provides.

Like autistic-contiguous experiencing, paranoid-schizoid is a mode of the present moment. There is little sense of continuity through time but rather a sense of the immediacy of the moment disconnected from past events. This is why a patient who is operating mainly from the paranoid-schizoid mode can experience the therapist one week as a different person from the therapist of the preceding week. The patient may, in fact, remember the last session and the way the therapist was perceived then but it does not have much psychic reality and is as if it were another person. Moreover, the person may "rewrite" the memory ("I thought that you were really concerned about me then but now I know it was just a sham"). The experience of self can be similarly discontinuous over time as well. The patient who was thrilled last week by a successful presentation at work, today feels like a total failure after a dispute with his boss. Each instance can be experienced as if that is the whole reality. What happened in the past and what the person thought of himself then seems very far away and unconnected to *now*.

Self is perceived in a manner that is beyond that of the sensory boundedness of the autistic-contiguous mode but it is "self as object." In Ogden's (1994) words: "In this experiential state there is very little sense of oneself as the author of one's thoughts and feelings. Instead, thoughts and feelings are experienced as forces and physical objects that occupy and bombard oneself" (p. 141). Projection and projective identification are dominant processes in this mode. Patients report subjective experiences such as "He made me angry," "I was forced to give in," "The pressure was too strong, so I had to get drunk." The sense of personal agency is lacking in the face of powerful forces that are felt to control, bombard, and pressure the person.

Evidence of all three modes of experience can be discerned in every person. Autistic-contiguous and paranoid-schizoid functioning can be particularly seen at times of high stress and trauma. Autistic-contiguous manifestations may be especially obvious in autistic and psychotic individuals. Paranoid-schizoid functioning is frequently the leading mode in borderline and narcissistic states.

Depressive Mode

This is the most mature and least primitive mode. There is the capacity for more symbolic and abstract thinking. The person is able to make multiple linkages of various sorts that do not occur in either of the other two modes. Whereas the paranoid-schizoid inner world is made up of split and part objects, the depressive inner world is characterized by whole objects. The person experiences self and others as being mixtures of positive and negative aspects. The relationship to the inner and external objects is one of ambivalence: the person both loves and hates, likes and dislikes self and others. These feelings coexist in relation to self and other. The person is able to maintain a relationship with someone even with such conflicting feelings.

> I have seen Victor in therapy for several years and he has angrily quit therapy eight times. After days or weeks, he decided each time to return. In these situations he is operating predominantly from the paranoid-schizoid mode: when he is angry with me, I am totally no good and Victor feels he has no option other than to get rid of me. Later, my "badness" recedes and he then returns, being

in touch at that time with how I am valuable to him but being out of touch with how frustrating I can be. Recently, however, I have seen more signs of the depressive mode and Victor has been able on a number of occasions to be furious with me but to still hold onto the sense of me as being partly a good object and has stayed with, and in, our relationship.

In the depressive mode, the person sustains a connection with the past. Present experience is not split off from the past but is perceived within the context of what occurred in the past and what is expected or hoped for in the future. This sense of continuity over time and with the multiple parts of self and others creates more of a sense of stability and cohesion of the self. Patients express sentiments such as "I hate that my wife left me but other women haven't seen me as being so awful"; "Even though I blew up yesterday at my kid, I'm still pretty good as a parent."

In this mode the self is a "self as subject." The person feels a sense of control and responsibility in living rather than feeling buffeted by powerful forces outside of the self. In Ogden's (1994) words: "One's thoughts and feelings are experienced as one's own creations that can be thought about and lived with and need not be immediately discharged in action or evacuated in omnipotent fantasy" (p. 143).

Depressive mode experiencing also includes the capacity for empathy. The person has an appreciation that the other is not just a thing but is a human being who has an inner world of experience, too. With concern for the other, the person also can feel guilt over hurting the other. The prime anxiety in the depressive mode is fear of harming or driving away the other. The person, though, also has a wish for and a sense of the possibility of realistically repairing the damage.

As already noted, while one mode may be predominant at a given moment, the other modes exist and affect the functioning and perception of the person. Ogden's view of these modes is of a dynamic, dialectic interplay among them rather than a consecutive, unconscious selection of which mode is manifested at a particular time.

To illustrate the interrelationships among the modes, I return to the case of Victor, who has repeatedly fired and rehired me. In a recent session he was furious at me for an interpretation that he perceived as a criticism of him. His rage was barely containable as he spit out how much he hated me and what a uniformly poor therapist I was (paranoid-schizoid experiencing). While he was attacking me he was repeatedly pressing his hand against the wall next to his chair and running his hand down the edge of the wall where it takes a ninety-degree angle away from him. He was clearly feeling under attack both by me and, I think, by the intensity of his own feelings. He was having difficulty holding himself together. His physical touching of the wall was autistic-contiguous functioning that was helping to keep him from psychologically disintegrating. It was an example of a relationship with an autistic object and it gave him a feeling of being protected and bounded. Despite the intensity of Victor's rage, he was resisting the urge to fire me again and walk out of the office, and he actually said, angrily, "You've helped me so much, why do you have to do such stupid things [like some of my interpretations]?" Victor's being able to hold onto my "goodness" in the midst of this tirade and resisting the urge to walk out suggests his movement toward depressive mode functioning.

Clearly the movement from the autistic-contiguous to the paranoid-schizoid to the depressive mode of experience is toward increasingly sophisticated and mature functioning. However, it would be erroneous to assume that the autistic-contiguous and paranoid-schizoid modes are bad and the depressive mode is good. It would not only be erroneous, it would also be an example of splitting. Each mode brings with it its own unique benefits and unique deficits. The *limitations* of the first two modes described above are perhaps obvious. On the positive side, the autistic-contiguous mode grounds the person in bodily, sensory experience. The paranoid-schizoid mode accentuates the intensity and vitality of moment-to-moment living. Alternatively, the *benefits* of the most mature mode stand out. However, preoccupation with depressive mode experience can lead to "a form of isolation of oneself from one's bodily sensations, and from the immediacy of one's lived experience, leaving one devoid of spontaneity and aliveness" (Ogden 1989, p. 46).

PROJECTIVE IDENTIFICATION

This is one of the most useful concepts to come out of object relations theory but also one of the slipperiest. Klein introduced the concept but many subsequent writers have developed it further. The concept goes back to early infant–mother interactions and it addresses how the internal world gets played out externally in the interpersonal world. The present discussion takes one look at projective identification but it should be noted that there are different views on what it is. For three excellent, in-depth examinations of projective identification I refer the reader to Grotstein (1981), Ogden (1982), and J. Scharff (1992).

Definition

This view of projective identification includes one part projection and two parts identification. This is a process that is part of the paranoid-schizoid mode and occurs basically at an unconscious level.

Projection

A person projects a part of his inner world onto someone else. The multiple motivations and functions for this activity are discussed below.

Introjective Identification

The person receiving the projection unconsciously identifies with it *and* feels subtle, unconscious interpersonal pressure to be and act like the projection.

Projector Identification

The projector unconsciously identifies with what he has projected onto the other person. As Ogden (1982) describes it, "The projector subjectively experiences a feeling of oneness with the recipient with regard to the expelled feeling, idea, or self-representation" (p. 34).

Clinical Example: Janet

This petite young woman came into my office for her first session making little eye contact and saying nothing. Despite my efforts to encourage her to talk, she remained withdrawn and quiet throughout the session. Her presentation of the material included little anxiety or other affect. In the few things that she did say, she revealed that her housemate had returned home early the previous evening and found Janet having cut her wrists. The friend took her to a hospital emergency room, where she was accurately assessed as not being suicidal. She was referred to the clinic where I worked at that time and I saw her for an initial evaluation. Reporting all of this in a detached manner, Janet said she was not suicidal nor did she have the urge presently to cut herself, but she expected she would cut herself at some point in the future. During the session, I found myself having two strong feelings. First, I was very, very anxious. My anxiety was disproportionate to the situation. She had said she was not suicidal, her wounds were not very deep, and she was willing to enter outpatient psychotherapy—all of this stated in her extremely calm, detached manner. I had worked before with other patients who had cut themselves, more deeply, but I had not had such an intensely anxious response. With Janet, I had thoughts of hospitalizing her, having her return to the clinic later in the day, having her call in later that evening, getting her medication—all excessive for the situation. Second, despite the discomfort of my anxiety, I found myself strongly wanting to work with her, more so than I do with most patients that I see during a first session.

These two countertransference reactions were based on both some internal issues of my own and on the projective identification process. The focus here is on the projective identification aspect of it but it is important to note that individuals have a valency (Bion 1961), or predisposition, to take in a particular projection. I will outline the steps of the projective identification process with each of my reactions. Much of my now-verbalizable understanding of Janet's internal state at the time came from subsequent sessions with her.

My Anxiety

PROJECTION

As noted, there was little overt indication of Janet's anxiety. Her anxiety was overwhelming for her and so she projected it into me to contain it for her (see below for a discussion of the process of containment). Remember, this is an unconscious process. This caused her to feel more comfortable since she had "gotten rid of" her anxiety.

INTROJECTIVE IDENTIFICATION

I unconsciously identified with the anxiety that she had projected into me. This "supercharged" my anxiety level. I would be somewhat anxious anyway with a patient who had recently mutilated herself but in this session I was now much more anxious because I was holding her anxiety as well as my own. Moreover, I felt a strong urge to act on my anxiety and be an anxious, intrusive, hovering therapist. As I later learned this is precisely how she experienced her mother.

If the therapist is aware of an unusual, uncanny response to the situation, it can be an important signal. It may indicate that a primitive projective identification process is occurring. However, it does not necessarily indicate projective identification. For example, it may have more to do with the therapist's own internal world largely separate from the interpersonal, intersubjective matrix with the patient. However, such strong reactions do signal a warning to consider the possibility of projective identification.

PROJECTOR IDENTIFICATION
Janet unconsciously identified with her anxiety that she had projected into me. She had a sense of "oneness" with me as I held her anxious feeling and her internal object derived from experience with her hovering mother.

My Wanting to Work with Her

PROJECTION
She projected into me some of her caregiving capacity, her ability and desire to be therapeutic to herself. As I later learned she had by now despaired of being able to take care of herself. She only felt aware of what she considered her innate badness overwhelming anything good about her. Therefore, she unconsciously projected the goodness into me for safekeeping. Note how this process and Janet's thinking exemplify the paranoid-schizoid mode's world of splitting and the personality as a battleground of good and bad. Also, this projection illustrates how not only negative parts of the personality but also positive elements can be projected, as in this instance, to keep the good protected and separated from the destructiveness of internal badness.

INTROJECTIVE IDENTIFICATION
I unconsciously identified with Janet's projected caregiving capacity. It intensified the desire to work with her that I would ordinarily have had anyway. I felt an increased pressure to be a good, protective therapist. This pressure felt so strong that, coupled with my anxiety, I felt compelled to even go further than my good judgment would indicate in "protecting" her (my thoughts about hospitalization, medication, phone calls, etc.). This was part of my identification with her anxious, hovering mother. Note the

paranoid-schizoid quality of my experience of being pressured and compelled (my self as an object of forces outside of me).

PROJECTOR IDENTIFICATION
Janet identified with the caregiving capacity that she had projected into me. In a sense, I contained it for her until she was able to do so herself. This unconscious identification helped her to maintain her relationship with me at subsequent times of anger and discouragement.

Functions of Projective Identification

Ogden (1982) has outlined four functions of this process.

1. *Defense*: To get away from painful affect and/or to regulate the functioning of the self, the person uses projective identification. This function is apparent in Janet's case.
2. *Communication*: Projective identification is a form of nonverbal, unconscious communication. Rather than telling the other about a part of her inner world, the person has the other *experience* it. Janet couldn't tell me about her intense anxiety so, through projective identification, she had me feel it. This dramatically illustrates the invaluable knowledge we get about our patients through our countertransference reactions, if we can attend to them and make some sense out of them.
3. *Object-relatedness*: This is a way of relating to another person, albeit a rather primitive (paranoid-schizoid) one. Projective identification was Janet's unconscious way of starting up a relationship with me. As Scharff and Scharff (1991) state, the recipient of the projection experiences an unconscious mixture of separateness and undifferentiation. The recipient is separate enough to receive the projection (Janet did "get rid of" those parts of her by putting them into me) but undifferentiated enough for there to be some misunderstanding—What was I feeling? Whose anxiety and

caregiving capacity was it anyway? This misperception promotes a sense of connection and oneness between the participants.

4. *Pathway for psychological change*: Projective identification can promote psychological growth or damage. Personal change occurs in a relationship through the cycle of projection, introjection, projection, and so on. In a healthy, positive relationship, the part that is projected into the recipient is unconsciously modified and the projector then reintrojects this as a more positive part. Janet's anxiety was overwhelming and she projected it into me. While I felt overwhelming anxiety, my anxious response to her was in a modulated manner. Over time, this "metabolizing" of her anxiety helped her to accept and to tolerate it herself. In a disturbed relationship, however, the recipient can modify the projection in a more toxic direction and the projector in that instance receives back a more disturbed projection. One can often see such a process in the accelerating anxiety between a therapist and patient or in the intensifying cycle between a persecuting spouse and victimized one.

Additional Points Concerning Projective Identification

Projective Identification Is A Two-Way Process

In the interests of brevity, my example of Janet focused on her projections into me. In fact, however, projective identification goes in both directions: from patient to therapist and from therapist to patient. In therapy, as in other relationships, we mutually affect each other through the process of projective identification. A frequent instance of a positive projective identification process is the therapist's projection of her hope into the patient as the patient comes to have more realistic hope for the future. A negative example, common in brief therapy, is the therapist projecting her disappointment over limited progress into the patient and the patient then undervaluing and discounting the substantial progress that he'd made.

Projective Identification Spotlights the Relationship
between the Intrapsychic and the Interpersonal

A particularly powerful aspect of the concept of projective identification is that it shows how a person's internal world can get played out between two (or more) people in the external world. What can simply appear to be an argument between two people may, in fact, be an externalization of inner conflicts and struggles within each of them. Projective identification bridges the intrapsychic and the interpersonal.

Projective Identification Can Evoke Exactly the Opposite
of What the Projector Consciously Wants

> Consider the dynamic between Ann and Ali, a married couple. As I have worked with them we have come to identify a common destructive interpersonal pattern that is a manifestation of mutual projective identification. Ann wants more emotional closeness with Ali. Ali wants Ann to respect his need for time to be alone. They have often been locked in a cycle in which Ann criticizes Ali for his distance and Ali coldly withdraws. The more he withdraws, the more Ann attacks. The more she attacks, the more Ali withdraws. This interpersonal pattern is driven by a mutual process of projections and introjections. Ali consciously wants her to "get out of my face" and Ann consciously wants him to "talk to me, be there for me." But their behavior is having exactly the opposite effect. It is very difficult to change this process until couples (husbands and wives, therapists and patients, etc.) see the pattern.

Just as Parts of Self and Object Can be Projected, the Recipient
Can Identify with Parts of Self and Object

I noted in my example of Paul that people project both self and object parts onto others. Similarly, the recipient can identify with self and/or object projections. Racker (1968) has elaborated on the role of these unconscious identifications by the therapist in countertransference. When the therapist identifies with a part of the patient's self, it is a *concordant identification*. When the therapist identifies with a part of the patient's objects, it is a *complementary identification*. To return to the example of Paul, at times I have felt inadequate and never quite good enough for him. I was identifying with his experience of self (a concordant identification) in relation to his harsh, critical father. At other times, I have felt disappointed with him and have thought that "he just doesn't have what it takes" to be successful in relationships. I was identifying with his internalized father (complementary identification) in relation to Paul.

In Janet's case, some of my intense anxiety came from both concordant and complementary identifications. I was feeling some of her overwhelming inner terror over her own badness and helplessness (a concordant identification). But my anxiety was also fueled by my identification with her anxious, intrusive, hovering mother (a complementary identification).

Projective Identification Is a Developmental Continuum, Not a Single Mechanism

For purposes of illustration, I used a rather primitive example of projective identification in the case of Janet. This is a process, though, that ranges from the primitive to the mature. Toward the primitive pole, there is self and object confusion and intense, large elements of the projector's inner world are projected. Toward the mature pole, self and object differentiation is not in question, and the projections are less intense or global. The most mature form of projective identification is empathy ("I put myself in his shoes").

HOLDING AND CONTAINMENT

A central therapy paradigm for the object relations therapist is that of the mother–child dyad. Just as the mother's relationship to her child fosters his growth and development, so too does the object relations therapist's relationship with her patient promote his development. Similarly, just as the infant also profoundly affects the mother, the patient also has a meaningful impact on the therapist. There are, of course, significant differences, but both relationships involve deep and authentic human encounters, empathy, gratification, and frustration.

Holding and containment refer to two aspects of the maternal/therapeutic function. *Holding* refers to the external interaction between mother and child while containment is about their internal states. *Holding* is the term Winnicott (1945) used for the actual, observable caregiving relationship between the mother and infant and the emotional holding it conveys. For example, a mother goes to her crying baby who is distraught, having been startled by a loud noise. The baby is very upset and, despite the mother's best efforts, does not calm down for several minutes. The mother holds and rocks the baby and hums to him (autistic-contiguous mode) and gradually he settles down. *Holding* is the general term used to describe the mother's provision of a physical environment that facilitates her child's growth and development. Similarly, the therapist "holds" her patient through the provision of an environment that promotes therapy such as a quiet, comfortable office, respectful demeanor, consistent frame and empathically based interpretations (I am not suggesting that the therapist physically holds the patient).

Containment (Bion 1967) is an internal state. It is a special state of being (Bion called it reverie) in which the mother is able to take in and tolerate experiences of the infant (e.g., anxiety, frustration) that the infant himself is unable to contain. Her introjection of this part of the infant is then modified and made less toxic and projected back to the child in a way that he can now contain it himself. To return to the example of the startled baby, the mother does more than the external holding described above. During the time that the infant continues to be flooded with anxiety, the mother feels (identifies with) some of the primitive anxiety but contains it within herself and stays empathically in relationship with the infant. The mother contains the anxiety and metabolizes it; the infant then takes it back (introjects it) in a less terrifyingly intense form. In this description of a positive, facilitating mother–infant interaction, I want to emphasize that the effective mothering involves not only the *external* actions of the mother (the holding) but also her *internal* responses (the containment).

I was referring to this process of containment in my discussion of projective identification when the therapist identifies with a projection of the patient, modifies it, and then the patient takes it back in a more tolerable form. Just as the mother bears and contains her child's psychological pain, so too the therapist bears and contains the patient's pain during treatment. Therapists often ask at this point, "What do you then do with what you've contained?" The process of containment does give the therapist additional, experiential insight into the patient and this can inform the therapist as to what to do. But, fundamentally, containment is not about *doing* but it is about *being* without having to act—being with the patient in his painful inner world. This issue speaks to some of the strains and demands of being both a mother and a therapist. It also speaks to the frequent necessity and benefits of our countertransference suffering. Sometimes, just being with the patient and serving the containing function with his rage, anxiety, hopelessness, and so on, without avoiding the pain, without allowing oneself to be abused and without being attacking—*just being there with the patient*—is what's needed.

THE ENVIRONMENTAL MOTHER AND THE OBJECT MOTHER: THE CONTEXTUAL AND FOCUSED TRANSFERENCES

Winnicott (1945, 1963) delineated two parts of the mother's interaction with her child. First, the *environmental mother* involves much of what was just described as the holding function of the mother. It is that element of mothering that is in the background, that provides an adequately secure environment for growth and development to take place. This is a crucially important aspect of mothering that is easy to overlook. However, if it is not adequately there, little else that is good can take place. This is the "arms around" relationship in which the mother provides the context for relating (Scharff and Scharff 1991).

Second, the *object mother* refers to the interactions with the mother in the foreground. When the child is relating to the object mother, he is directly dealing with his experience of her as an object, not to the background atmosphere that she has provided. As such, she is the direct object of love and hate, affection and aggression. This is the "eye to eye" and the "I to I" relationship (Scharff and Scharff 1991).

These two types of mothering are the basis for two different types of transference (Scharff and Scharff 1991, J. S. Scharff 1992). Based on past experiences with environmental mothering (with the actual mother as well as with subsequent relationships), the patient reacts in a particular way to the therapist's office and manner and has expectations about the way he will be treated that are separate from the direct relating between the therapist and patient. The Scharffs call these reactions to the therapist the *contextual transference*. This type of transference is prominent in the early phases of treatment and in brief therapy it may well be predominant throughout. In *focused transference* reactions, the patient's responses are based on past experiences with the object mother (and on subsequent "centered relating" with others). The therapist is then more directly a focus of the patient's thoughts and feelings. Focused transference reactions reveal more about the unique aspects of the patient's inner object world since they show the play of those inner structures in relation to the person of the therapist.

In my experience, when the contextual transference takes center stage, therapy usually is not verbally very interpretive. Therapy that addresses the focused transference tends to be more interpretive. The case of Alan (see Chapter 5) exemplifies a brief therapy in which the transference was mainly contextual. The therapies with Ronald and Diane (see Chapters 6, 8, and 9) involved more focused transference material.

FAIRBAIRN'S INTRAPSYCHIC SYSTEM

Fairbairn (1952, 1958, 1963) stands out among the various object relations theorists as providing, I believe, the most comprehensive, fully relational theory of personality and intrapsychic functioning. He starts with the premise that psychic energy (libido) is not inherently pleasure-seeking, as Freud argued. Rather, libido is fundamentally relationship-seeking. This changes the primary question in understanding psychological development and dysfunction. The central question is no longer the drive model question of "How do the person's attempts to seek pleasure and reduce tension determine her psychological health?" The question now becomes relational: "How do the person's efforts in dealing with her need for human relatedness determine psychological health?"

Fairbairn theorizes that each person has an intrapsychic system made up of three self and object configurations. The relative power and the relationships among these structures (degree of aggression and/or attraction to each other) are determined by the person's past history. Figure 3-1 gives a visual outline of this system. Each part object is in primary relationship with a particular part of the self (Fairbairn uses the term *ego*). Each pair forms the

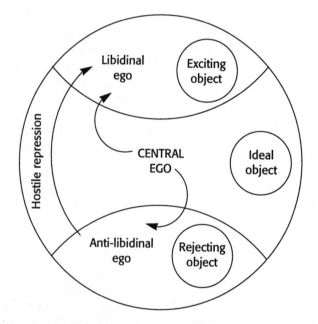

Figure 3-1. Fairbairn's model of psychic organization. (From Scharff 1982. Reprinted courtesy Routledge and Kegan Paul and David E. Scharff.)

template for different types of relationships with people in the external world. Relationship is so central to his theory that all parts of the ego are inevitably attached to some internal object. Just as Winnicott wrote that there are no infants without mothers (infants cannot survive without mothering individuals), there are no egos without objects in Fairbairn's theory.

The Central Ego-Ideal Object

This is the segment of the personality formed by the good, satisfying aspects of early development. The ideal object represents those experiences of the mother in which she appropriately met the needs of the developing infant. Its primary connection is with the central ego, which is oriented toward effectively interacting with the external world. This part of the self is similar to Freud's conception of the ego. It is that part of the personality that serves the executive function of enabling the person to get needs met in the external world. Since the central ego is primarily connected with the object that represents satisfying interpersonal experiences, it makes sense that it would be oriented toward outside relationships. Dominant affects associated with ideal object relationships include comfort, security, satisfaction, and positive relatedness. The central ego-ideal object is the most conscious of the three dyads. The other two dyads are generated by frustrating, unsatisfying experiences with the mother.

The Antilibidinal Ego-Rejecting Object

This portion of the personality develops from experiences when the mother does not meet the infant's needs and the infant feels unwanted, abandoned, angry, and/or frustrated. These are also the dominant affects associated with rejecting object relationships. The antilibidinal ego attacks the person's attempts at developing relationships. Actually, Fairbairn's earlier term for the antilibidinal ego was the *internal saboteur*. The attacks upon relationships are understandable from the antilibidinal ego's primary connection with an internal object that is rejecting, abandoning, frustrating, and unsatisfying.

The Libidinal Ego-Exciting Object

Despite its name, this part of the personality also forms a paradigm for bad (unsatisfying) object relationships. The libidinal ego longs for satisfaction in relationships and seeks out relationships. However, it is in a constant state of yearning due to its connection with the exciting object that was formed by early experiences of having hopes raised for satisfactory relatedness that were ultimately frustrated. The mother produces this by being overly attentive and trying to satisfy a need that is not there yet. She also can create exciting object experience through inconsistency or the transmission of anxiety, so that the infant expects a satisfying interaction but then the mother does not come through. These are tantalizing, enticing but eventually rejecting encounters. "The promise is kept alive but fulfillment is impossible" (Greenberg and Mitchell 1983, p. 166).

Exciting object relationships are often more difficult than rejecting object ones. As painful as rejecting object relationships are, there is a clarity and eventual predictability about the rejection—the person knows where he stands (albeit painfully) in the relationship. In exciting object relationships the pain is often more excruciating because the disappointment is greater. The person's hopes and longings are raised but then dashed. So the experience of exciting object relationships is of unfulfilled need and desperate yearning. As discussed in Chapter 2, brief therapy has a great deal of potential for evoking exciting object relating in the patient and the brief therapist needs to be cognizant of it.

While relationships can be characterized as being either predominantly ideal, rejecting, or exciting, relationships are, in fact, more complex than that and involve mixtures of these three different paradigms of relating. The following example illustrates this in a brief therapy case.

Clinical Example: Rita

This articulate, divorced college instructor in her early thirties began therapy with a highly motivated, hopeful, cooperative demeanor. She wanted help in dealing with her 7-year-old son's relationship with his father and with her own loneliness. Since she was moving to another city in a few months, we had time for only nine sessions. For four sessions we worked very productively on these two foci. Our relationship during this period was predominantly an ideal object one. She had realistic optimism that I could help her and we collaborated effectively—central ego-ideal object interactions.

In the fifth session, Rita confided a secret to me that she had never told anyone before. She had been sexually promiscuous for much of her adult life, felt humiliated by this "immoral, out of control" activity, and feared that she might continue to do it. As the session ended, she expressed relief and gratitude that she had been able to share that with me. It was therefore jarring when Rita came in the following week enraged with me. She felt I had led her to believe that it would be okay to talk about the secret. But, as she considered the session later, she questioned why she should have felt better telling me, and she said she had realized that I was really critical and condemning of what she had revealed. For my part, I had not consciously felt any of those responses and did not feel that I had given more than minimal encouragement for her to discuss her secret, if she wanted. Furthermore, she began attacking herself for having been so foolish as to confide this to me. As she emotionally talked about all of this, I kept silent about my own reactions.

The ideal object interactions of the first four sessions had given way to first an exciting object then rejecting object dynamic. Encouraged, I think, by the help that I had provided, she came to hope that I could accept her secret (which I could) and resolve its damaging impact on her sense of self (which I couldn't in such a short period of time). This was libidinal ego functioning. Initially feeling good about her revelation but then sensing the incomplete nature of what we could do she began doubting herself and me—I was an exciting but frustrating object.

She then came to see me as a rejecting object—a critical judge who viewed her as being bad. Her attacks on me were the attacks of her antilibidinal ego on the rejecting object and her attacks on herself were antilibidinal ego attacks on her libidinal ego for trying to deeply relate to me.

Fortunately, the central ego functioning that had been so helpful in the beginning of therapy helped her to stick with the pain of this encounter and to process it with me. We looked at how her relationships with men had been a series of primarily exciting object relationships. Each promiscuous relationship had not been simply a sexual fling but had been an effort to connect more deeply and positively with a man. The relationships were stormy, with her being wildly happy at times but more often painfully yearning for more. Eventually, most of the men in her life left her and she was furious with them and herself for having been so trusting. Her view then was that they were simply rejecting objects. Clearly, this dynamic pattern was repeated with me and we were able to explore it for a few sessions. Rita had never before identified this pattern and the fact that she *experienced* it with me was a powerful event. We also investigated why it was that she delayed entering therapy until she had such little time left (she had been in the area for over three years). The very brevity of the therapy evoked more exciting object experience. I recommended to her that she begin open-ended treatment at her new location. She called two months later to tell me that she had.

I think this example illustrates a dynamic that is quite frequent in both brief and long-term treatment. The patient and therapist have a particularly good, close session followed by one in which the patient is angry and attacking toward either herself, the therapist, or both. Fairbairn's intrapsychic system is particularly helpful in understanding this clinical phenomenon. It helps us understand the complex and dynamic interplay between libidinal (longing) relationships and antilibidinal (rejecting) ones.

THE REGRESSED LIBIDINAL EGO

Guntrip (1961, 1969) further elaborated on Fairbairn's intrapsychic system and theorized that there existed an even deeper layer of personality that was a split-off part of the libidinal ego. He called this the regressed libidinal ego. It is the only part of the self not connected to an internal object. Just as a schizoid person finds the world of external object relations too threatening and withdraws from human interaction, so too does the regressed ego find the inner world too threatening and withdraws from internal objects.

There are two aspects to the regressed ego: it functions as both a tomb and a womb. Through this retreat the person can have a sizable portion of his personality inaccessible to him for relating and for living. In that sense the regressed ego is a tomb. "It is the true source of all passive and regressive phenomena, exhaustion and fatigue, compulsive sleep, agoraphobic anxieties and the claustrophobias which are a reaction from them, phantasies of a return to the womb and retirement and escapist phantasies and longings in real life" (Guntrip 1961, pp. 432–433).

However, there is another side to the regressed ego. It is a retreat to a womblike state of isolation and safety wherein regrowth is possible. Guntrip (1961) states, "Whereas all the other parts of the psyche tend to the rigidities characteristic of defensive structures, the regressed libidinal ego retains the primary capacity for spontaneous and vigorous growth once it has been freed from fears. There lies the ultimate hope of psychotherapy" (p. 433). In this sense Guntrip saw the regressed ego as similar to Winnicott's (1960) concept of the true self.

Guntrip (1969) states that for psychotherapy to produce "radical" change—personality change—it needed to address all of the levels of intrapsychic structure:

1. Support for the patient's ego functioning of everyday life (the central ego) while the deeper issues are being dealt with.
2. Analysis of the internal world of bad object relations (the antilibidinal ego-rejecting object and libidinal ego-exciting object dyads) and uncovering of the regressed ego.

3. A "safe symbolic womb" for the regressed ego as the patient struggles to reintegrate his psyche and to slowly move toward growth.

In brief therapy it is usually not possible to reach the level of the regressed ego, and patient and therapist must accept less "radical" change. In Rita's case, described above, I believe that her secret was a regressed ego phenomenon. She felt safe enough (a "safe symbolic womb") with me to bring it into the object world. She did then become afraid that she had gone too far, that she could not trust me with it and that I was attacking this very private part of her. While our work on this regressed libidinal ego material and on her subsequent experience of me (as an exciting and rejecting object) was very meaningful, we did not have the time to actually work it through. We can hope she did so with her subsequent therapist. The following is a more detailed example of regressed ego phenomena from a long-term case.

Clinical Example: Donald

When Donald began therapy he described feeling hopeless about romantic relationships. This narcissistic 27-year-old lawyer would often choose unattainable women for love objects and then feel rejected by them. Less frequently, he would find a woman who was interested in him but as soon as he felt secure in the relationship he would begin to feel dissatisfied with her. These two patterns kept him from having an enduring relationship with a woman. I will describe a dream he had in the second year of a three-year therapy, but first I must describe one piece of background information. As a child he was prone to shame. When he felt embarrassed at or near his home he literally retreated into a closet. He would stay there until his shame had subsided and then he would come out and resume his interactions. This closet was the external equivalent of his regressed ego. He reported several dreams in therapy about closets and he was always alone in them—until this dream:

"I'm in the closet again but different than it's ever been before. Susan's in it, too! The closet's not peaceful this time. Somebody's coming to attack us, I don't know who. We're trying to clear off shelves—there are shelves in the closet—so we can move. You know, so we can maneuver when they attack us. But she's getting in the way! She's not helping at all and I'm thinking, Christ Jesus, we're going to die! All because of her. I'm furious at her and I'm scared shitless. It wakes me up."

At the time Donald had this dream, he had been dating Susan for four months. He was feeling secure and accepted by her and was at his characteristic point of thinking that she wasn't good enough for him. However, he was resisting this urge to break up with her. His dream represented his beginning to let his regressed ego reconnect with the object world (internal and external). However, he was terrified about this intrusion into his "womb" and feared he might not survive (feared his regressed ego or true self would not survive). He did persist in the relationship with Susan and seemed to be able to be more connected with parts of himself and with other people as well. He and Susan eventually married.

The dream also represented his struggle with closeness with me. We had gone through a progression (as with his girlfriends) in which he had initially idealized me and then been disappointed. However, he had come to sense that I was *good enough* to continue with and *safe enough* to bring in deeper, more private material.

While regressed libidinal ego material does not frequently emerge directly in brief therapy, it sometimes does, as in Rita's therapy. When it does, it often takes the form of revealing a secret action or fantasy and must be dealt with very carefully since it represents a communication from the part of the personality that is most split off and isolated from relatedness. Even when it does not surface, it is important for the brief therapist to be aware of the presence of the regressed libidinal ego as a part of the personality. First, attention to this concept can cause the therapist to be more sensitive to creating a safe space for the patient in therapy whether it is brief or long-term. Second, the concept of the regressed libidinal ego reminds the therapist not to assume that what we are working with in brief therapy (or in long-term therapy, for that matter) is the entire picture. We are always dealing with only a part of the complexity of a human personality.

THE CONCEPT OF SELF
IN OBJECT RELATIONS THEORY

Guntrip's concept of the regressed libidinal ego touches on the issue of self in the personality and in relationships. I noted that Guntrip sees his concept as similar to another conceptualization of self, Winnicott's (1960) true self. The term *self* has had a myriad of uses: a set of ideas in the mind, an experience, something one does, a structure in the mind, and so on (Mitchell 1993). Mitchell comments that even Kohut (1977), the father of self psychology, admits to having trouble clearly defining the concept of self.

> The self has been the central and most important concept in psychoanalytic theorizing of the past several decades. The most striking thing about the concept of self within current psychoanalytic thought is precisely the startling contrast between the centrality of concern with self and the enormous variability and lack of consensus about what the term even means. [Mitchell 1993, p. 99]

An important development of the past several years is that writers from both the object relations tradition (e.g., Ogden 1994, D. E. Scharff 1992, J. S. Scharff 1994) and the self psychology tradition (e.g., Stolorow and Atwood 1992) have been combining the emphasis on the concept of self with its relational, intersubjective context. While there are certainly many differences in these perspectives, this convergence is providing a richer look at the self-in-relationship.

The object relations perspective situates the self as having developed inextricably within a relational context. The basic units of the personality are self and object representational dyads. Even

Guntrip's (1961, 1969) regressed ego and Winnicott's (1960) true self developed within relationship and retreated from object relatedness to achieve safety. "Paradoxically, when we feel most private, most deeply 'into' ourselves, we are in some other sense most deeply connected with others through whom we have learned to become a self" (Mitchell 1993, p. 112).

I agree with Mitchell (1993) that object relations theory sees self as multiple and discontinuous, changing and developing, within particular and diverse relational contexts. For example, I have somewhat different experiences of myself when I am with my wife, when I am with a friend, when I was with Rita, when I was with Donald, when I am alone *with myself,* and so on. I also experience a continuity that makes up "Michael Stadter," but that continuity consists of my collection of experiences of these multiple self and object dyads.

A Tibetan Buddhist parable captures this conception of self and

> likens the individual to a sort of crowded town meeting. Once in a while somebody in the assembly gets up and makes a speech and carries the majority along with him on a certain course of action. Sometimes everybody has different ideas of what to do, and there are violent disputes. Sometimes members of the group leave or are forced out, die, or lose their voices. New ones come along, become bolder, and gain influence—even to the point of setting themselves up as dictators over the rest. . . . Put together, in whatever order they may happen to be in at any given moment they make up the "person." [Anderson 1990, p. 215]

My approach to brief therapy attempts to be attentive to the patient's experience of self, even when the therapist and patient are dealing with rather circumscribed symptoms. In Chapter 5, I describe an interpretive schema that acknowledges the way the patient deals with his own self.

THE RECEPTIVE CAPACITY

How does the therapist come to know herself, the patient, and their relationship more fully? How does the patient come to appreciate himself and his relationships (including the one with the therapist) at a deeper level? Bollas (1987) has written about the therapist's (and patient's) receptive capacity. What is needed is a state whereby the "noise" of directed, purposeful thought is suspended. In its place is a receptive, not active, state of mind "for the arrival of news from within the self" (p. 239). There is time and space allowed for mulling over the narrative of the patient before trying to organize it into a form so that interpretations and other interventions can be made. The receptive capacity is a state of *being* and *experiencing* that must precede *knowing*. "For here lies a paradox: this aspect of mental life activates when tranquillity is achieved. Reception of news from within (in the form of dream, phantasy, or inspired self observation for instance) arrives through evocation, a mental action characterized by a relaxed, not vigilant, state of mind" (Bollas 1987, p. 239). Such a receptive capacity will tune the therapist and patient into subtle transference and countertransference states and other experiences. In this way, truly new news is seen by the patient and therapist rather than news that has been around for some time.

Bollas is primarily writing about psychoanalysis and the need for analysts not to be too directed toward interpreting and being too diligent and vigilant. These activities can limit and even eliminate a receptive capacity. How much more difficult this issue is in brief therapy! And, yet, how important it is if brief therapy is to offer penetrating therapeutic help. The limits of time in brief therapy often evoke a hurried impatience on the part of both the therapist and patient that can lead to superficiality. Brief therapy is typically focused around one or a few issues. Determining this focus and then adhering to it is valuable, but it can prevent both patient and therapist from being receptive to "news from within the self." Even in brief therapy, a period of being and experiencing is crucial before knowing can begin.

4

Historical Review: A Sampling

The utility of living consists not in the length of days, but in the use of time; a man may have lived long, and yet lived but a little.

Michel de Montaigne (cited in Nuland 1994)

Montaigne's point about life can also be made about psychotherapy and the use of time. The history of the development of brief psychodynamic psychotherapy is rich and complex and starts with Freud himself. While it is beyond the scope of the present book to comprehensively survey these developments, I will, in the spirit of brief therapy, briefly sample some of the major models that are representative of brief dynamic psychotherapy. I will then offer some thoughts on what these models have in common. Crits-Christoph and Barber (1991) have organized the models of dynamic brief therapy according to first, second, and third generations and

I will follow this outline. I will then discuss two other recent models under the heading of Pragmatic Models and also consider the creative contributions of Balint and Winnicott. The crucial topic of selection will be taken up in a separate section at the end of the chapter.

FIRST GENERATION:
FREUD, ALEXANDER, AND FRENCH

Freud was the first dynamic psychotherapist and was the first dynamic brief psychotherapist. It is easy to forget that psychoanalysis began as a relatively short form of treatment. I looked at some of the reasons for the lengthening of psychoanalysis and psychotherapy in Chapter 2. There are five cases in *Studies on Hysteria* (Breuer and Freud 1895) of five- to ten-session duration. Some of Freud's most celebrated cases were very brief. The conductor Bruno Walter was treated for six sessions for a chronic cramp in his right arm. The composer Gustav Mahler was treated for obsessional neurosis and severe marital problems in a single four-hour session (Jones 1955). In his analysis of the Wolfman, Freud (1918) described the benefits of therapy being time-limited for some patients. Freud stated, "Treatments often reach a point where the patient's will to be cured is outweighed by his wish to be treated" (cited by Eisenstein 1980, p. 31). While brief treatment characterized Freud's early work, he later moved progressively toward analyses of longer and longer durations.

As Freud was moving toward longer analyses, several members of his group explored the possibilities of shortening the time involved in therapy. Ferenczi (1926) recommended an "active" therapy that involved directive techniques. Some of these active techniques were controversial and have been discredited (e.g., hugging and kissing patients). However, his use of here-and-now transference interpretations and encouragement of phobic patients to confront the object of their phobia have been useful contributions. Rank (1929) also advocated frequent use of here-and-now interpretations and wrote of the benefits of having a set termination date for therapy. Both Ferenczi and Rank emphasized present experience and did not feel it was necessary for the therapist to become deeply involved in analyzing and uncovering the past.

While Freud, Ferenczi, and Rank all contributed to the development of brief therapy, most students of the field would identify Alexander and French's (1946) *Psychoanalytic Therapy* as the first organized presentation of a brief dynamic therapy. In that book, Alexander and French directly questioned some of the tenets of psychoanalytic orthodoxy. One of the key notions that they developed is the corrective emotional experience, which emphasizes affective experience in the here and now over intellectual analysis.

In writing of the contributions of Alexander, Eisenstein (1980) provided an insightful, concise description of the corrective emotional experience:

> He [Alexander] felt that the difference between the old childhood relationship with the parents and the present relationship between patient and therapist is the central therapeutic element in therapy. The therapist's reaction to the patient's feelings in therapy is completely different from the reactions of the parents during the patient's childhood. . . . This difference allows the patient to understand the sources of his conflicts. What is more important, the patient becomes aware of the inappropriateness of his emotional experiences. The ego of the patient is afforded a second chance, so to speak; it is helped to adapt to changed situations and to adjust to new and entirely different reality conditions. [p. 29]

Alexander and French (1946) recommended that the therapist actively behave in a manner that disconfirms what the patient expects from past experience with parents. This makes the corrective emotional experience much more likely to occur and to occur more quickly. This became (and still is) a controversial technique. The power of such an experiential confrontation with what was expected from the past and what is experienced in the present is undeniable. However, the concept of the therapist consciously acting in a manner different from the past objects has struck many therapists as being manipulative and inauthentic.

In reviewing Eisenstein's (1980) excellent summary of Alexander and French's (1946) and Alexander's (1956) work, it is striking how many fundamental contributions they made to the practice of brief therapy. Consider the following:

1. Active analysis of the dependency needs of the patient. They recommended that the therapist decrease the frequency of sessions from time to time to confront the patient's dependency.
2. "Experimental temporary interruptions" to determine how the patient might deal with termination.
3. Emphasis on the present but appreciation of the importance of historical material.
4. Limitation of the patient's regression in the transference.
5. The importance of countertransference reactions in brief therapy.
6. Planning on the part of the therapist outside of therapy.
7. Direct encouragement of the patient to face conflicts.
8. Selection criteria that are based on ego strength rather than on the symptomatic presentation.

Note how many of these points continue to be relevant to the practice of brief therapy today.

SECOND GENERATION: MALAN, DAVANLOO, SIFNEOS, MANN

All four of these models developed at about the same time. Malan, Davanloo, and Sifneos share the characteristics of being vigorously interpretive, having strict patient selection criteria, utilizing classical psychoanalytic concepts, and demonstrating impressive outcomes through extensive research on their approaches.

Malan's Intensive Brief Psychotherapy

Malan was a member of Balint's group that investigated the idea of focal psychotherapy (Balint et al. 1972) at the Tavistock Clinic in London, and he published two books on this model of brief psychotherapy (1963, 1976). The 1976 book, *The Frontier of Brief Psycho-*

therapy, is a classic that provides a penetrating look at brief dynamic therapy, psychotherapy technique in general, specific cases (including some failures), and research on psychotherapy outcome. Balint and Malan were a very synergistic team. Balint provided the intuitively brilliant approach to brief encounters with patients and Malan contributed the precise and systematic study and elaboration of the model permitting specific elements to be identified (Gustafson 1981). Some of Balint's contributions to brief therapy will be discussed later in this chapter.

This model emphasizes careful patient selection, precise development and execution of a therapeutic focus and plan, and the primacy of interpretation as the agent of therapeutic change. Trial interpretations are an important part of the assessment process. The presence of a suitable focus, high patient motivation, and curiosity about his inner world are seen as especially desirable. The focus usually is a rather traditional psychoanalytic theme and although it guides the therapist it is not explicitly discussed with the patient as the focus. Examples of focus include guilt over aggressive feelings toward parents, fear of oedipal triumph, passivity in response to fear of aggressive or sexual impulses being deregulated, and defenses against loneliness and depression.

The therapist's aim is to work through a particular limited conflict (or a few conflicts, at most). It is expected that successful work on this particular conflict can begin a therapeutic process that can have a positive, cascading effect on other problem areas not directly addressed. I view this point as indicating that the patient not only learns to change in a particular focal area but also learns a *process* of change that he internalizes and then applies to other areas of his life (consciously or unconsciously). In any event, the therapist's goal is a formidable one: "The aim is really to *resolve* either the patient's central problem or at least an important aspect of his psychopathology" (Malan 1976, p. 248). This therapy is, indeed, intensive: "The aim of every moment of every session is to put the patient in touch with as much of his true feelings as he can bear" (Malan 1979, p. 74).

Drawing on earlier work by Menninger, Malan developed an interpretive schema that helps to guide the therapist in interpreting the focal issues to the patient within the time constraints of brief treatment. It involves linking the parts of two thematic triangles that I discuss in detail in Chapter 5. Davanloo (1980), who also uses the schema, has labeled the two triangles the triangle of conflict and the triangle of person. The triangle of conflict looks at the connections among impulse, anxiety, and defense. The triangle of person centers interpretation on the interpersonal patterns the patient has with the therapist, important past objects (especially parents), and significant present relationships. Groves (1992) has noted that the therapists in Malan's studies tended to emphasize themes of dependency and depression and focused more on the repetitive object relations patterns than on the impulses. Malan found that the most powerful type of interpretation involved linking the transference with the relationship with the patient's parents (see Chapter 7).

Malan recommended early setting of a termination date rather than a specific number of sessions. However, he did suggest twenty sessions as a reasonable brief contract with an experienced therapist and thirty for therapy conducted by a therapist-in-training. His approach to termination is flexible and he found that effective dealing with issues of loss and grief (including loss of the therapist) was associated with successful outcomes.

Davanloo's Intensive Short-Term Dynamic Psychotherapy

Davanloo (1978, 1980, 1991) developed his approach at McGill University in Montreal and uncompromisingly remains faithful to the basic concepts of drive-oriented psychoanalytic psychology. Like Malan's approach it is characterized by a careful selection process, by a highly interpretive approach, and by extensive research study of its effectiveness. However, a broader range of patients are accepted for Davanloo's approach and his interpretive technique is much more forceful and persistent. (His own word for it is *relentless*.) It is the most vigorous and intense of the dynamic brief therapies. Critics have used terms such as *bullying* and *remorseless* (Hildebrand 1986) to describe his approach. Davanloo's response to such criticism is that (1) his assessment procedure screens out patients who do not have the ego strength to tolerate his model; (2) the research indicates the high degree of success with the patients selected; and (3) most of his patients experience the therapy as supportive despite the intense confrontations, challenges, and interpretations. His supporters have also responded that it is crueler to have a patient suffer for years in long-term treatment than it is to relentlessly confront resistances in intensive short-term dynamic therapy. Without question, this approach provides most patients with an affectively powerful experience.

The evaluation process can take up to six hours and is typically performed in a single day. A key feature of the assessment is the use of trial interpretations to see if the patient can tolerate and use them. As Davanloo (1980) put it, "This technique of initial interview really consists of *trial therapy*, and is the only reliable method of finding out whether the patient is likely to respond" (p. 47). The focus is determined in the assessment process, is directly presented to the patient, and is persistently pursued. Resistances to the examination of the focus are actively noted and interpreted. Davanloo's focus often involves looking at the patient's passivity, avoidance of intimacy, repressed rage, and how she keeps herself "crippled" (a term he seems to use with many patients). The therapist interprets transference early and frequently, not only to keep the therapy moving expeditiously, but also to prevent the formation of powerful dependent transferences. Like Malan, Davanloo's interpretive approach is organized around the triangles of conflict and person.

The goal of the therapy is the "unlocking of the unconscious" of the patient. The therapist persistently interprets and confronts the patient's resistances which

> produces an intrapsychic crisis by exposing the self-destructiveness of long-standing ego syntonic character patterns. This crisis produces intense affects, which tap into a reservoir of unconscious thoughts, memories, and feelings and activate the unconscious alliance. This dynamic flow speeds and compresses the psychoanalytic process [Laikin et al. 1991, p. 83]

The number of sessions that the patient receives is determined by the patient's degree of pathology and progress. One to ten sessions is usually adequate for highly motivated patients with a single, circumscribed oedipal focus. For patients with moderate resistance and complicated oedipal issues, ten to twenty sessions is the norm.

Highly resistant patients with diffuse character pathology and neuroses require twenty to thirty sessions. Thirty to forty sessions are needed for patients with massive resistances who have significant ego syntonic character pathology. Note the emphasis that Davanloo has placed on psychodynamic diagnosis.

Davanloo has described termination as being a rather simple and straightforward process that, in most cases, requires only a session or two. In some of the more complicated cases termination may take from three to five sessions. Perhaps even more than Malan, Davanloo's approach is very ambitious. The therapist aims for "the total resolution of the patient's core neurosis. . . . Everything is experienced so intensely that the neurosis is dissolved" (Davanloo 1980, p. 70). Clearly, Davanloo is one of the most optimistic of the brief therapy developers (Horowitz et al. 1984) and he and his colleagues have reported significant character change even in patients with severe character pathology.

Sifneos' Short-Term Anxiety-Provoking Psychotherapy

The management of anxiety is the central theme in Sifneos's approach to brief therapy (1972, 1987), which he developed at Beth Israel Hospital in Boston. The underlying theory is psychoanalytic and drive-oriented. Sifneos has written that the level of anxiety in therapy is crucial in fostering change. With some patients therapy needs to reduce anxiety, while for other patients it is therapeutic to increase anxiety. He has developed two types of therapy for these two groups of patients: anxiety-suppressing therapy and anxiety-provoking therapy. It is his anxiety-provoking model that has been most innovative and it is this model that is summarized here.

This is the most selective of all the brief dynamic therapy models with the criteria including only 2 to 10 percent of the patients in an average clinic (Flegenheimer 1982). Only patients with oedipal-level conflicts or patients who are dealing with uncomplicated grief reactions and who have good ego strength and who can rapidly develop a therapeutic alliance are accepted for treatment. Trial interpretations are used to assess the patient's ability to do psychodynamic work. I will discuss this selection paradigm in detail as an example of the exclusive school of patient selection later in this chapter.

Neither number of sessions nor termination date is set at the beginning of therapy but most cases are in the seven- to twenty-session range. A focus that deals with oedipal dynamics is explicitly agreed upon between therapist and patient and specific goals are also discussed and set. Examples of focus would be repeated triangular relationship problems or unassertiveness due to fear of oedipal victory and guilt over "selfishness." Sifneos' technique is characterized by active and early interpretation of transference (including positive transference feelings) and resistance. The therapist persistently confronts the patient on the focal oedipal material but avoids pregenital issues (e.g., narcissism, dependency). The stance of the therapist is one of therapist-teacher but the reeducation provided is more effective than simple intellectual learning because it is within the affectively (and experientially) charged atmosphere of the therapeutic encounter.

The goal of therapy is resolution of intrapsychic conflict through the patient's facing in therapy material that has been avoided in the past. When clear evidence of improvement has occurred, a termination date is set. Signs of progress may include reduction in symptoms, greater patient ease in the sessions, changes in the area of focus, and some generalization of progress to other areas. Unlike Mann's approach, separation and loss issues are not emphasized at termination but instead the therapist focuses on what the patient has been able to accomplish.

Mann's Time-Limited Psychotherapy

No other brief dynamic model places as much emphasis on how profoundly time affects human experience and psychopathology. This approach was developed by Mann at Boston University (Mann 1973, 1991, Mann and Goldman 1994) and it centers around the experience of time, negative self-image, and separation/loss issues. People experience time in two ways: categorical and existential. Categorical time is reality-based, has beginnings and endings, and can be measured by clocks, calendars, and the aging process. This is the time experience of the adult world. Existential time is simply experienced or "lived in"; it is the time of early childhood—timeless, time as endless, without limits. "Our current life consists of memories of things past and expectations of the future; it is a fusion of eternal *child time* and finite *adult time*. Thus, we are caught in a neverending conflict between the reality of death and our denial of it, our expectation of immortality" (Mann and Goldman 1994, pp. 2–3).

Long-term dynamic psychotherapy and time-limited therapy evoke predominantly different types of time. In long-term work, the open-endedness of treatment and the therapist's abstinence promote existential or child time. Regression and transference are therefore facilitated. By contrast, time-limited brief therapy orients the patient toward categorical or adult time and tends to reduce regressive trends. "The more specific the duration of treatment is, the more rapidly is child time confronted with real time and the work to be done" (Mann 1991, p. 24). I will elaborate on the concept of time in brief therapy later in this chapter.

The deadline for Mann is invariably twelve sessions and is presented to the patient at the beginning of therapy. This follows the assessment process, which is usually accomplished within three sessions. During the assessment phase the central issue (focus of therapy) is determined and discussed with the patient. It is typically different from what the patient brought in as the presenting problem. The central issue has to do with the patient's self-image. The therapist tries to get a clear idea of what the patient's self-representations are as his narrative unfolds and repeatedly asks herself how was the patient experiencing himself as these events occurred? "The statement of the central issue in these terms directly links past, present, and future: that is, the patient's private time line and the affects that accompany memories, regressions, fantasies, developmental arrests, and spurts—all of which eventually emerge as the unspoken, painful self-image. It is this time-bound self-image that brings the patient to us for help" (Mann and Goldman 1994, pp. 23–24).

The concept of the patient's self is central and the goal of Mann's Time-Limited Psychotherapy is to help the patient to decrease his negative self-image. The technique is psychodynamic and interpretive but its goal is not primarily to make the unconscious conscious other than to clarify the meanings and extent of the patient's defect in self-esteem. It is the definition of the central issue and the setting of the end point of therapy at the start of treatment that provides the ingredients for change. No matter what specific self-image elements are defined in the particular patient's central issue, the therapist will also focus on the key concepts of time and separation. Mann (1991) believes this is essential since the patient's self-image is, to a great extent, formed by the separations and losses that are an integral part of the human condition.

As such, processing of termination of therapy and loss of the therapist is a crucial part of this approach. Kupers (1988) has described the entirety of Mann's approach as termination-phase psychotherapy. The ending is inflexible in the sense that the patient is not given sessions beyond the twelve nor is given the option of returning to the therapist at some future point. Ending is "unequivocal" (Mann and Goldman 1994). To do otherwise would imply that more time may be available and would undermine the patient's progress in dealing with adult time. No other model places such an emphasis (and demand on patient and therapist) on the finality of termination. I will later examine the pros and cons of this approach. My own opinion is that the benefits of patient return for future treatment with the therapist (serial brief therapy) outweigh the benefits of Mann's model but one cannot deny the power of his approach to termination.

THIRD GENERATION: HOROWITZ
AND COLLEAGUES, AND STRUPP AND BINDER

Horowitz and Colleagues's Short-Term Dynamic Therapy of Stress Response Syndromes

Horowitz and his colleagues at the Langley Porter Psychiatric Institute of the University of California (Horowitz 1986, 1991, Horowitz et al. 1984) have developed an eclectic system of brief therapy that begins with a twelve-session model not unlike Mann's Time-Limited Psychotherapy. They add to it knowledge about acute stress reactions, a tailoring of their approach to different personality styles, and a paradigm of cognitive functioning and processing to create a very rich and multileveled model. Moreover, this model and its efficacy have been the subject of systematic research, referenced and briefly summarized in Horowitz (1991).

This approach is designed for patients who are struggling with an acutely stressful situation, such as a death of a loved one or a loss of a job. A major advantage of this model is that a focus is quite clearly and easily definable—the response to the stressful event and the working through of this response. Additionally, though, the acute subjective distress experienced by the patient in the situation intensifies other issues (self-esteem, relationships) and increases motivation. Therefore, someone going through such an acute incident and response might be in a particularly productive state to be able to make some personal, emotional changes—defenses may be "shaken up."

As a psychodynamic brief therapy, this approach views the particular form and intensity of the patient's stress response as being related to the patient's unique intrapsychic issues and makeup. While the model is oriented toward patients dealing with recent stressful events, Horowitz has recommended its use with other conditions as well. The therapist's activity is informed by three theories of psychological functioning (Horowitz 1988).

> *States of mind theory* examines how a stressful experience evokes psychological states different from those present before the event. States of feeling either overwhelmed by affect or numbed and deadened are common examples.
>
> *Person schemas theory* has to do with enduring but slowly changing views of self and of other, and with scripts for transactions between self and other" (Horowitz 1991, p. 169). In dealing with a stressful event, especially something traumatic, patients may not have a schema to help them adapt to the new reality and may need to develop new or modified schemas of self and other.
>
> *Control process theory* suggests that people use different types of controls to facilitate or inhibit conscious recognition or communication of conflicts between preexisting schemas and the new traumatic situation. . . . The therapist's choice

of technique depends on what type of controls the patient is using, is capable of, or is capable of learning" (Horowitz 1991, p. 170).

All three of these theories direct the therapist to individualize her approach to the unique modes of psychological functioning of the particular patient seated before her. This thinking underlies Horowitz and colleagues's (1984) efforts to modify technique depending on the particular personality style of the patient, and they describe brief therapy with four types: hysteric, compulsive, narcissistic, and borderline. The goals of the therapist are, minimally, to help the patient return to his previous level of functioning. More ambitiously, the therapist attempts to help the patient work through and modify underlying psychological mechanisms—his "inner model" (e.g., change in schemas and in control processes). An outline of how the twelve-session model typically unfolds is presented in Table 4–1. Note that this outline explicitly gives attention to relationship issues. However, like most brief therapy models the emphasis in the writing is on technique (or in Horowitz's work, emphasis is also placed on building a detailed conceptual framework). Also, the contributions of countertransference to the relationship do not receive much attention. Transference interpretations are employed but are primarily connected with the reaction to the stressor rather than with early parental experiences. During the termination phase of treatment, the therapist attends to this being another loss for the patient and helps him look at the meaning of this loss within the context of other material. Also, there is more flexibility than in Mann's approach concerning additional sessions or further contact with the therapist.

Strupp and Binder's Time-Limited Dynamic Psychotherapy

Of all the brief therapies surveyed in this chapter, Strupp and Binder's (Binder and Strupp 1991, Strupp 1993, Strupp and Binder 1984) places the most emphasis on the therapeutic relationship. While this is not the case in most brief therapy models it is not surprising in their approach since their theory is based on interpersonal theories of personality (e.g., Sullivan 1953). Additionally,

Table 4–1. Sample Twelve-Session Dynamic Therapy for Stress Disorders

Session	Relationship issues	Patient activity	Therapist activity
1	Initial positive feeling for helper	Patient tells story of event	Preliminary focus is discussed
2	Lull as sense of pressure is reduced	Event is related to previous life	Takes psychiatric history; gives patient realistic appraisal of syndrome
3	Patient testing therapist for various relationship possibilities	Patient adds associations to indicate expanded meaning of event	Focus is realigned; resistances to contemplating stress-related themes are interpreted
4	Therapeutic alliance deepened	Implications of event in the present are contemplated	Defenses and warded-off contents are interpreted, linking of latter to stress event and responses
5		Themes that have been avoided are worked on	Active confrontation with feared topics and reengagement in feared activities are encouraged
6		The future is contemplated	Time of termination is discussed
7–11	Transference reactions interpreted and linked to other configurations; acknowledgment of pending separation	The working through of central conflicts and issues of termination, as related to the life event and reactions to it, is continued	Central conflicts, termination, unfinished issues, and recommendations all are clarified and interpreted
12	Saying good-bye	Work to be continued on own and plans for the future are discussed	Real gains and summary of future work for patient to do on own are acknowledged

From Horowitz 1986. Used by permission of Jason Aronson Inc.

like Horowitz's, their approach is extensively influenced by insights from psychotherapy research. Strupp is one of the most internationally respected psychotherapy researchers of the past several decades. Developed at Vanderbilt University in Nashville, the model "stresses the careful monitoring, exploration, and use of the therapeutic relationship as a technical strategy in its own right, merging so-called relationship factors with technique" (Strupp 1993, p. 432). With its research background, this approach is characterized by the clear definition of technique and the measurable, observable nature of its goals for patient change.

The selection process is not as elaborate as Davanloo's or Malan's. My impression from the literature is that assessment in their model can be generally accomplished in a single session of about 90 minutes. Following the selection process, the patient's presenting problem is conceptualized in interpersonal terms and a focus is set, the Cyclical Maladaptive Pattern (CMP). This focus is a recurring pattern of interpersonal interactions that interfere with relationships and affect the patient's self-image as well. Examples of the focus include being victimized, being overly passive/dependent, being critical in relationships, and remaining emotionally distant in relationships. The goal of Time-Limited Dynamic Psychotherapy is to improve interpersonal functioning. However, Strupp and Binder have found that extensive change also occurs in other areas (symptoms, self-esteem). Once the CMP has been selected, a termination date is set and therapy duration is commonly about twenty-five sessions.

This approach stresses the individuality of each patient. Strupp and Binder found that no single, particular therapeutic intervention consistently produces the most improvement. However, the model does emphasize the analysis of transference and countertransference, which are conceptualized in interpersonal terms. The therapist's attention to her own countertransference is seen as a powerful and productive part of the therapist's work. They (Binder and Strupp 1991) outlined the therapeutic process as having four central elements. First, the therapist tries to create an atmosphere of safety to permit the emergence of the patient's problematic interaction patterns. Second, the patterns emerge within the limits of the therapeutic relationship and are experienced by both the patient and the therapist. Third, the therapist draws the patient's attention toward the patterns as they are occurring. Fourth, the patient is invited to examine and explore the underlying beliefs involved in the maladaptive interpersonal patterns. In each session the therapist tries to designate themes that are related to the CMP and to especially highlight their manifestations within the therapeutic relationship.

An additional contribution of their model is its attention to the role in therapy of both the patient's and therapist's hostility. In summarizing research in this area, Strupp (1993) observed that patients who entered treatment with attitudes of "negativism, hostility, and resistance" generally did not do as well in therapy. Moreover, many instances of unconscious acting out on the part of the therapist were noted with such patients. Strupp and Binder (1984) have recommended early confrontation of negative transference reactions and that the therapist give much attention herself (including consulting with colleagues or supervisors) to managing and containing negative countertransferences.

Strupp and Binder's model shares many elements with my own approach and I will frequently refer to additional aspects of their work throughout this book. Readers interested in further exploration of brief therapy models that, like Strupp and Binder's, direct attention to the therapeutic relationship are referred to the models of Gustafson (1986) and Luborsky (Luborsky 1984, Luborsky and Crits-Christoph 1990, Luborsky and Mark 1991).

PRAGMATIC MODELS: BLOOM, AND BUDMAN AND GURMAN

Bloom's Focused Single-Session Therapy

Bloom's (1981, 1992) jumping-off point for a model of single-session therapy is a very pragmatic one: many patients presenting in outpatient clinics come for only one session. Could therapy be organized in such a way as to provide some meaningful interventions in one session? He has noted that the idea of single-session therapy may seem "outrageous." However, many other models recommend that each session be conceptualized as a micro-therapy in and of itself and that there is an extensive anecdotal literature (dating back to Freud) that reports successful single-session therapies. Working at the University of Colorado in Boulder, Bloom has described his therapy as being psychodynamic in that he has two guiding principles. The model tries, first, to help patients become aware of something that was previously unconscious, and, second, to initiate a process that promotes psychological health after termination.

The single session is two hours in duration and identifying a focus is of crucial importance. He does not seem to find history-taking to be productive in the session. Examples of Bloom's focus are a patient coming to see that his marital dissatisfaction was related to his low self-esteem or a graduate student frustrated with her lack of academic progress realizing that this experience has evoked anger toward her parents for their lack of support. The therapist also respects the simple power of the patient having a session to share his painful experience with a concerned listener.

Some additional guidelines in Bloom's (1992) single session approach are presented below:

1. *Do not be overambitious*. The therapist attempts to focus on only one or two issues and to keep them simple. Bloom describes his own personal guideline as trying to make comments in ten words or less.
2. *Be prudently active* especially in the later part of the interview.
3. *Explore, then present interpretations tentatively.*
4. *Encourage the expression of affect*. Primarily, the therapist does this through the explicit recognition of the patient's affective states.
5. *Keep track of time.*
6. *Keep factual questions to a minimum.*
7. *Do not be overly concerned about the precipitating event.*
8. *Avoid detours*. The therapist is dedicated to maintaining the focus.
9. *Do not overestimate a patient's self-awareness.*
10. *Use the interview to start a problem-solving process.*
11. *Do not underestimate patients' strengths.*

12. *Help mobilize social supports.*
13. *Educate when patients appear to lack information.* Lectures are not viewed as being useful but short explanations (e.g., the role of stress in psychological functioning) can be quite helpful.
14. *Build in a follow-up plan.* If the patient doesn't call, the therapist does. The patient is encouraged to return for subsequent sessions, as needed. Consider how similar this approach is to that of a primary care physician.

The guiding principle of pragmatic models such as Bloom's and the following one (Budman and Gurman's) is a practical emphasis on what works within the sessions and a lack of emphasis on a theoretical conceptualization of the patient. I will further discuss single-session therapy in the chapter on very brief therapy. I appreciate the acute scarcity of time in Bloom's approach but I do question the lack of attention to factual and subjective historical information and I especially question his lack of concern with the precipitating event. In my experience this often provides a key to the meaning of the patient's problem. People are frequently unhappy and in pain yet they seek out treatment only at particular times. Why now? is a crucially important question.

Budman and Gurman's I-D-E Therapy

Perhaps the two words that best characterize Budman and Gurman's (1988, 1992) model are *flexibility* and *eclecticism*. Their model was developed through their work in health maintenance organizations (notably the Harvard Community Health Plan). "We are convinced, however, that most therapists who do brief therapy (whom, we believe, are *most* therapists) are rarely theoretical or technical purists. Rather, they are pragmatic and eclectic, if not integrative, in method and technique" (Budman and Gurman 1988, p. ix). They have developed a paradigm that they acknowledge utilizes elements of many other brief therapies: "Thus, in a certain sense, the model of therapy presented here is not particularly unique, but reflects what we see as the essential and common elements in effective brief therapy-as-most-often-practiced. It is a distillation of what we believe to be the central features of any effective brief therapy, even those aspects of the treatment that may not be completely articulated by the therapist" (Budman and Gurman 1988, p. ix). While their approach does address underlying psychodynamic issues, it is not strongly interpretive. With their flexibility in technique, variable number of sessions, variable duration of sessions, and ease of patient return for additional therapy after termination, Budman and Gurman's brief therapy is most different from Mann's.

The question of selection (see below) is not a major concern in this model since the approach is individualized to the particular patient. Unlike Bloom's model, this one emphasizes the question of why the patient comes into treatment at this particular point in time. Why now? Focus, too, is a major concern, and Budman and Gurman have identified five issues as the most common foci in their brief therapy: loss, developmental dysynchronies (the patient feeling out of step with expected life milestones), specific symptoms, interpersonal problems, and personality disorders. As an indication of the centrality of these foci to their approach, these topics comprise seven of twelve chapters in their 1988 book. (I will discuss and define these foci in Chapter 6.) The therapist and patient then examine the chosen focus from the standpoint of three dimensions: the *interpersonal* component of the patient's distress, the stage of *development* in his life, and the *existential* meaning of his symptoms and situation. This is called the I-D-E approach (see Chapter 6).

Duration is quite variable, with many therapies appearing to be within the twenty- to forty-session range. Techniques of many different schools of psychotherapy are employed. Budman and Gurman have highlighted the use of hypnosis and work with other family members in individual therapy. They also seem to frequently use cognitive restructuring and reframing techniques. The termination phase of therapy is similarly flexible and the patient is encouraged to return to therapy in the future if needed. They have written that the "finality" of termination is actually a myth and research backs them up (see Chapter 9): many patients return for therapy at different points in their lives for further work. They have placed great emphasis on the patient's capacity to grow and change outside of therapy.

In their more recent writing, Budman and Gurman (1992) have described elaborations of their model around issues of patient readiness for therapy, the "reauthoring" of the patient's narrative, and the use of control mastery theory (how patients use therapy to confirm or disconfirm their expectations).

THE BRIEF, CREATIVE STYLES OF BALINT AND WINNICOTT

It would be impossible to adequately discuss brief therapy and object relations concepts without acknowledging the contributions of Balint and Winnicott. Two master clinicians and British object relations theorists, they are well known for their long-term work but have also contributed insightfully to brief therapy. I use the word *style* in the heading both to denote their characteristic *manner* and also their *flair* for clinical brilliance.

Balint

I want to highlight three major contributions Balint made to the field of brief therapy. First, as already indicated, Balint started the Tavistock investigation into brief focal psychotherapy (Balint et al. 1972). Malan's intensive brief psychotherapy model came out of that work.

Second, he trained primary care physicians in brief psychotherapy or counseling techniques (Balint 1957). The doctor–patient interaction was conceptualized as part of an *interpersonal relationship*. While the interactions might be very brief, the doctor–patient relationship might continue over a long period of time. In these interactions, there is a dynamic of the patient's making an offer (symptoms) and the physician's making a counteroffer (treatment). He trained physicians to not just make the counteroffer of traditional physical medicine (medication or other prescriptive measures) but also to engage the patient in discussion of her experience of her symptoms to deepen both patient's and doctor's understanding of the illness. While this discussion could be extended, it usually was quite short, 5 to 15 minutes. In fact, Balint (Balint and Norell 1973) intensively studied interactions of 6 minutes in length, which was the average amount of time that a physician spent with patients (talk about brief therapy!).

The "flash" method came out of this investigation. A therapeutic opportunity is created by the patient's distress and the physician's invitation to talk about it and about herself. The intensity created by this quick interaction can make a comment by the physician very effective and powerful. What the doctor tries to do in the flash method is to provide an insight, to provide something new to the patient, during this very brief encounter.

Third, Balint emphasized the unique interpersonal elements of human experience in his descriptions of his brief therapy cases. As Stewart (1993b) put it, Balint's therapy was characterized by "the application of his own person to the individuality of the patient." Concerning brief therapy, "Balint provided the generative idea that patients could be offered new kinds of relationships" (Gustafson 1981, p. 120). Balint (Balint et al. 1972) clearly viewed change occurring in therapy as coming not simply from interpretation but also from the new relationship the patient experienced with the therapist. This is similar to the idea of "new endings for old experience" described in the next chapter.

Winnicott

Winnicott's work is also characterized by a highly developed respect for the uniqueness of the individual patient. As a child and adult analyst with a background in pediatrics, he focused on the conditions necessary for the emergence of a sound sense of self. In therapy he would concentrate on the impediments to normal development and on the unique power and vitality of the patient. Interestingly, some of his most moving cases are brief ones. He saw "The Piggle," a young girl who was one of his most famous cases, for only fourteen sessions (Winnicott 1977).

In his role as a consultant with the British National Health Service, he provided thousands of consultations for general practitioners and pediatricians. "In terms of brevity, he could apparently remove important blocks to development in only one session. *Therapeutic Consultations in Child Psychiatry* (1971) provides examples where one, two, or three sessions are sufficient to help the individual push through a block and resume normal development" (Groves 1992, p. 53).

Two aspects of Winnicott's brief therapy bear mention. First, even within the constraints of very brief interventions, he was a master at creating psychological space for the patient to use to examine himself. When I read his brief therapy descriptions, I am struck by how unhurried they seem. Winnicott's writing frequently involves paradoxes and this is one of them: how for a *limited time* (Mann's categorical time) the therapist and patient can create a *timeless, unbounded space* (Mann's existential time) within which to "play" and explore. His concept of play is an important one and it refers to the patient and therapist experiencing themselves and each other in a mode of openness and discovery, looking at the experience from varying perspectives and not having to "do" something about it. Play occurs when patient and therapist are exercising their receptive capacities (see the previous chapter). Winnicott's work is a reminder to us that time-limited and time-sensitive do not have to mean rushed and pressured.

Second, if the therapy is to be infrequent, he argued for it to be provided "on demand," when the patient needs it and requests it (Winnicott 1971). The therapy can then capitalize on the readiness and timely motivation of the patient.

COMMONALITIES AMONG BRIEF PSYCHODYNAMIC THERAPY MODELS

Obviously, there are many differences among the various psychodynamic models of brief therapy. The following are elements that they have in common.

Focus

Brief therapy is brief. To be able to effectively use the limited time available in brief therapy, the therapist and patient cannot follow every topic in a leisurely, exploratory manner. To do so would permit everything to be touched upon but nothing to be dealt with adequately. Developing a focus or foci is the defining characteristic that distinguishes brief therapy from long-term work. All models of brief therapy, psychodynamic and others, require that the work center on particular issues. The focus could be a prominent symptom, a selected intrapsychic conflict, a dysfunctional interpersonal pattern, or other theme. When the focus is exclusively symptomatic the therapy tends to be supportive rather than expressive.

The focus may be conceptualized differently by different dynamic therapists but an attempt is made to center on some of the patient's underlying dynamics. For example, Sifneos focuses on neurotic-level oedipal conflicts, Davanloo's focus often emphasizes split-off rage and the patient's attempts to avoid hostility and aggression, Malan frequently highlights dependency issues, Strupp and Binder emphasize interpersonal patterns and dynamics, Mann often centers on separation-individuation issues and always has the metafocus of time, and Budman and Gurman focus on five issues ranging from loss to personality disorder.

More extensive discussions on focus setting in brief therapy are presented in Chapters 5 and 6.

Unique Meaning of Time in Brief Therapy

The brevity of brief therapy causes time to be experienced in a distinctive way. The particular manner is different for different patients. Similarly, brief therapy writers have described the differing impact on the experience of the therapy—some positive, some negative.

As a starting point for this discussion, I would suggest that the ten sessions in a ten-session contract are going to be experienced very differently than the first ten sessions of an open-ended treatment. Consider the following example.

> When I first saw Jackie, a 35-year-old director of human resources, I recommended that we meet weekly in open-ended psychotherapy. She wanted help in dealing with the end of her second marriage and with what she felt was a

series of failed relationships with men. She said she was wary of getting stuck in therapy (as she had in other relationships with men) and wanted to commit herself to only ten sessions. This seemed to give her a greater sense of control over the therapy and helped her to deal with her fear of becoming too dependent on me. Viewing the holding environment as being only ten sessions helped her to feel safer and less confined, and actually freed her to *more intensively* deal with her difficult issues concerning intimate relationships and self-esteem. In the ninth session she said that she was pleased with the progress we had made and wanted to "reenlist" for another ten sessions. She did this once again in the nineteenth session. After the thirtieth session, we met in weekly, time-unlimited therapy and I eventually saw her for four years. For Jackie as for many patients (see Alan in Chapter 5), viewing therapy as a short-term experience reduced her anxiety and permitted her to feel safer as she began therapy. Of course, the brevity of brief therapy can also cause some patients to be more defensive and resist "really getting into it" because it will end fairly soon and the loss would be more painful.

Binder (1977) has eloquently described the positive impact that the scarcity of time can have on therapy when both patient and therapist are aware of the brevity of the treatment.

This awareness seems to impel the participants to greater efforts in striving toward their goals, and imbues their relationship with a high emotional intensity, which could be unbearable in longer term treatment. . . . The high emotional pitch of these relationships also heightens the therapeutic influence of interpretations that lack extensive genetic connections and the opportunity for working through. The intense affective pitch of the relationship may produce a combination of unusual therapist empathic acuity, access to more intense and fluid affect states in the patient, and the rapid internalization of therapist as good object leading to a new and enduring self-object configuration. [p. 240]

No author has written more compellingly about the unique meaning of time in brief therapy than Mann (1973). He has emphasized that the very experience of brief therapy revives difficult and complex feelings about time, loss, and separation in both patient and therapist. These powerful evocations can be key elements in both therapeutic change and resistance to it.

Engelman and his colleagues (1992) have thoughtfully examined the nature of time when time-limited therapy shifts to long-term treatment and how brief therapy can constrict clinical material. They described different types of time. *Sequential time* involves the past, present, and future and is measured by clocks and calendars. This is similar to Mann's categorical time and it is unidirectional. Two other types of time transform sequential time. *Nonlinear time* condenses and expands sequential time through the use of symbolization. It is a way that the past enters the present (through, for example, transference) and the present enters the past (through, for example, the changing quality of remembered experience). Nonlinear time is multidirectional.

Engelman and colleagues (1992) define *epochal time* as being made up of events or epochs that have a dramatic effect upon the individual or even upon an entire culture. Epochal time transforms and transcends the experience of sequential time—the past and the future are changed by epochal time. A historical example would be the birth of Christ, which had such an enormous impact on Western civilization that it is the marker for the passage of years (B.C. and A.D.). They gave the following examples of epochal time in the lives of individuals: separation-individuation, the birth of siblings, oedipal events, and loss. Traumatic events might be examples of the transformation of sequential time into epochal time. For instance, a patient told me of "a tear (a rip) in time" when his mother was shot to death in front of him at age 12. He described having one life prior to that time and one life after and these two lives seemed to be separate and distinct.

Engelman and colleagues (1992) observe, "While time-limited therapy enhances conformity to sequential time, it short-circuits the ability to experience and explore other dimensions of clinical experience that are governed by these (nonlinear and epochal) aspects of time" (p. 124). They state that the transference can rarely be in the forefront of time-limited therapeutic work because it provides insufficient access to epochal and nonlinear time. They give some examples of how transference exploration became more possible when therapy shifted to long-term.

Clearly, the unique quality of time in brief therapy can both facilitate and impede the therapeutic process. I would list the following as some of the ways that the experience of time in brief therapy frequently affects the participants. Some of these issues are further examined in the following chapters.

Positive Impact

1. Motivated by time urgency the patient may bring difficult issues in more rapidly and may work on them in a more persistent manner.
2. The therapy may have a more intense affective tone.
3. There is less opportunity for therapist and patient to collude in the denial that the time in therapy and in life is, in fact, limited (a major point of Mann's).
4. As with Jackie, brief therapy may feel safer and less likely to intrude on the patient's personal space or evoke intense dependency needs that cannot be met.
5. Less malignant regression (Balint 1968) may arise. The structure of the therapist maintaining the focus and reminders of the impending termination frustrate the wish to return to infantile dependency states. This frequently limits pathological regression and makes it possible to treat personality-disordered patients. For instance, in my experience, borderline patients often regress and act out less in brief therapy than in long-term work.

Negative Impact

1. Both the therapist and the patient may feel so pressured by the brevity of the treatment that they may focus monomaniacally on *the* identified problem and not allow sufficient

space for nonlinear thinking (e.g., receptive capacities). The therapy becomes too centered in sequential time.

2. The material may stay more connected to immediate problems and be superficial. The limited time and space of brief therapy may be experienced as an inadequate holding environment within which to take risks. Little work in nonlinear and epochal time may take place. Less regression in the service of therapy may occur. The transference may be more constrained or altered in other ways (e.g., an exciting object or rejecting object experience). The patient might not bring dreams into the treatment.

3. The therapist and/or patient may communicate a heightened impatience to each other, which constricts their receptive capacities.

4. The therapy may be predominantly cognitive and include little affective involvement (on the part of either the patient or the therapist).

As a final point in this section on time, I support Budman and Gurman's (1988) challenge to brief therapists to be more creative in their use of time. They noted Alexander and French's (1946) novel experiments in this regard and recommended that therapists consider changes in duration and frequency of sessions to enhance the treatment on a case by case basis.

Greater Therapist Activity

Typically, transcripts and recordings of brief therapy show a higher activity level on the part of the therapist than is usually the case in those of long-term therapists. Similarly, therapists I know who do both brief and long-term work indicate that they are more active in brief therapy than they are when they are conducting long-term treatment. This is certainly the case for me. It makes sense, of course, since the brief therapist does not have the luxury of extended time to allow issues to develop. So, she attempts through her activity to quicken the process. Greater therapist activity should not be construed as meaning that the therapist is inevitably more directive. The increased activity may take the form of more frequent interpretations, confrontations, empathic reflections, and clarifications rather than direction-giving.

Planning on the Part of the Therapist

Two factors—the focus and the time constrictions—require that, between sessions, the therapist put some organized thought into the progression of the brief therapy. The brief therapist needs to periodically examine the status of the focus—progress on it, how it may be changing over the course of treatment, what that may mean, its continued relevance, and so on. Also, he needs to be aware of where he and the patient are in the life span of this brief therapy contract—how much time is left and what may be realistic to try to accomplish. While competent long-term therapists periodically review their cases outside of sessions, as well, these two issues in brief therapy require especially careful attention on the part of the therapist. My own practice is to write down the focus (or foci), modify it as we go, and review it before each session. Similarly, when therapy is time-limited, I will check before each session to see how many more sessions I expect to have. If therapy is not time-limited but is brief for other reasons, I regularly try to roughly estimate the amount of future therapy time we will have relative to what we have done so far.

An interesting related question is, Does brief therapy require more outside of the therapy sessions of the patient as well? I think it probably does. Since the duration of therapy is condensed, it is particularly helpful for the patient to engage in the following efforts between sessions:

1. Maintain a receptive capacity to dynamic material such as dreams, fantasies, and associations, especially if they are related to the foci of therapy.
2. Be aware of interactional patterns and symptomatic variation as they occur in everyday life.
3. Try out, when possible, new responses outside of the sessions and then discuss them with the therapist.

I have sometimes suggested to patients to consider the short time that we have available to us as a time to put their psyches in "intensive care," to make this exploration a very high priority during the brief therapy.

Greater Technical Flexibility

Most brief dynamic therapists describe modifications to long-term technique, although the degree and type of changes vary considerably. Davanloo (1991), for instance, has described his active, confronting interpretive technical approach and stressed that it should be followed in a very careful, systematic manner with little or no deviation from his guidelines. Budman and Gurman (1988), on the other hand, have argued for a very eclectic approach on the part of the therapist that makes use of any of that particular therapist's therapeutic skills.

My own training has included behavioral, cognitive, and Gestalt approaches, and, as discussed in the following chapter, I incorporate these nondynamic techniques with many brief patients. Especially in very brief therapy (see Chapter 10) I am guided by "Think dynamically and do what you can." The problem with an eclectic approach is that it can become a hodgepodge of interventions that pull the therapy in a variety of disparate directions rather than a dynamically informed approach that integrates techniques from different theories into a coherent treatment. The therapist needs to be thinking about when and why to use different interventions and how they may affect the therapeutic relationship.

THE QUESTION OF SELECTION

Which patients can benefit from brief psychodynamic therapy and which ones cannot? If a brief approach is used, should the patient be seen using a supportive model or can a more demanding expressive approach be taken? Which patients should be excluded from brief therapy? Do certain types of patients benefit more from a particular model than from others? The issue of selection is a highly controversial one and the answers to these questions depend on the model used and which brief therapist is asked.

In general, however, there are two schools of thought, one of which is quite *exclusive* and restricts the model to patients who meet various restrictive criteria. There are, of course, varying degrees of exclusivity among these models. The other school of thought is *inclusive* and tends to see brief therapy as being of benefit for most, if not almost all, patients. Table 4–2 summarizes the positions of the models discussed above. Alexander and French (1946) did not directly address the selection question but the spirit of their writing suggests that their approach fits more into the inclusive school.

The Exclusive School

Some analytically oriented therapists view brief therapy as a treatment that provides only supportive help and should be utilized only for uncomplicated mourning, situational adjustment problems, and some traumatic and post-traumatic stress reactions. All of the models previously discussed in this chapter are directed toward a broader range of patients than this view but some are still quite restrictive. Of the models discussed, the ones that are the most exclusive are the ones that are the most intensely interpretive—the models of Malan, Davanloo, and Sifneos. These brief therapists hold that it is very important to accept only patients who can tolerate the demands of highly interpretive, anxiety-provoking work. Mann's approach is less restrictive in terms of patient selection but still rules out a number of the patients that commonly present at an outpatient clinic or private practice.

Table 4–2. Patient Selection: The Exclusive and Inclusive Schools

Exclusive	Inclusive
Malan	Alexander and French
Davanloo	Horowitz and colleagues
Sifneos (anxiety-provoking)	Strupp and Binder
Mann	Bloom
	Budman and Gurman

I will discuss Sifneos' selection paradigm first since it is, by far, the most restrictive. Flegenheimer (1982) has estimated that only 2 to 10 percent of individuals presenting at outpatient clinics would meet the selection criteria. Sifneos' selection requirements include five dimensions (Neilsen and Barth 1991). The patient must:

1. Be able to define a *focus*
2. Have had at least one *"meaningful" relationship* during childhood
3. Interact with the therapist in a manner that indicates the ability to *experience and express affect* in the sessions
4. Evidence *psychological-mindedness*
5. Demonstrate *motivation* for change beyond simple symptom relief

The patient must meet all five of these criteria in the selection interviews. Criterion 5 (motivation) is seen as the single most important criterion and can be further specified according to seven issues (Neilsen and Barth 1991). Does the patient:

1. See the symptoms as having a *psychological cause*
2. *Honestly* present the material
3. *Actively participate* in the selection interview(s)
4. Display *curiosity* about self
5. Demonstrate some *receptivity to new ideas* suggested by the therapist
6. Have goals for therapy that are *realistic*
7. Evidence adequate motivation by a willingness to *make reasonable accommodations* concerning scheduling and payment issues

The patient must meet five of these seven subcriteria. It is very easy to see how most patients would be excluded by this selection process and that the patients who remain could likely withstand the intense, confrontive interpretive therapy that makes up Sifneos' approach (1972, 1987).

Malan's (1976) careful selection process (which involves extensive psychological testing) would accept a broader range of patients than Sifneos' but narrower than Davanloo's (see below). Malan's selection criteria would exclude patients with any of the following:

1. Previous serious suicide attempts
2. Drug or alcohol addiction
3. Long-term hospitalization
4. More than one course of electroconvulsive therapy
5. Incapacitating chronic obsessive-compulsive or phobic symptoms
6. Gross destructive or self-destructive acting out

He also notes that if the therapist believes that more than six sessions are necessary for a trial therapy to see if the patient can benefit from brief therapy, then the patient should probably not be accepted for it. Once such patients were excluded from consideration, he indicates that he would accept the patient if a focus could be identified, if the patient responded positively to it, and if motivation seemed to be adequate. One of the valuable contributions of Malan's (1976) work is his presentation of cases that failed (e.g., an error in selection and lack of therapist flexibility in modifying the technique to accommodate the patient).

Davanloo's (1978, 1980, 1991) model selects for a broader group of patients and, as noted earlier, ranges from highly motivated patients with a single, circumscribed oedipal focus to individuals with massive resistances who have significant ego syntonic character pathology. It is estimated that 30 to 35 percent of outpatients (Flegenheimer 1982) would meet his criteria. Laiken and his colleagues (1991) have stated that it is applicable for patients with personality disorders in the DSM C cluster (avoidant, dependent, obsessive-compulsive, passive-aggressive) as well as for histrionic personalities (B cluster). Contraindications for this model would be major affective disorder, psychotic breakdown, borderline personality disorder, severe and active substance abuse, serious sociopathic tendencies, and certain life-threatening psychosomatic conditions. Davanloo has noted some modification of his technique and efforts to apply it to some borderline patients.

Mann and Goldman (1994) have described their criteria for patient selection as "lower than the Malan-Sifneos criteria, in some respects very much lower" (p. 26). A priori high motivation for change is not seen as crucial since that will be affected by the appreciation for and containment of the patient's anxiety during treatment. What they presented as being the most important variables affecting outcome were the capacity for rapid affective involvement and ability to tolerate loss (a measure of ego strength). They did not feel that their approach was suitable for psychotic or borderline patients or other patients with strong, primitive dependency or narcissistic issues. They also would not see patients with severe psychosomatic complaints. Mann (1991) has reported that certain borderline patients who have some effective neurotic defenses have been helped by his approach. He noted that they were often then referred for long-term treatment. So, while Mann and Goldman would accept for treatment many patients that other models in the exclusive school would not, there is still a sizable group of patients that they would not see in their Time-Limited Psychotherapy.

The Inclusive School

Strupp and Binder (1984) have noted that, historically, brief dynamic therapy has centered on selecting the most promising patients and excluding the majority. There is an important issue here of social and professional responsibility since many, if not most, of the most disturbed patients are, in fact, seen in various forms of brief rather than long-term treatment. One reason for this (there are other reasons as well) has to do with the impaired quality of object relatedness of many such patients (see Chapter 11). Strupp and Binder conclude: "In order for psychotherapy to meet more adequately the needs of patients as well as society, it is essential to focus attention upon patients who have typically been rejected as suitable candidates for short-term psychotherapy and to explore systematically the extent to which such patients can be treated more effectively by a well-defined, time-limited approach" (p. 276).

The inclusive school of selection is varied but all use rather liberal criteria. It would appear that there is a trend in the more recent writing on brief therapy for inclusion of a broader range of patients. This is due to a variety of factors: (1) the increased interest in brief therapy, (2) research and clinical experience on the successful treatment of more difficult and challenging patients, and (3) the improvements in brief dynamic therapy. This mirrors the development of intensive psychoanalytic psychotherapy, which is being utilized with a much greater range of patients than was the case initially. As the array of models sampled in this chapter demonstrates, brief dynamic therapy is not a unitary treatment approach. There are significant differences among the different models. Therefore, it makes sense that various selection criteria would be much more important for some models than for others. The whole question of matching particular patients to particular models is an intriguing one that bears further serious study (Groves 1992, Piper et al. 1990, Steenbarger 1994). However, even more important is the effective matching of the specific therapist to the specific patient given the uniqueness of the relationship that the two will develop at a particular time.

Of the models discussed in this chapter, I would put the approaches of Alexander and French, Horowitz and colleagues, Strupp and Binder, Bloom, and Budman and Gurman in the inclusive school. Alexander and French (1946) did not direct much attention toward selection criteria in their pioneering work. They did note that a life history of adaptability was a positive prognostic sign and that adequate intelligence should be considered. Sensory disturbances, severe neurological problems, crippling somatic conditions, and advanced age were cited as conditions that may make the patient unsuitable for their therapy.

Horowitz and colleagues (1984) designed their approach for patients presenting with stress response syndromes. When that is the presenting problem almost any nonpsychotic patient who could benefit from psychotherapy would be eligible for their twelve-session approach. As already noted, they explicitly have included personality-disordered patients within their patient population. However, in a more recent description of the model, Horowitz (1991) excludes borderline personality disorders in his research studies. Although patients with chronic, delayed, or chronic stress response patterns can be treated in this approach, time-unlimited psychotherapy is the treatment of choice for them, in his opinion.

Strupp and Binder (1984) have stated that once severe pathology is ruled out, ". . . we advocate greater latitude with respect to levels of functioning that others might consider too impaired" (p. 58). In fact, in some earlier work, Binder (1979) described the brief treatment of a patient with a narcissistic personality disorder. The patient need not evidence the capacity to display feelings or to have a "good" relationship with the therapist. Both of these qualities, however, would be seen as very desirable. As a major part of the focus on interpersonal relationship patterns, obstacles to effective relating would usually be carefully explored. Butler and his colleagues (1992) have stated that this approach is most successful when patients view their distress as the outcome of interpersonal patterns and conflicts. While Strupp and Binder (1984) would not rule out nearly as many patients as those in the exclusive school would, they still attend to similar factors that would indicate suitability for treatment:

1. Emotional discomfort
2. Basic trust
3. Willingness to consider conflicts in interpersonal terms
4. Willingness to examine feelings
5. Capacity for mature relationships
6. Motivation for the treatment offered [pp. 57–58]

Bloom (1981) does not specify selection criteria other than requiring that the patient have the capacity to work on an identified focus and possess "adequate" ego strength. He also states that severely depressed patients would probably not benefit from single-session therapy.

The eclecticism and flexibility of Budman and Gurman's (1988) approach is well illustrated in their views on selection. They have contended that many patients who present as poor candidates for brief therapy "do extremely well" with the right patient–therapist and brief modality match. They state that they were unable to come up with a list of contraindications for brief therapy and summarized their thoughts on the matter as follows:

> Our recommendations in patient selection are to monitor the patient's response to treatment on a trial basis; to be prepared to make creative modifications as necessary (two such modifications may involve the patient's seeing another therapist or includ-

ing the patient's family); and to be prepared to use various alternatives, including longer and more open-ended treatment. [p. 25]

Concluding Comments on Patient Selection

How can we pull together these disparate and complex ideas on patient selection? In a summary of various brief dynamic approaches to it, Barber and Crits-Christoph (1991) conclude that the most important criterion for many is the assessment of the patient's ability to form a collaborative therapeutic relationship. This is interesting for a number of reasons. First, while it does seem to be a central criterion in most models, once it has been identified, most of the writers then sparingly or indirectly refer to the relationship, highlighting instead the technical interventions or theoretical conceptualizations. The relationship, when discussed, is often presented as a static entity rather than a living transference–countertransference matrix. Strupp and Binder are an exception to this.

Second, it is precisely in the area of forming collaborative relationships of various sorts that many of our patients (especially our most challenging patients) have profound difficulty. Even when a patient cannot form much of a collaborative relationship, the work around his difficulty in that area of human experience can be very important. The work involved may simply be the therapist's maintaining the limits of the therapy and her role in a warm but firm manner. Or, after a shaky start, the therapist and patient may be able to examine and interpret the presence and significance in the transference and countertransference of some recurring patterns of disturbance. This is the area in which an object relations perspective proves to be particularly valuable.

Barber and Crits-Christoph (1991) summarize the following as the most emphasized qualities dynamic therapists look for in candidates for brief therapy:

1. A history of a good relationship (at least one)
2. A degree of psychological-mindedness
3. Some motivation to change beyond the level of symptomatic relief
4. A good response to the therapist's trial interpretations.

They conclude that most dynamic models are not designed for patients who abuse drugs or alcohol, have severe personality disorders, might regress to psychotic states, or are inclined toward frequent acting out.

Piper and his colleagues (1985) studied fifteen of the variables frequently used in the selection of patients for brief therapy. They found that defensive style and quality of object relations were the only two variables that predicted outcome. As might be expected, more mature defensive styles and higher quality of object relationships were associated with more positive outcomes. However, other variables that are almost ubiquitous in the literature such as focality of complaint, psychological-mindedness, and degree of motivation did not significantly correlate with outcome.

From my own clinical and supervisory experience I believe that focus, psychological-mindedness, and motivation are major factors in determining outcome. It is, however, a worthy effort to constantly question such "truths" that we see as being "self-evident" as we do our work. In effect, doesn't the clearly documented success of brief therapy itself challenge and question some of our basic assumptions about the practice of psychotherapy in general? In the chapter on beginning a brief therapy, I will present my own approach to selection.

5

Overview of the Approach

> I have long held that "brief" psychotherapy was to be
> achieved by improving the utilization of the psycho-
> therapeutic minute. If one is governed by no principles,
> but only by some vague beliefs—as in something like
> "free association"—I think brief psychotherapy is very
> likely to be measured in terms of decades. But if one is
> interested in a precisely defined, recurrent difficulty
> that people have in significant relations to others, it is
> quite possible that a good deal can be done in a rather
> short time.
>
> Harry Stack Sullivan, 1954

As I discussed in Chapter 1, my intent in this book is not to propose a new model of brief psychodynamic therapy. There is already
an impressive array of brief dynamic models. Many of the compo-

nents of these models can be selected and used synergistically. Rather, I am outlining in this chapter a brief therapy approach that combines four elements. I believe this approach, which is described in more detail in subsequent chapters, can be especially powerful with a broad range of patients. The four elements are:

1. The depth of understanding of human experience that comes from an object relations perspective
2. The insight and experiential vitality of attention to the therapeutic relationship including its real, transferential, and countertransferential elements
3. The impact of the psychodynamic techniques that have been carefully studied and delineated by brief therapy writers (especially Davanloo 1978, 1980, 1991, Horowitz et al. 1984, Malan 1963, 1976, Strupp and Binder 1984)
4. The flexibility of an eclectic approach that thoughtfully and selectively incorporates nonpsychodynamic interventions

THE OBJECT RELATIONS PERSPECTIVE

Chapter 3 presented key object relations concepts and their relevance to brief therapy. The central points are:

1. Attention to the unique holding and containing functions of the particular therapeutic relationship can very much enhance therapeutic effectiveness.
2. This is especially the case with difficult, resistant patients who are frequently viewed as not being "good" brief therapy patients.
3. Even in very brief therapy (e.g., one to three sessions) the therapist's awareness and use of the therapeutic relationship is important.
4. With the focus in the literature on technique and protocols, the crucial role of the relationship in brief therapy has been largely ignored.

Clinical Example: Alan

Alan, an 18-year-old college freshman, referred himself to the Student Health Clinic. His clothing was very unstylish for a college student and he interacted stiffly and awkwardly. He presented his situation in a flat, affectless manner reminding me of how the weather report is read over the phone. He made almost no eye contact. As we sat down, he reminded me of a stereotypic computer wonk and I was vaguely uneasy.

In his flat, matter-of-fact style Alan began to tell me that he came for therapy because he has been fighting with himself for the past two weeks over whether or not to kill himself. He had bought a rope and had figured out how to rig it in his dormitory room and when to do it so as not to be interrupted by his roommate. He had actually practiced it. Listening to him, I was feeling very anxious and pressured that "I've got to do something fast." However, I was also somewhat disoriented by the disparity between his calm, almost boring narrative style and the alarming nature of what he was describing.

He had been feeling the sometimes overwhelming urge to kill himself since he had asked another classmate, a man, to join him for lunch and the classmate said no. He reported never having had any friends and his only peer play was with his two brothers (he is the middle child). He was feeling intense shame both because he thought this other student would join him for lunch and also because he thought he himself might enjoy it. Alan later said he probably wouldn't have enjoyed it and he really doesn't like people other than his family.

Despite the fact that his suicidal feelings started shortly after this incident with the other student, he was not convinced that the two were fundamentally connected. He just knew that he felt intensely anxious and vaguely self-punitive. On the one hand, he felt that his life was pointless and it would be good to end the pain that he was currently feeling. On the other hand, he felt he had a lot to live for—he believed that he could accomplish a lot in his professional field (physics, as it turned out). Alan told me that he had read that many people stay in therapy for years and years and that he didn't want that. He needed help in controlling his suicidal feelings and he wanted to work on them in the shortest amount of time possible and asked if I would be willing to do that. I said that I would but I cautioned him that it is difficult to know how much time it will actually take. He repeated that he didn't want to be in therapy for a long time.

I was feeling very worried about this young man with very flat affect who had a continuing strong urge to kill himself. He had a well-defined suicide plan and the means, and had actually rehearsed it. I was thinking that it was my bad luck that he came in on my intake time—why couldn't another clinic staff member have seen him! I was also thinking that I want him to go into a hospital— *now*! These uncomfortable countertransference reactions proved very important for me to attend to since these were frequent reactions that others had to him—my reactions were complementary identifications. Alan seemed to often make people uncomfortable and they would respond by either trying to get away from him or by rushing in to take control. His father seemed to be a man who was generally uninvolved with him but who would infrequently and un-predictably rush in and try to control his life.

My anxiety was tempered, though, by his willingness (and, I hoped, ability) to make an alliance with me to resist his suicidal impulses. It was a positive prognostic sign in itself that such a schizoid man would come in for treat-ment on his own. I did not raise hospitalization with him (although that seemed like a reasonable option) because, in addition to his willingness to make an alliance, he appeared to be extremely sensitive to being intruded upon and controlled and I wanted to respect that and not cause him to retreat.

I developed an outpatient anti-suicide plan with Alan that involved seeing him the next day and a third time during the first week of treatment. He was also given the clinic's emergency phone number. I saw him twice weekly the next two weeks and then once per week after that for a total of twenty sessions. In almost every session he repeated his desire to end therapy as quickly as possible and I frequently would wonder whether each session would be our last one. His acute suicidal feelings rapidly diminished and he did come to see that the rejection from the classmate had triggered his suicidal crisis. He also somewhat (but not totally) accepted the notion that he might actually want relationships with other people. In the nineteenth session, Alan said that he had gotten what he wanted from therapy and thanked me, but he wanted to stop. I recommended to him that he stay in treatment but he seemed to be firm and I thought it best not to push too hard on continuing. I did recommend that we at least have one more session and he agreed to that. As we will see later, this was not to be the last time that I saw Alan in treatment.

Alan was a young man who was clearly in need of some therapy and benefited from these twenty sessions. I liked him and respected his schizoid mode of being. I believe that these factors and my willingness to work in the way that he asked and my care in responding to his sensitivity to his boundaries being violated were crucial in creating a relatively safe intersubjective space that in turn produced a positive therapeutic outcome. My impression is that Alan came to see me as less of a rejecting object during the therapy and more as someone he could trust, to some extent. In short, I believe that what was most helpful to Alan was the experience of the therapeutic relationship rather than any particular technical strategies I used.

DUAL FOCUS: SYMPTOMATIC AND DYNAMIC

Setting a therapeutic focus is the single most important and ubiquitous difference between brief and long-term dynamic psychotherapy. There are many different types of focus that can be set. For example, Schacht and colleagues (1984) list the following:

1. A cardinal symptom
2. A specific intrapsychic conflict
3. A developmental impasse
4. A maladaptive conviction about the self
5. An essential interpretive theme
6. A persistent interpersonal dilemma
7. A pattern of maladaptive functioning [p. 66]

When different therapists examine the same clinical material, they often come up with different foci depending on therapeutic orientation, experience, and other variables. Since I discuss the proposed focus explicitly with patients, the patient's conscious and unconscious willingness to make an alliance to work on a particular focus is crucial. The limits of the particular therapeutic contract also influence focus selection. For instance, a different focus might be set if the contract is for three versus twenty-five sessions.

I try to set a focus on two levels—symptomatic and dynamic. The symptomatic focus typically addresses the psychological pain or the functional impairment that brought the patient in. Sometimes this is all that can be done. However, whenever possible, I also propose a dynamic focus that centers on the patient's underlying psychodynamic structure. While it is not always obvious, the two foci are usually connected and work on the dynamic focus assists in the work on the symptomatic focus. The therapist should at least be struggling to understand a link between the symptomatic focus and the patient's dynamics. If an appropriate dynamic focus cannot be found, the therapy is usually limited to being a supportive rather than expressive intervention (see Chapter 6).

Clinical Example: Alan

The focus of the therapy with Alan was to reduce the anxiety causing his suicidal impulses and to control the impulses. The therapy had an exclusively symptomatic focus and was, I felt, an example of supportive therapy. While I was certainly pleased at termination that Alan was alive and no longer suicidal, I also felt disappointed that little had been done to address the underlying issues that were driving the anxiety and expected that he would again be struggling with similar issues in the future.

So, I was heartened when Alan called me eighteen months later to ask for an appointment. I was not surprised that he was unfortunately again in acute distress. Since we had last met he had become depressed and was spending much of his time in his room. His parents obtained a therapist referral from their family doctor. Alan indicated that the therapy had not gone well. He said the therapist had told him that he was seriously disturbed and that he required at least six months of twice weekly therapy. When Alan told the therapist that he only wanted to feel better and wanted to be quickly finished with treatment, he said the therapist brushed him off saying, "This is what you need." Alan indicated that he met with the therapist for a few months but became increasingly anxious, feeling that the therapist was trying to control him and was phony—acting like he liked him but really didn't.

I suggested that such feelings often come up in therapy and don't necessarily mean the therapy is bad but in fact are quite useful despite their painful nature if they can be discussed. He was adamant that he would not return. I agreed to meet with him in weekly therapy and he again reiterated his desire to have therapy end as quickly as possible. We met for ten sessions.

During this period of therapy, however, we were able to set a dynamic focus in addition to the symptomatic focus of anxiety reduction. His anxiety diminished rather rapidly as we talked of his experience of being overwhelmed by and almost "invaded" by the other therapist. He brought in short pieces of writing that he asked me to read. Each of these had themes of conflict over interpersonal relationships. They described his fears of being overwhelmed, rejected, controlled, and losing his own identity. However, they also (but less directly) dealt with his desire for relationships. The writing had a depth of feeling and pain that was in marked contrast with the way he presented himself to me. Our dynamic focus became his conflict about personal relationships, especially trust and his fear of being controlled and losing himself.

Just as had been the case in the first installment of

therapy, Alan had made it clear that he wanted treatment to be as brief as possible. In the ninth session he said that he was grateful for the help that I had given him and that he wanted to stop. I suggested that his desire to stop so quickly was perhaps related to fears about closeness and being controlled by me but he calmly said no, therapy with me was for a specific purpose and he had gotten what he came for. We were probably both accurate. One of the frustrating elements of working with Alan was that he almost invariably would reject any interpretations that I made. I didn't push him to stay since I had, by now, gotten even more indications of the great sensitivity that he had concerning being controlled and impinged upon. I felt better about this termination since I believed that we had begun to deal overtly with the underlying issue of his conflicts over interpersonal relationships. But, I was somewhat frustrated over his suddenly coming back into my life in crisis, working very intensively and then, almost as suddenly, leaving. I thought that this was a projective identification and I was feeling like he did with his father (a concordant identification). Perhaps, like Alan in relation to his father, I was feeling that more was possible and was frustrated with the in-and-out quality of our relationship.

Alan's return for a second installment of therapy and the further work that we were able to do illustrate the underlying impact of the uninterpreted holding and understanding in the first twenty sessions. Like a mother who has to contain the anxiety of early, first steps while hoping for further growth later, I was containing uninterpreted issues and anxiety in our beginning work and hoping that Alan could use it later. He clearly did.

INTERPRETIVE EMPHASIS

The key technique in psychodynamic psychotherapy is interpretation. Langs (1973) defines interpretation as "verbal interventions through which the therapist makes material previously unconscious in the patient, conscious for him in a meaningful and affective way" (p. 451). Scharff and Scharff (1992) describe interpretation as "a continuum of therapist interventions, from complex formulations that are mutative to simple comments, on the way to building shared understanding" (p. 113). What is interpreted? Different therapists and different orientations emphasize different themes. Some of the differences among dynamic brief therapists were discussed in the previous chapter. From an object relations perspective, Scharff and Scharff (1992) have stated:

> Interpretation begins with linking and clarifying and proceeds all the way to understanding how whatever happened long ago in the patient's life influences current difficulties in relation-ships. The most effective interpretation begins with the current reenactment in the transference and countertransference and proceeds to the reconstruction of repressed internal object relationships. [p.114]

A basic interpretation can be simply pointing out to a patient how he is relating to the therapist. Additionally, the therapist can attempt to make various connections between and among internal representations and/or responses. I briefly discuss these linking interpretations below and will discuss interpretation in further detail in Chapter 7.

Triangle of Conflict

Malan (1976) has presented a conceptual model that I find quite helpful in thinking clearly about interpretations. Davanloo (1980) also makes use of this model in his approach as well. Malan's inter-pretive schema (Figure 5–1) consists of two triangles, with the thera-pist attempting to make connections between and among the three points on each triangle.

The first triangle, which Davanloo (1980) has called the "tri-angle of conflict," is the classical drive theory constellation of impulse (or drive), the anxiety that arises from the drive, and the defense against the anxiety.

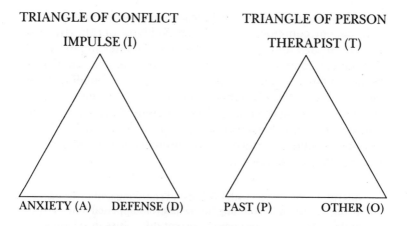

Figure 5–1. Malan's interpretive schema. (Adapted from Malan 1976, and used by permission of Plenum Press and David Malan.)

For example, Robert was a married man in his early forties who unconciously was strongly sexually attracted to a female co-worker, Jean. This caused anxiety (unconscious thoughts included: "She'll reject me anyway," "She's off-limits," "I'm married") and he unconsciously defended against this by being and feeling angry toward her.

The following are examples of possible interpretations that a therapist might make to link the points of this triangle of conflict:

I-A interpretation: "From what you've said it may be that you feel attracted to Jean [I] but this makes you very uncomfortable [A]."

I-D interpretation: "I think your anger [D] keeps you from being aware of how attractive you find Jean to be [I]."

A-D interpretation: "I have this thought that Jean makes you uneasy [A] for some reason and that causes you to be mad at her a lot [D]."

I-A-D interpretation: "You know, from everything we've been talking about, it may be that your strong feelings for Jean [I] make you so uneasy [A] that, without knowing it, you frequently pick fights with her [D]."

Triangle of Person

The triangle of conflict can be quite helpful in organizing one's thinking about the patient's issues. My own work, however, emphasizes the object relational reenactments in patient's lives and this is the domain of the second triangle, which Menninger (Malan 1976) termed the triangle of insight and Davanloo (1980) referred to as the triangle of person. This triangle connects the patient's feelings and actions toward the therapist (T); toward important figures from the past, frequently parents (P); and toward others (O) in the present or recent past.

Cindy was a widowed woman in her mid-forties who had been repeatedly sexually abused by her father during most of her early teen years. While she had great fears of men controlling her, once she got into a relationship with a man she alternated between being very compliant and demanding that the man treat her in special and inappropriate ways.

The following are some interpretations using the triangle of person:

T-P interpretation: "While your father abused you it also made you feel special. I think your desire for me to go to bed with you [T] might be based in part on your very natural desire to be special to me—like you were to your father [P]. But it would also abuse you [P]."

P-O interpretation: "You seem to be feeling that you can't say no to Neil [new boyfriend] [O]—just like you couldn't say no to your dad [P]."

T-O interpretation: "When I was 5 minutes late today, you felt that I might have gotten tired of you [T]. It's a bit similar to the way you described your fears about Neil when he didn't call you back for two days [O]."

T-P-O interpretation: "This hurt you have about only being special behind closed doors really does seem to go all the way back to your father [P]. In the group, you also felt that I didn't respond to you like I do in individual [T] [she was also in a therapy group that I co-led]. I wonder, too, if that was part of your feeling discounted by Neil when you were with his friends on Saturday [O]."

The Self and the Triangle of Person

As I discussed in Chapter 3, the self is a central concept in psychoanalytic theory. It is important for the therapist and patient to direct their attention toward *how the patient treats her own self*. Therefore, the therapist also interprets self phenomena and connects them with past, other, and therapist material as well. I have subsequently concluded that an addition to the triangle of person should be made to include interpretations that are directed toward how the patient's relationship with her own self is connected with her relationship to other objects. My addition to the triangle is presented in Figure 5–2.

> James (married, mid-forties) was a very successful CEO/ owner of a small business. He came into therapy due to difficulty in his relationships with his partners. He had very high standards for himself and others and was frequently disappointed with both. His own father was very stingy with praise and seemed to usually take him for granted. James often felt he was disappointed in him.

The following are some examples of linkages to self using the interpretive schema in Figure 5–2:

T-S interpretation: "You're frequently feeling that what I'm offering you isn't helpful enough—it should be better [T]. This is often how you describe feeling about yourself [S]."

P-S interpretation: "I was impressed by how little credit you gave yourself for landing that large contract with the Green

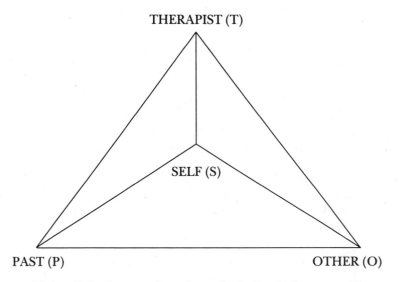

THERAPIST (T)

SELF (S)

PAST (P)

OTHER (O)

Figure 5–2. Interpretive schema including linkage to self.

> Corporation [S]. It seems to me that you were treating your-
> self the way your father treated you [P]."
>
> O-S interpretation: "I was thinking about how, so often, you
> feel that no matter what you do, it's not good enough [S].
> This came to mind as you were describing the Thursday
> meeting in which you said to yourself that Len [one of
> his partners] really had met you more than halfway in that
> Thursday meeting—more than he had ever done before.
> But you were still disappointed in him and took some jabs
> at him [O]."

NEW ENDINGS FOR OLD EXPERIENCE

Many patients, especially character-disordered patients, actually live
very little in the present. Their lives are strangled by the inability
to truly encounter another person as is. Instead, they experience
the person through the distorted prism of past experience. Also,
friends and partners may be unconsciously selected on the basis of

their similarity to important past people. The unconscious reenactments of past relationships with others dramatically limit and
trouble the lives of many of our patients. Awareness of it and then
experimentation with new modes of relating in and during therapy
may be the most important part of therapy for these patients.

Given that old, repetitive experiences are being replayed by the
patient in the relationship with the therapist, the brief therapist
attempts to respond in a manner that is different from that of important past objects. In this way a new outcome to the old experiences
can be brought about. As Guntrip (1969) puts it, "The therapist must
be more than just a projection of good elements in the patient's own
superego. He must, in his own reality as a person, bring something
new that the patient has not experienced before" (p. 346).

> For instance, Linda was a divorced, 30-year-old attorney
> with strong borderline features in her personality. Procras-
> tination was her presenting and long-standing complaint.
> Her history was dominated by relationships in which she
> was either abused or in which she was abusive or, less fre-
> quently, in which someone dramatically rescued her from
> a crisis situation. Within the first several sessions, I encoun-
> tered all of these experiences. She was a very attractive and
> seductive woman and I found the atmosphere of the ses-
> sions becoming sexualized. I also felt abused by her late-
> ness and her tendency to no-show or cancel at the last
> minute. I thought, however, it's hard enough for her to
> get to therapy and maybe I should tolerate her inconsis-
> tent attendance. Lastly, I found myself being powerfully
> sympathetic toward her inability to adequately handle her
> job and fantasized about intervening with her employer
> (e.g., a letter to him validating the psychological stress she
> was under and recommending that she be excused from
> the project that she was working on).
>
> These reactions gave me dramatic glimpses (much
> about her was dramatic) into her inner world but to act
> on them would have simply repeated what she had expe-
> rienced with previous people (especially men) in her life.

How, then, could a therapist respond to her in a way that made possible a new ending for these old experiences that were being brought into our sessions? I periodically would think "How can I be useful to her without abusing her, being abused by her, or rescuing her?"

The roots of this therapeutic stance go back to Alexander and French's (1946) seminal book relating to brief therapy. They put forth the well-known but poorly understood concept of a "corrective emotional experience." The patient has suffered painful or traumatic events in the past. Through the process of transference, those experiences are replayed in the relationship with the therapist, who then tries to respond in a manner that gives the patient an object relationship different from what he had had in the past. The concept has tended to be discredited in psychoanalytic circles due to Alexander and French's active and rather manipulative approach to bringing this corrective emotional experience about. Also, Alexander and French seem to suggest that the therapist could make up for the earlier failures of nurturance and empathy in the patient's life. With our current psychological knowledge, it seems clear that it is impossible to fully compensate for serious trauma or parental deficits when the patient was a child, no matter how good the relationship with the therapist is.

However, it can be profoundly therapeutic when the therapist can disconfirm the patient's belief (unconscious or conscious) that she will be responded to in a particular way. The patient can then come to believe that other types of relationships are possible. Moreover, the patient's experience of herself in such a relationship may be different since distinct aspects of oneself are evoked in different relationships. In writing about Malan's brief therapy model, Gustafson (1981) noted one way in which the therapist's difference is "corrective":

> Indeed, one cannot make up for this failure [inadequate parental nurturance]. But one can help the patient to experience the longings, giving up those that are impossible and seeking what satisfactions life can offer. The good therapist fails to nurture the patient as much as the latter would like to be nurtured. The

therapist is "corrective" in that, unlike the parents, he or she is willing to face this failure and help the patient bear it. [p. 106]

USE OF NONPSYCHODYNAMIC TECHNIQUES

To conduct brief therapy from an object relations perspective, the therapist does not need to restrict his technique to exclusively psychodynamic ones (e.g., interpretation, silence, confrontation, dream work, etc.). In fact, the use of other interventions such as hypnosis or techniques from cognitive, Gestalt, or behavior therapy can very much complement the psychodynamic perspective. Budman and Gurman's (1988) very eclectic approach actively incorporates techniques from different schools of psychotherapy. Strupp and Binder (1984) have indicated that their brief therapy sometimes involves techniques that are similar to cognitive restructuring. Horowitz and colleagues' (1984) approach clearly includes elements similar to those in cognitive therapy.

One does, of course, need to be aware of the effect of the role shift when the therapist gives directive instructions to the patient. For instance, how does the fact that the therapist was able to teach the patient to quickly reduce anxiety through deep muscle relaxation affect the transference? How does the patient feel when the therapist at one point in the treatment recommended a cognitive therapy technique to deal with guilt while at another time remains more passive, permitting the patient to "stay with" the guilt?

These are examples of the types of questions that therapists need to keep in mind and, at times, to explore with the patient when integrating different therapeutic approaches. However, in my experience, the merger of dynamic with nondynamic approaches usually enhances the work, if done thoughtfully. The nondynamic interventions often serve to expedite the therapeutic progress on symptoms and particular issues. The dynamic perspective attends to the meaning of the patient's suffering and symptoms within the context of who this particular person is. It also provides knowledge about the nature of the patient's resistance.

This last point can be crucial with any form of therapy. As a behavior therapist once said to me when he referred a former patient of his, "This patient would have benefited enormously from behavior therapy—if he had only done his assignments." Understanding the unconscious dynamics involved in noncompliance is often a necessary condition for effective treatment. In work with many patients, the knowledge that comes from attention to transference, countertransference, and unconscious processes in general is frequently required to facilitate change. Even when using, say, a behavioral intervention, the therapist should remember Heimann's questions (Bollas 1987) that orient the therapist toward the inner world: "Who is speaking?"—what part of the patient's inner world is being given expression at that particular moment?; and "To whom is the person speaking?"—what part of the patient's inner world is being represented by the therapist at that moment?

The therapy with Ronald, described in detail in Chapters 6, 8, and 9, included behavioral (relaxation training, anxiety management training) and cognitive interventions (cognitive challenging, cognitive restructuring, three-column technique) to reduce his anxiety. His anxiety was preventing him from being able to adequately function as a law student and he was rapidly falling behind in his studies. However, I do not believe that they would have been as successful without attention to his underlying narcissism and the way it manifested itself in the relationship between us.

SERIAL BRIEF THERAPY

Brief therapy contracts are often viewed simply as isolated interventions related to the focus worked upon. I would suggest that a more useful perspective is to consider a specific brief therapy contract as only a part of a *process* of therapy. It not only will continue, we hope, within the patient after the contract has ended, but also permit the patient to return to therapy in the future for another episode of treatment, if needed. In fact, many patients return to therapy several times in their lives to continue the personal growth that had been stimulated by previous work (Budman and Gurman 1988).

The brief therapist needs to consider not only the present work with the patient but also how this experience may affect his continuing growth and development. Attention to the dynamic focus is very helpful in this regard in that it works on a theme or issue that usually has potency well beyond the more limited focus of the particular brief therapy contract. Seen from this perspective, an individual piece of brief therapy work is a part of a much larger process of change that may include periodic brief episodes of therapy that occur throughout the patient's life. In a successful brief therapy the patient has experienced help at a time of distress through the relationship with a good, reliable object. He has experienced a process of change in the context of a unique relationship. Why should he not return to the therapist or to the therapeutic process at difficult times in the future? In this way, I believe that individual episodes of therapy can build upon earlier episodes and "the whole is greater than the sum of its parts"—the whole process takes on a power beyond each episode.

This perspective does hold that the therapy for many, but not all, patients does not need to be continuous but rather can be made up of episodes of discontinuous brief therapies. This perspective also has the advantage of being compatible with many managed care plans. I have termed this process *serial brief therapy*. Hoyt (1990) has used the term *serial short-term therapy* to describe periodic brief therapy contracts.

This is a different perspective for dynamically trained therapists. We are trained to work intensively with the patient for a continuous, extended period of time. The therapy should not end until the crucial dynamics have been fully analyzed—but are they ever *fully* analyzed? In writing about this attitude and the problems that flow from it Cummings and VandenBos (1979) state: "Any recontact with a former mental health patient is labeled a 'relapse' and is viewed as evidence that the earlier intervention was either unsuccessful or incomplete. . . . No other field of health care holds this conceptualization of treatment outcome" (p. 433). This attitude by therapists that return to therapy is bad, a "relapse," may be unconsciously communicated and can discourage patients from returning to the therapist for further work. When this is unconsciously communicated, the patient may feel shame in facing the therapist again and so seek out a different therapist.

Other writers have described a process similar to serial brief therapy. Budman and Gurman (1988) have written about the "(frequent) interminability of brief therapy" and report seeing the same patient periodically over many years:

> Patients return to therapy at various points in their lives. Assuming that as a therapist one can (or should) provide a patient with a "definitive" treatment is like assuming that a teacher should provide the definitive class, that a physician should provide the definitive antibiotic, or that a travel agent should provide the definitive vacation. [p. 248]

Concerning patients returning to therapy, Bennett (1989) has noted:

> This orientation is entirely consistent with the way patients seek to use therapists: repeatedly, over time, at points of life transition. Episodes of treatment that are keyed to developmental readiness and that build on change-promoting forces within the patient's own environment are likely to be discontinuous rather than continuous, brief rather than diffuse, and modest in scope. [p. 352]

Pollack and colleagues (1991) have suggested that their approach to brief therapy (Brief Adaptive Psychotherapy) might effectively use brief courses of treatment that alternate with planned periods of no therapy for such challenging patients as narcissistic and borderline characters.

While it is a different perspective for dynamically trained therapists, it is a common experience in clinic work (and in many private practices) to see the same patient returning to therapy at irregular intervals over extended periods of time. To distinguish among various types of patient returns to therapy, consider the following admittedly simplified list of causes (frequently the patient returns due to more than one cause):

1. The patient did not feel she received adequate help previously. Fortunately, many patients do not give up on therapy when they've had a negative or nonproductive experience.

They try again—sometimes repeating the old unsatisfying patterns, sometimes collaborating to create more positive outcomes (new endings for old experiences).

2. The patient received symptom relief but underlying issues were not addressed. Symptom relief is certainly a noble goal in and of itself. However, when therapy provides only the alleviation of suffering and no personal change, the patient often returns again and again whenever a new crisis or problem crops up. Clinic staffs frequently describe patients who return time and time again over the years dealing with similar problems but without much evidence of having learned any ways to more effectively handle them. One clinic told me of patients that had been seen over twenty years who had not learned to handle their lives any better but whose pain had been reduced each time they came in for a few sessions. Yet these patients had been seen for a total of over 150 sessions over two decades. If some of these patients had been seen for a more extended period in the early years, might they have been able to learn more effective coping mechanisms by looking at some dynamic issues and ultimately have been seen, perhaps, for fewer sessions over the long run?

This is a significant problem in the way that many managed care organizations direct mental health care. The emphasis is so much on *immediate* cost containment and *rapid* symptom relief that patients return again and again without having learned how to better manage their lives.

3. The patient is facing a new problem, crisis, or developmental challenge in her life.

4. The patient wants to work further on the dynamic themes dealt with previously. She has already made progress and wants the assistance of the therapeutic relationship to further that change.

5. The patient wants to work on new dynamic issues. Having found therapy to be a process that effectively addressed the issues that were the focus of the previous therapy, she now wants to resume it to evoke movement on additional underlying themes.

Certainly, when a patient returns to therapy because she was not helped in the first place (cause 1) this is no cause for self-congratulations by therapists. Similarly, while we can take some satisfaction in contributing to the alleviation of the patient's pain in supportive therapy (2), it is reasonable to challenge ourselves on whether something of more lasting value could have been done. However, it is remarkable that patient return after positive but limited change (4 and 5) is often viewed as treatment failure. This is frequently due to therapists' narcissism—the therapist is disappointed with the delimited nature of the improvement. It also is related to an attitude toward therapy (and life?) that implies that the patient can actually get to the end of therapy and be fully analyzed or fully developed. Therapy, like life, is a process of becoming rather than a process of arriving.

The occurrence of patients returning for further treatment following an episode of brief therapy is sometimes cited by long-term therapy proponents as evidence of brief therapy's inadequacy relative to long-term work. However, additional therapy experience following intensive psychotherapy or psychoanalysis is also common. Hartlaub and colleagues (1986) surveyed psychoanalysts of the Denver Psychoanalytic Society. They found that of these analysts' successfully analyzed patients, fully two-thirds had consulted their analyst again within the following three years. Their study didn't provide any evidence on what percent of the successfully treated patients consulted other mental health professionals during this period, but we might safely speculate that there were some additional contacts of this sort as well.

Clinical Example: Alan

I have already described Alan's return to therapy after eighteen months for a second period of work with me. Over an eight-year period I saw him for a total of fifty sessions. We met for five therapeutic installments of twenty-, ten-, three-, five-, and twelve-session durations. The dynamic focus of conflict about personal relationships, especially trust and his fear of being controlled and losing himself, continued to center the work throughout this time. I will briefly discuss these three subsequent episodes of therapy.

Two years after the second episode of therapy, Alan returned again in crisis. He had become more involved with his parents' harsh religion and simultaneously had become more aware of strong sexual feelings. The religion had a strong prohibition against sex in any form other than sex in marriage for the purpose of procreation. Fearing that he would act on his sexual feelings, he considered self-mutilation or suicide as preventative measures. He presented all of this in his characteristically unemotional narrative and said the purpose of his seeing me was to get my advice on whether he should do this (suicide or self-mutilation).

In the second session I advised him, of course, not to do either. He thanked me for this consultation and said he would follow my advice. Although I recommended that he continue seeing me to deal further with this, he declined and stopped in the third session. I was very unsettled by the brevity of this contact with him, coupled with the extreme actions he had been contemplating. However, my anxiety was moderated by my experience with him in that he had always followed through on his word and had effectively worked collaboratively with me. Once again I felt it was very important that he not experience me as intruding on him or invading him. Still, I found it very difficult to see him walk out the door in the third session. I once again thought that, through projective identification, I was being made to feel as he had in his relationship with his father. Also, I was experiencing his projected anxiety about suicide and self-mutilation. I did think (and hoped) that I would see him again.

I subsequently saw Alan several years later for two more brief therapy episodes. He was not in crisis during either of these therapies. He had developed a small group of friends and it was noteworthy how much more socially skillful and stylishly dressed he was. As he had become more oriented toward and open to the interpersonal world, he had directed his high intelligence to this arena and the results were rather impressive. Both times he requested help for the stress of trying to get a high-level job in the highly competitive business consultant field. He was, in essence, marketing himself and while he was experiencing some success as well as much frustration, the process was very depleting and lonely. Our supportive focus was on practical stress management and the dynamic focus continued to be interpersonal trust and boundaries—these times focusing on professional as well as personal relationships.

I have not seen Alan since the fifth installment of therapy, which ended seven years ago as of this writing. He has written to me twice to tell me that he was doing well. He indicated that he is successful professionally and is married and has a child. I believe that each segment of this serial brief therapy did build upon previous ones and that this clearly was a therapeutic process of at least eight years' duration for him (probably, I think, much longer than that).

FOLLOW-UP SESSIONS

In recent years a number of brief therapists (e.g., Budman and Stone 1983, Goldsmith 1986) have recommended planned follow-up sessions as a means of furthering change and preventing symptom relapse. I believe that follow-up sessions as well as lengthening the duration between the last several sessions in a brief therapy contract can be helpful for some patients. First, it can help in dealing more gradually with termination and strong dependency issues. Second, it permits more time for working through of the issues outside of the sessions. Third, the additional time between sessions allows for additional life events to occur that then may be usefully dealt with in the therapy. However, planned follow-up sessions and less frequent sessions can dilute both the work on the clinical material in general and on the termination experience, in particular. Therefore, they should not be automatically suggested but should be used selectively. I discuss these issues further in Chapter 9. In Chapter 10, I present a case (Sharon) in which I believe my offering a follow-up session was a mistake.

Two Abridged Clinical Examples: Ronald and Bill

Ronald was an anxious, narcissistic 24-year-old law student whose therapy is described in detail in Chapters 6, 8, and 9. Therapy was limited by insurance coverage to fifteen sessions. While the therapy was helpful rather quickly in reducing his anxiety and addressed some of his narcissistic issues, he was uneasy at the twelfth session about not yet having landed a summer job. At this point in his progression through law school, getting a good summer job was very important for possible future permanent job prospects. Ronald requested that our final three sessions be held every two weeks rather than weekly to allow more opportunity to address his anxiety related to the job search. I also thought that this was a way for him to delay and diffuse termination although I didn't interpret this to him. I believe that he would have rejected it given his counterdependent approach to me and the therapy. I believe that ending therapy was difficult for him although he could not admit it to himself. The spacing out of the sessions permitted him to more gradually deal with the loss of me and the therapy. Also, it was helpful to have the support during his difficult job search process.

Bill was a 55-year-old married university professor. He entered therapy very depressed following the breakup with a woman that he had been having an affair with over the past several years. The thirty-two sessions of therapy focused on his great difficulty in setting and accepting limits and the connection of this to his self-esteem. I suggested a follow-up session three months after termination to revisit the limit setting/self-esteem issue. This follow-up session took place shortly after the academic year had ended and permitted us also to examine how he was coping with a period of relatively unstructured time. During the three months that had intervened since our last session, Bill had been aware of many instances of how when he accepted limits he felt weak, inadequate, and "unmanly." We had an opportunity in the follow-up session to further explore the meaning of this dynamic for him.

6

The Beginning

To be brief is almost a condition of being inspired.

George Santayana

SELECTION

Which patients can benefit from object relations brief psychotherapy and which ones cannot? If a brief approach is used, should
the patient be seen in a supportive model or can a more demanding expressive approach be taken? Which patients should be
excluded from brief therapy? In Chapter 4, I discussed two schools
of thought, one that is quite *exclusive* (e.g., Sifneos 1987) and
restricts the approach to patients who meet various restrictive
criteria. The other school of thought is *inclusive* (e.g., Budman and
Gurman 1988) and tends to see brief therapy as being of benefit
for most, if not almost all, patients.

My own thinking places me in the inclusive school. I believe that object relations brief psychotherapy can be of benefit to most patients. Wolberg (1965) states:

> The best strategy in my opinion is to assume that every patient irrespective of diagnosis will respond to short-term treatment unless he proves himself refractory to it. If the therapist approaches each patient with the idea of doing as much as he can do for him within the space of, say, up to 20 treatment sessions he will give the patient an opportunity to take advantage of short-term treatment to the limit of his potential. If this fails, he can always resort to prolonged treatment. [p. 140]

This idea of considering brief therapy for potentially every patient is sound. It is consistent with the fact that most treatment is brief and with the research that brief therapy is generally highly effective. Moreover, it is compatible with the reality of the managed care models within which much psychotherapy is now conducted. However, qualifications are in order. While the brief therapy may be beneficial, it may not be as extensively or as intensively helpful or growth-promoting as long-term therapy. Consider, for instance, the following different levels of therapeutic effectiveness: symptom improvement, symptom elimination, improved coping abilities, increased self-awareness and understanding, and characterological change. Symptom improvement is certainly a valuable therapy outcome but it is quite different from the depth of enhanced self-awareness and personality change. Usually, but not always, there is more opportunity for personality change in long-term than in brief therapy.

As discussed in Chapter 2, the nature of time is different (Engelman et al. 1992) when the patient and therapist experience the number of sessions as being limited and brief. Twenty sessions that are viewed as being the total time available for therapy will produce qualitatively different clinical material than twenty sessions that are seen as only part of a potentially open-ended contract. In some cases, patients may regress less in the service of the work and unconscious material is less available (dreams, fantasies, associations) in the sessions. In other instances, the brevity creates an affectively intensified atmosphere that brings out latent material.

Some patients will require extended treatment to permit mutative material to either emerge or to be worked through.

> Lee (single, 26 years old) sought therapy because of her difficulty in completing assignments in her position as a research assistant for a health care policy institute. Her therapy was limited by financial resources and she could afford to come for only twelve sessions. The therapy was successful in that she was able at termination to complete her job assignments in a timely manner but she still struggled with serious problems of low and fragile self-esteem. The self-esteem issues were only touched upon in the brief therapy contract but we did identify her relationship with her mother as an important component of her self-esteem problems. Six months later, Lee returned to treatment, this time asking for an open-ended approach. Only at this point did she settle in and develop more of a receptive capacity. This permitted us to explore the painful material of her childhood with a severely borderline, suicidal mother and her unconscious identification with the mother. In so doing, we began to address her disturbance in the area of self-esteem.

This case exemplifies an additional benefit of brief therapy that sometimes occurs—namely, that the experience of a positive, beneficial but limited therapeutic relationship in brief therapy can serve as a catalyst for longer term work. A positive outcome of some brief therapies is that the patient then enters a long-term therapy process.

Six Selection Questions

I approach selection from a pragmatic rather than theoretical standpoint: Can this particular person at this particular point in time benefit from brief therapy with me? Binder and colleagues (1987) have argued that the stringent selection criteria of the exclusive models, while theoretically appealing, do not actually predict course and outcome of brief therapy very well. Object relations brief therapy can be helpful at least in a limited way if the patient can meet the following criteria:

1. Can the patient benefit from psychotherapy?
2. Can a clear focus be defined?
3. Can the patient quickly develop a positive, collaborative relationship with the therapist?
4. Can the patient tolerate the frustration of a brief approach?
5. Has the patient responded positively to trial interpretations or interventions in the evaluation session(s)?
6. Can the patient benefit from brief discontinuous courses of therapy (as opposed to needing a continuous long-term relationship with a therapist in order to change in ways that are significant)?

If the answers to all of these questions are yes, then I would accept the patient for brief therapy. As I discussed in Chapter 4, Crits-Christoph and Barber (1991) conclude in their review of selection criteria for brief psychodynamic therapy that the patient's ability to form a positive, collaborative relationship was the most important criterion.

SETTING A FOCUS

This is the aspect of brief therapy that most distinguishes it from long-term work. To be able to use the limited time available in brief approaches effectively, the therapist and patient cannot follow every topic in an open, reflective manner. To do so allows everything to be touched upon and nothing to be adequately dealt with. In fact, a patient's persistent resistance to staying with a focus is often a defense against intimacy—staying at a distance and surveying the field but never getting close to the material or to the therapist.

In doing brief dynamic work, I try to set two types of focus. The first type is a *symptomatic* focus that directs the work toward the patient's distress and the present-oriented issues driving the distress. The second focus is a *dynamic* one that selects a part of the patient's underlying psychodynamic structure to concentrate on. It is usually the case (but not always obvious) that the two foci are connected and that work on the dynamic focus will aid in the symptomatic work. It is the therapist's job to strive to understand the possible links between the foci. Most patients in my experience will readily agree to work on the symptomatic focus but this is sometimes not the case with the dynamic one. For either focus to be suitable for treatment, it must possess two elements. First, the focus must be limited enough for gains to be made within the constraints of the particular brief contract. Second, it must be something that engages the patient's motivation and curiosity sufficiently so that she is willing to work on it.

The therapist may not be able to determine a dynamic focus within the first few sessions, although it may emerge as the therapy progresses. Whether or not a suitable dynamic focus can be found determines if the therapy will be supportive or expressive.

Sifneos (1989) has described brief supportive psychotherapy. The goal is to return the patient to the previous level of adaptation even if it was not very stable. Insight and transference are not utilized very prominently or actively. "One would expect a diminution in the intensity of the symptoms, an improved self-esteem, and a confidence in the treatment as a therapeutic modality that can be sought in times of future trouble" (p. 1564).

Expressive psychotherapy aims for more, and insight is a major goal. The therapist attempts to explore transference and it may become a major focus of the therapy. Depending on the individual situation and the particular dynamic brief therapy model, the therapist and patient may have the following goals beyond symptomatic and functional improvement: more enduring strength and maturity of self-esteem, greater awareness of self and others, and, perhaps, significant character change.

BUDMAN AND GURMAN'S I-D-E APPROACH
TO SETTING A FOCUS

Budman and Gurman (1988) listed the following as the five most common foci in their approach to brief therapy:

> *Losses:* past, present, and anticipated losses; losses of significant others; losses of health, job, status, self-image

Developmental dysynchronies: when expectations at particular transition points have not been met, when one's cohorts are seen as having advanced toward their goals more than oneself (e.g., "I thought I'd be married by now"; "All my friends are managers in their companies, what's wrong with me?")

Interpersonal conflicts: most commonly with intimate relationships (couple and family issues), authority figures and co-workers

Symptomatic presentation: patient wants help with specific symptoms—depression, anxiety, insomnia, phobia, sexual dysfunction, and so on

Personality disorder: persistent patterns of self and relational pathology

Budman and Gurman (1988) have suggested a flow chart (Table 6–1) to assist in selecting among these focal themes.

The focus that is selected is then examined along interpersonal, developmental and existential dimensions. As Budman and Gurman (1988) state:

> The I-D-E approach in brief treatment is an attempt to capture and understand the core interpersonal life issues that are leading the patient to seek psychotherapy at a given moment in time, and to relate these issues to the patient's stage of life development and to his or her existential concerns. (Existential concerns include factors such as the meaning and values of one's life, and ultimately the issue of confronting one's own mortality.) [p. 27]

I think this is a useful schema to organize our thinking about focus-setting. To compare it to my own conceptualization of two levels of focus, what I have described as a symptomatic focus includes, but is not limited to, Budman and Gurman's first four foci—losses, developmental dysynchronies, interpersonal conflicts, and symptomatic presentation. What I have described as a dynamic focus is similar to their personality disorder focus but I would broaden it to include underlying personality issues in general, disordered or otherwise.

Table 6–1. Focal Flow Chart

Key question: Why now?
Is this visit related to any of the following?

⋮	⋮	⋮
	Developmental	Interpersonal
Loss	dysynchrony	conflict

If the patient does not view the above focal areas as relevant, or if the patient defines the symptom itself as the major issue,

⋮

Symptomatic focus

If the patient has had repeated presentations around any or all of the foci above, without clear benefit, or if character issues preclude these foci because of constant interference with the therapeutic process,

⋮

Character focus

Warning: Under circumstances of active alcohol or drug abuse, this problem must be addressed before or simultaneously with the development of any other focal area.

From Budman and Gurman 1988. Copyright © 1988 Guilford Press. Used with permission.

STRUPP AND BINDER'S APPROACH TO SETTING A FOCUS

Strupp and Binder's approach is organized around the concept of the Cyclical Maladaptive Pattern (CMP). They state: "The CMP is a working model . . . of a central or salient pattern of interpersonal roles in which patients unconsciously cast themselves; the complementary roles in which they cast others; and the maladaptive interaction sequences, self-defeating expectations, negative self-appraisals, and unpleasant affects that result" (Binder and Strupp 1991, p. 140). To develop the CMP, the therapist and patient examine four areas:

1. *Acts of self.* Both observable and covert (e.g., feelings) behaviors and both conscious and unconscious actions are included in this category.

2. *Expectations about others' reactions.* These include conscious and unconscious beliefs about the ways other people react to the person.

3. *Acts of others toward the self.* This category looks at the actions of others that appear to be connected in some way with acts of self.

4. *Acts of self toward self (introject).* These are actions that indicate the ways that a person relates to him/herself (e.g., self-soothing, self-deprecating, self-attacking, etc.).

The CMP is used as a collaboratively developed working focus that becomes more fine-tuned as therapy progresses. An example of a CMP would be a pattern of interpersonal passivity coupled with expectation of rejection. The foregoing summary of Strupp and Binder's ideas illustrates how grounded their work is in the relational life of their patients. While they emphasize interpersonal conceptualizations their work also addresses the world of internal objects relations (e.g., acts of self toward self).

HOW TO SET A FOCUS

Setting a meaningful focus within a short time is one of the most challenging tasks for therapist and patient. Binder (1977) has criticized several models (e.g., Sifneos, Mann) for, in effect, avoiding this problem by having predetermined the focal theme for their patients. He writes, "They tend to circumvent the problem of focusing by presetting it. Either they cull out those patients who don't fit, or they make all patients fit a procrustean focus" (Binder 1977, p. 233). What I am suggesting is that the brief therapist not initiate the process of focus-setting with preconceived notions of what the focus should be. Rather, she should approach it as a process of mutual discovery that places the highest priority on the uniqueness of the patient. It can be very easy for therapist and patient to deal with the anxiety of "not knowing" by jumping prematurely to a readily available but superficial focus. Balint and colleagues (1972) quote a former supervisor of Balint's, Max Eitingon, as remarking, "Every new patient must be treated as if he had come directly from Mars; and as no one has met a Martian, everything about each patient must be considered as utterly unknown" (p. 126).

A brief therapist and patient may develop an initial focus within the first session or can spend many hours to develop it. Malan (1976) has presented one of the most detailed and thorough approaches to selecting a dynamic focus. He investigates the question through the following:

1. Psychiatric history
2. Psychodynamic history
3. History of interpersonal relationships
4. The patient's present outside relationships
5. The relationship made with the therapist
6. Projective tests.

When he finds a common theme running through most of these six areas of inquiry, he then has identified the focal conflict for the therapy.

Attention to all of these areas is usually beneficial. In practice, however, such rigor is usually not necessary to identify a suitable initial focus to launch treatment. The brief therapist often does not need to invest the amount of time and energy that Malan does if she is willing to use the initial foci as working tools that will be fine-tuned as therapy progresses and is also willing to be flexible with technique as the therapy unfolds in its own unique manner. Selection and highly fine-tuned focus are most important when the therapist is planning to approach the patient from a strongly and actively interpretive model.

If one takes a more flexible approach in working with the patient, the following considerations often prove adequate in developing working foci and can usually be accomplished in one to three hours. The therapist strives to have the patient be an active participant in the focus-setting.

History

In even very brief therapy, for example a three-session employee assistance program (EAP) contract, it is essential to develop an understanding of the patient through taking a history. In a typical brief therapy contract I would spend at least an hour obtaining historical information. If I had only, say, three sessions, I'd try to devote at least twenty minutes to it. Among the most important issues to address:

1. Patient's impressions of parents, other members of the family of origin, and other important figures that contributed to the patient's personality structure
2. Recurring patterns of interpersonal interactions (e.g., repeatedly being in an abused position in relationships)
3. Best and worst levels of past functioning
4. Previous experience with therapy
5. Family history of psychological disturbance including substance abuse
6. Past suicidal, self-defeating, psychotic, or other regressive behavior.

Malan (1976) has noted that often taking a history itself can be therapeutic. The patient is able to see (sometimes for the first time) that there are some understandable patterns in his life while it had before seemed chaotic and inscrutable.

Present Level of Functioning

How well is the patient functioning in the arenas of work, school, friendships, intimate relationships, and other interpersonal interactions? What is the patient's presenting problem and current level of distress? What is the patient's view of himself?

Relationship with the Therapist

Ask the patient what she thinks the problem is, how she understands it, and what she wants to emphasize. What is it like sitting with this patient? What types of responses does she evoke in the therapist? To what extent is the patient able to interpersonally connect with the therapist?

Trial Foci

One way to assess the suitability of a focus is to tentatively present it to the patient and see what the response is. Does the focus seem to make sense to the patient in terms of his present understanding of the problem? Is his curiosity engaged by the focus? Does the patient seem to be defensive and resistant to it? Does the patient seem to be able to respond only to the symptomatic level of the focus—if so, he may at that point, only be able to do supportive therapeutic work.

Psychological Testing

In my experience, usually the previously listed considerations will yield preliminary foci and I do not regularly use psychological testing. However, if the brief therapist is struggling to develop a dynamic focus with a particular patient, psychological testing (especially projective testing) can be very useful. An example of this is presented below in the case of Diane.

SETTING A FOCUS: UNCOMPLICATED CASE—RONALD

Ronald, a 24-year-old single man, had just begun his second semester in law school and was acutely anxious because of his so-so performance during the first semester. He was having great difficulty sleeping, he couldn't concentrate on his studies, he felt out of control, and was viciously self-critical about this reaction. He felt humiliated for being so out of control. His insurance would cover only fifteen sessions of psychotherapy and he wanted therapy to be conducted within that amount of time. Ronald said that he expected it would take less time than that "if it helps at all."

In the first session with Ronald I was impressed by his narcissistic issues and was aware of a number of feelings and reactions. First, I felt saddened by how hard he was on himself and by how difficult it seemed to be for him to accept himself. He talked movingly about almost always being disappointed with himself. I found my own thoughts going toward some of my own lack of self-acceptance (a concordant identification, see Chapter 3). I was feeling some moderately strong sense that I'm going to be disappointing to him because I won't meet his standards (another concordant identification). Lastly, I was feeling some irritation at an arrogant, entitled quality to him (a complementary identification). For example, when I explained to him that I expected my patients to file their own insurance forms, he replied, "I realize that that's the way you do it for other people, but couldn't you make an exception for me?"

At the end of the first session we agreed to work on the symptomatic focus of trying to get his anxiety to a more manageable level and to help him be able to concentrate well enough to study. In law school, a student can easily fall hopelessly behind in just a few weeks. I also made a tentative suggestion to Ronald that I was impressed by the extremely high standards that he set for himself and thought that they may be connected "in some way" with the intensity of his anxiety reaction. He seemed to accept that idea, and the issue of his high or "all or nothing" standards became the beginning of our dynamic focus to examine a part of his narcissistic character.

In the second session, I took a history with Ronald and we began to see some of the formative factors affecting his personality. (Ronald's history and course of treatment [fifteen sessions] are described in Chapters 8 and 9.)

SETTING A FOCUS: COMPLICATED CASE—DIANE

When she came into my office, this 32-year-old mother was depressed and said that she would have killed herself were it not for the fact that she couldn't do such a terrible thing to her four children (ages 7 to 12). She had been acutely suicidal for the past two weeks. This followed her arrest for embezzling $30,000 from her employer. The stealing occurred dozens of times over the course of two years in dissociated states. These actions were particularly ironic since she was married to a "nail 'em and jail 'em" prosecuting attorney. The husband had had some limited contact with me during the previous year when I had done some consulting with his organization. Money was understandably tight and her insurance would not cover seeing me (their insurance was through an HMO). Also, she still hoped that she and the family could follow through on their plans to move to rural North Carolina in about six months.

The dominant feeling I had in this first session was one of feeling overwhelmed—What in the world can I do in six months? As a concordant identification, this gave me an experiential sample of some of the overwhelming feelings she was experiencing. This feeling was intensified when I took a history in the next session and learned the following. She was the oldest of four siblings and was the custodial child after her father left the family when she was 7. She often denied herself ("as the substitute parent") in deference to the other children. Her mother was described as being nice but also a perfectionist who would beat Diane for small things (e.g., not cleaning up her room adequately). The first time Diane stole from her company was to get money to save her mother from being evicted from her apartment. She described her father as being a rotten man who was alcoholic and who beat her mother. She had little to do with her father after he moved out.

When Diane was 7 she was sexually abused by the nephew of a babysitter. From 15 to 19 she had a steady boyfriend whom she described as the love of her life despite the fact that he would beat her. He died in a motorcycle accident when she was 19. Also, her father died of a heart attack when she was 19 following an argument with him (her paternal grandmother blamed her for his death). Additionally, she had a history of episodes of impulsive, sometimes violent self-destructive behavior that punctuated (punctured, I thought) generally responsible, conventional behavior. Diane had never stolen before but reported a history of overspending.

The symptomatic focus was straightforward: we decided to work on diminishing her suicidal feelings and to deal with the stress of the impending legal proceedings against her. But what would be a realistic dynamic focus over the next six months? This was a woman with a history of multiple traumas involving loss and abuse who had serious problems with impulsivity and perhaps a borderline character structure. To try to determine this fairly quickly, I referred her to another psychologist for testing. I also felt that it would perhaps be useful in the legal proceedings for testing to be done.

The results of the psychological testing indicated that she did in fact have a borderline personality disorder with her ego being characterized by multiple splits and particularly a split between a self with strict self-punitive perfectionism (unconscious identification with her mother) and another self that was impulse-ridden and irresponsible (unconscious identification with her father). The testing also revealed a high degree of conscious suppression of painful experience and much shame but little guilt.

I received the test results from the testing psychologist and interpreted them to Diane. In the interpretation, I explained what the diagnosis of borderline personality meant. I said that, in part, it was a personality characterized by many portions that are unconscious and not integrated together so that the split parts clash and sudden changes can occur that seem baffling to the person. Such a personality structure causes the person to often feel overwhelmed and out of control. I gave the following illustration: "How can we understand how a person who is so dedicated to her family can suddenly, without thinking, do things that are so destructive to her and to them?"

This description of her personality seemed to be quite poignant for her and she said tearfully that she had been very troubled for a long time about the chaotic nature of her personality and that it had caused her to feel crazy. The preliminary dynamic focus we set, then, was to explore the meaning and impact of these splits and the "emotional storms" (as she called them) that were a consequence of them. She was clearly motivated to explore this particular theme due in part to its being connected in her own mind with feelings of being overwhelmed and out of control. It is noteworthy that these were strong feelings that I had had in the first session with her and were, as already noted, a concordant projective identification. As the therapy proceeded over a course of twenty-five sessions this focus became more finely tuned and is described in Chapters 8 and 9.

DEVELOPING THE WORKING ALLIANCE

I believe that good brief therapy is very similar to good long-term work. Too much has been made of the differences between the two. The differences are significant but much of what is helpful in long-term work is also helpful in brief therapy. This point applies to developing the working alliance. The importance of the therapist operating from a stance of empathic attunement, sensitively and nonjudgmentally trying to understand the patient's concerns, and interacting with the patient in a manner that conveys respect, competence, and compassion cannot be exaggerated in its role in developing a working alliance in any form of psychotherapy.

However, time is limited and at a premium in brief therapy and it raises the challenge to not only develop a working alliance but to do so quickly. The following are some elements that can facilitate the swift development of a working alliance.

Be Aware of the Common Countertransference of Impatience

The therapist needs to take care to not push this process faster than the patient can tolerate. When he tries to speed up the therapy without adequate responsiveness to the patient's readiness, the patient may experience a repetition of earlier unempathic relationships or the patient may defensively idealize the therapist. As discussed in Chapter 2, the brief therapist must be aware of the common countertransference of impatience in the face of the time and resource constraints. A rapid development of the working alliance is different from a hasty development. I have had the opportunity over the last few years to supervise a number of therapists doing brief work. As might be expected, less experienced therapists tend to err on the side of setting a focus quickly and running with it before the patient has truly made an adequate alliance. On the other hand, more experienced, predominantly long-term therapists tend to err on the side of needing a great deal of evidence of an alliance before proceeding with a focus, consuming much of the limited time they have.

Direct Attention to the Patient's Pain and His View of It

When it is clear to the patient that the focus will speak to his pain and suffering, the focus strongly promotes the therapeutic alliance. Acknowledgment of the patient's suffering and his understanding of it certainly help the patient to believe that this is someone that will take him seriously. What is less obvious is that the therapist may internally be aware of it but only overtly inform the patient of what she thinks is *really* going on.

> For example, a married man arrives for his first session saying, "I don't see any reason for being here, my wife said I had to come or she'd leave me. . . . I think therapy is ridiculous." The therapist learns that the patient can be very verbally abusive and was the target of much verbal abuse himself as a child. To move the therapy along the therapist says, "It sounds like your wife is angry with you because you seem to verbally attack her a lot. This may come from your own childhood and we need to understand this better." While this statement may be quite accurate, it is so far from the patient's own experience at this moment (he doesn't think that he's abusive toward her) that he feels criticized and misunderstood and is even

less likely to make a therapeutic alliance. The patient's own definition of the problem is that he's afraid of losing his marriage, and he doesn't clearly know why but his wife is upset with him.

A more useful therapeutic intervention at this point might be, "Your wife is threatening to leave you and you're baffled by this, let's see if we can understand this better. You really don't want her to leave and want to find some way to get her off of your back." The patient might feel more understood with this intervention and be more willing to explore his interactions with his wife in this context. Eventually, of course, he will need to take some responsibility himself for the problems but that can emerge more gradually. This issue of working with the patient within his perspective is particularly important with personality-disordered patients because quite frequently the therapist rather quickly can see aspects of the problem more clearly than the patient does. The only catch is that the therapist's view is so different from that of the patient that it is unusable as a direct intervention (although it may be quite valuable as a piece of understanding that the therapist contains for the time being).

Take the History as a Shared Process of Discovery

The very act of taking the history can be therapeutic. In Chapter 3 I described some of the brief therapy with Rita, a 32-year-old college instructor who entered therapy depressed over her relationships with men. As part of the history-taking, I ask patients to give me personality sketches of important people in their lives and I asked her about her father and two husbands. Rita was surprised by how similar her descriptions were. They were all rather exciting objects—engaging, interested in many pursuits, sexually flirtatious, but also very self-involved, with limited interest (or capacity?) for empathy or emotional giving. Rita had never before seen these similarities and it gave her hope in two ways. First, now that the pattern was identified she could work toward changing it. Second, if a major part of her problem involved selecting men with certain characteristics, she felt that perhaps there were other men out there who might be able to better meet her needs. The meaning of her selection of such men in her life became the dynamic focus of the therapy.

The Collaborative Process of Setting the Focus Can Assist in Alliance Building

In a brief therapy context, I typically indicate that, for the therapy to be useful within the limits that we have, we will need to decide what we can realistically accomplish. Moreover, I state that this will involve deciding what issues we can focus on and what we will not be able to address. Especially with therapeutically naive patients the process of focus-setting is frequently a holding and containing experience in that it can make the therapeutic process seem less vague and formless. Patients with strong fears about intimacy and dependency may find the emphasis on a focus to be anxiety-reducing since it directs the patient to center on a shared, somewhat structured task. The focus-setting described previously with Ronald and Diane helped to build therapeutic alliances with them.

Utilize the Knowledge of the Patient from Transference and Countertransference Reactions

The early contacts with a patient can often provide the therapist with important information that can be useful in solidifying a working alliance. Rita had a history of sexually charged, exciting object relationships with men, and I found myself in the first session thinking something along these lines: What a compelling, sexy woman; I wish I hadn't met her in therapy. Oh, I'd disappoint her anyway.

The quick erotization of the therapeutic relationship and my sense that I'd ultimately disappoint her were projective identifications that alerted me to erotic and exciting object issues being prominent for her intrapsychically and interpersonally. Her description of the presenting problem did not overtly include those elements. They did come out, as noted above, in the history taking. I didn't initially interpret what I saw but rather sat with it and tried to make some sense of it. In my experience, early interpretation of such material often impedes alliance-building. As I discussed in Chapter 3, Rita did come to see me by the sixth session as yet another disappointing, exciting, and ultimately rejecting man. Some of the most important work that we did was around this transference to me. I was able to be more responsive to it through my awareness of the countertransference fantasies I had had in the first session.

7

The Middle: I

> I take it for granted that interpretation is a form of object relationship and that object relationship is a form of interpretation (in the sense that every object relationship conveys an aspect of the subject's understanding of the latent content of the interaction with the object).
>
> Thomas Ogden, 1994

In the beginning phase of brief therapy the therapist and patient have developed an alliance and have identified a focus to work on together. In the middle phase of treatment they use these tools to promote change and growth. Of course, my outline of a beginning, middle, and end phase of therapy is simply a heuristic device—there is much overlap among the three phases. In some ways, the middle phase of brief therapy is very much the same as in long-term work. The patient and therapist create transitional space and receptive capacities to explore the material that develops. In other ways, the constraints of the limited holding and containing of brief therapy require a modification of approach.

This chapter especially highlights the roles of transference-countertransference and interpretation and examines some of the issues that arise during the middle phase of brief therapy. The middle phase may last dozens of sessions or part of only one session (very brief therapy is discussed in Chapter 10). Chapter 8 further explores middle-phase issues and concludes with descriptions of the middle of the therapies with Ronald and Diane, whose brief therapy beginnings were described in Chapter 6.

MAINTAINING THE FOCUS

Having set the focus, the therapist needs to work with the patient to keep the treatment related to it. (In the interests of simplicity, I will use the word *focus* generically to refer to the focused areas of therapy even if there are multiple foci or dynamic as well as symptomatic foci.) This is a balancing activity. If the therapy is too rigidly attached to the focus, it can have a dead, plodding, mechanistic quality to it. Worse, the patient may feel that she is only being related to as a part object and this may repeat previous experiences of not being adequately responded to in an empathic way. Alternatively, if the therapy follows every interesting lead that develops, much will have been surveyed but little will have been adequately dealt with. In this case, the patient may well feel that she had an experience that made her hungry but didn't really satisfy or nourish her—an exciting object experience. I suggest that the focus not be regarded as a road map that has to be followed meticulously and inflexibly. Rather, it might be considered as a navigational beacon so that when the clinical material meanders away from the focus, the therapist asks himself, "Where are we in relation to the focus?"

Related useful questions for the therapist to consider (and at times to collaboratively explore with the patient) when the material does not seem related to the focus include:

1. Is this in some subtle way related to the focus?
2. Is this an issue that needs to be addressed in its own right at this point?

3. What is the meaning of this coming up at this time? What is its meaning from the perspectives of the relational context, of the therapeutic process, and of the clinical material?
4. What is my subjective experience as this material comes up?

HOW DOES BRIEF THERAPY PROMOTE CHANGE?

This is obviously an enormous question that goes well beyond the scope of this book. For our present purposes I would make the following four points.

1. Brief therapy promotes change in many of the same ways that long-term therapy does. The two modalities have much in common.
2. The unique characteristics of the scarcity of time and attention to focal issues are important ingredients in change (see Chapters 2 and 4).
3. The nature and quality of the patient–therapist relationship as a positive, growth-promoting presence is key (see Chapters 3 and 5).
4. Depending on the particular approach taken, certain components of the therapy may be more important with some patients than with others. Burke and his colleagues (1979) have suggested that brief therapies be categorized according to which elements are emphasized as the agents of change. They define three types: interpretative, existential, and corrective. *Interpretative* therapy emphasizes interpretation of behavior and dynamics to increase the patient's self-understanding. *Existential* therapy primarily promotes change through the healing effects of a meaningful human relationship characterized by clear limits and empathic attunement. *Corrective* therapy brings about change through directive therapist interventions. Hypnosis and cognitive/behavioral exercises would be examples of corrective therapy.

Certainly, most therapies do not fit exclusively into one of these categories and are a mixture. Moreover, the existential element is almost always an important part of successful treatment even if interpretive or corrective interventions are emphasized. In some instances (Alan in Chapter 5), it *is* the therapy.

THE KEY IMPORTANCE OF TRANSFERENCE AND COUNTERTRANSFERENCE

A central question in the brief therapy literature is what, if anything, to do with transference and countertransference phenomena. As Malan (1976) notes, "Thus, whereas the need for planning and focusing remains as before an area of striking convergence, the role of transference [in brief therapy] remains an area of total disagreement" (p. 40). Opinions range from one extreme to the other: from the perspective that it should be ignored, to the therapist should be internally aware of it but should not work with it with the patient, to it should be actively and frequently interpreted. The disparity of opinion about countertransference is even greater. Therapists such as Sifneos (1987) and Davanloo (1980, 1991) have described countertransference as problem reactions on the part of the therapist that should be minimized. Strupp and Binder (1984), on the other hand, discuss countertransference reactions as inevitable and crucial elements of their treatment process.

From an object relations perspective the transference-countertransference interactions are at the core of all technique. It is crucial in brief therapy, even very brief therapy. This stance flows from an emphasis on both the unique relationship formed between the patient and the therapist and the unconscious repetitions of the past enacted by the patient. As discussed below, the actual management of the transference-countertransference will vary considerably. Barber and Crits-Christoph (1991) have described a number of reasons why attention to the transference is so important:

1. The therapist, in the patient–therapist relationship, can simultaneously disconfirm the patient's expectations of others and monitor it.
2. The monitoring permits the therapist to both be part of the reenactment *and* step back and examine it.

3. The transference can be a particularly effective way for change to occur since "the more something is experientially learned, the better it is learned" (p. 349).
4. The therapist models for the patient how one deals with difficult issues and intense affect.

So, through the here-and-now experience of the therapist–patient relationship the patient can learn how she reenacts old relationship patterns and how the therapist may be "really" responding in ways other than what's been expected, experienced, and perceived over the past. Also, the patient can see, in the therapist's attitude and behavior, new modes of handling emotionally difficult experience. In this way, new endings for old experience can come about.

STRUPP AND BINDER'S CONTRIBUTIONS

Among the writers on brief therapy, Strupp and Binder (1984) have perhaps written the most eloquently on it and I find their thinking to be particularly important. The principal technique of Time-Limited Dynamic Psychotherapy (TLDP) is "elaboration of the patient–therapist interactions" (p. 142). They noted that this frequently is a surprise to the patient since he usually does not expect his relationship with the therapist to receive much concentrated attention. Actually, the transference typically becomes part of the focus because a major goal in their treatment is for the interpersonal conflicts that trouble the patient to be enacted within the therapeutic relationship. Thus, the patient's cyclical maladaptive pattern can be observed and interpreted within the here and now as well as in past and present outside relationships. In TLDP, "analysis of the current transactions between patient and therapist (traditionally called the analysis of the transference and of the countertransference) constitutes the most effective means for dealing with chronic patterns of interpersonal conflict" (Strupp and Binder 1984, p. 144).

Strupp and Binder's emphasis is on the interpretation of present phenomena rather than linking them to the past. Past connections are made but they are not emphasized. This is different from Davanloo, Malan, and Sifneos, who have recommended frequently interpreting linkages between responses to the therapist with past experiences (T-P interpretations). The patient's resistance to forming a positive, collaborative relationship with the therapist is closely explored. This resistance sheds light on the obstacles the patient experiences in other relationships as well.

While Malan, Sifneos, Davanloo, and Mann have characterized countertransference reactions as problems to be minimized, Strupp and Binder describe them as an inevitable and valuable part of the therapy. Countertransference can be considered as a trial identification with the patient that the therapist is making consciously and often unconsciously. This is very much in keeping with the thinking of Racker (1968) on complementary and concordant identifications. Moreover, especially with many difficult patients, the therapist cannot help but become involved to some extent in the patient's maladaptive interpersonal patterns. A key aspect of the therapist's art and power as a change agent resides in her awareness of these countertransference reactions, their meaning, the degree to which she is involved with enactment of the patient's maladaptive patterns and the examination of these enactments. The enactments are, of course, *reenactments* of other relationships. In describing their approach Strupp and Binder (1984) write that the therapist becomes "immersed" in the patient's experience and then tries to "work his way out."

Note in this model how profoundly experiential the therapy is for both the therapist and the patient. Fromm-Reichmann (1950) wrote almost fifty years ago that our patients mainly need experiences with us, not explanations. In both TLDP and in the approach that I am proposing the experiential dimension for the therapist as well as for the patient is central.

TRANSFERENCE INTERPRETATIONS

Fairbairn (1958) and Guntrip (1961, 1969) were among the first theorists to emphasize the crucial significance and power of transference interpretations, in particular identifying the patient's responses to the therapist and connecting them to past relationships (therapist-past [T-P] interpretations). In his 1963 brief therapy study, Malan (1976) reports several important findings on transference interpretations and outcome. He found that T-P interpretations were the technical intervention that was most correlated with positive outcome. He concludes that "the most important factor in *technique* seemed to be interpretation of the *transference* [italics are Malan's] throughout the whole of therapy, with special reference to linking the transference with childhood (T-P interpretations) and to working through anger and grief about the loss of the therapist at termination" (p. 20). Additional support for this connection between T-P interpretations and outcome has been reported through more rigorous research by Marziali and Sullivan (1980) and Marziali (1984). Malan (1976) also feels that prognosis tended to be best when transference occurred early and when it was a major feature of the treatment. More recently, Joyce and Piper (1993) strongly argue for the effectiveness of careful transference interpretations in brief therapy. "Interpreting transference reactions explicitly invites attention to both the patient's interpersonal scripts and his/her experience of the therapist . . . and . . . also carries the impact of emotional immediacy" (p. 509).

It would be preferable with most patients for the transference phenomena to be directly analyzed and interpreted, if it can be tolerated. Growth and change can be greatly facilitated by the experiences being put into words within a meaningful context. This is often possible in brief therapy, as in the examples of Ronald and Diane. Sometimes it is not possible, as in the case of Alan, who resisted and at least overtly ignored almost all of the interpretative work and yet seemed to benefit from the *experience* of a different type of relationship. Yet, my own awareness of the tranference-countertransference matrix (Ogden 1994) permitted me to relate to him within my role as therapist in a deeper and more meaningful way.

Many dynamic therapists see interpretation in general and transference interpretation in particular as the highest level of therapeutic intervention. Accordingly, they may feel they are not conducting "real psychodynamic therapy" unless their sessions are dense with such interpretive work. Such an internal reaction may cause the therapist to "push" interpretations on the patient before the patient is ready to accept them. This can be an especially serious problem in brief therapy given the shortness of the time and the countertransference of impatience that may arise.

Transference Interpretations: How Much?

Consider the following findings from a recent study investigating the impact of transference interpretations in brief therapy. In an outpatient clinic sample, Piper and his colleagues (1993) studied what they termed the concentration and correspondence of transference interpretations. Their study also examined the quality of the patients' object relationships. They describe their approach as being similar to Malan's and Strupp and Binder's, and therapy duration was about twenty sessions. Piper and colleagues define concentration as the frequency of transference interpretations divided by the frequency of total interventions. Correspondence was a measure of the correctness of the transference interpretations. Quality of object relations referred to the patient's ability to form certain types of relationships ranging from primitive to mature. They found that "high" doses of transference interpretations were connected with poor outcomes. Only "low" concentrations of transference interpretations were associated with positive response to therapy. Low concentrations were defined as equal to or less than one tranference interpretation per every twelve total interventions. Hoglend (1993b) also has reported similar results concerning transference interpretations.

Piper and colleagues (1993) note that their conclusions are tentative. However, the results suggest that high concentrations of transference interpretations are to be avoided with patients in brief therapy (or at least in Piper and colleagues' approach). With patients who have a high (relatively mature) object relations capability, they recommend that the therapist offer low concentrations of highly correspondent transference interpretations. With patients who have a low (relatively primitive) object relations capability, highly correspondent interpretations should be avoided.

These results seem to run counter to Malan's finding that transference interpretations were positively correlated with successful outcomes. How can we understand this discrepancy? The findings also run counter to the experience of dynamic brief therapists who find that, with certain patients, transference interpretations are instrumental in facilitating change. Referring to an earlier report (Piper et al. 1991b), Piper and his colleagues (1991a) suggest two possible explanations for such findings. High concentrations of transference interpretations may cause the patient to feel criticized and then withdraw. The second hypothesis that they offer is that therapists may start interpreting more and more when it appears that therapy is not progressing. The increased use of transference interpretations may be an attempt to break a stalemate or to confront a weak therapeutic alliance. Piper and colleagues (1991a) state, "Consistent with both explanations . . . was an alternating cycle of silences and transference interpretations that was particularly apparent for patients who were exposed to the highest concentration of transference interpretations" (p. 951). They also report that the correlation between high concentrations of transference interpretations and poor therapeutic alliance became stronger over the course of therapy.

These studies suggest a number of cautionary notes concerning clinical practice. First, they illustrate the dangers of too aggressive interpretive activity, especially with patients who have a poor quality of object relations. Countertransferences of impatience, of needing to feel "psychodynamic," and of intolerance of the level of therapeutic alliance that the patient can make can all lead the therapist to interpret at levels and/or intensities that do not productively connect with the patient. In fact, the effect is often deleterious. Second, I think these studies confirm the wisdom of the restrictive selection criteria of the energetically interpretative approaches of Sifneos, Davanloo, and Malan. If the therapist is to actively and frequently interpret transference experience, the patient should have object relations functioning that can tolerate that degree of strain.

What I am advocating is an integrated approach that draws on the transference-countertransference matrix to interpret past and present experience both inside and outside of therapy. I am not recommending an approach that intensively makes transference interpretations but ignores the rest. While we need to look for opportunities to make T-P, T-S (therapist-self), and T-O (therapist-other) interpretations, we need to be careful not to "overinterpret," given where the patient is and given the limits of the brief therapy contract. Many a brief therapy (and long-term therapy, for that matter) has been sabotaged by the therapist's need to feel competent, intelligent, and/or useful. Strupp and Binder (1992) have reported that much research indicates that negative therapeutic outcomes arise from "subtle pejorative communications" on the part of the therapist. Subtle cues that the patient has not done "enough" can seriously undermine therapeutic progress.

Interpretations-in-Action

We need both to respect the limits of the individual patient and therapy and to appreciate the profound psychological change that can occur without much direct verbal interpretative work. In fact, I think that much of the beneficial effect from the therapeutic relationship in brief therapy comes from what Ogden (1994) has termed "interpretations-in-action." These are actions on the part of the therapist that constitute a transference-countertransference interpretation. These actions have to do with the way the therapy is conducted—for example, the management of the frame and the therapist's attitude, demeanor, and facial expressions. Ogden (1994), in writing about psychoanalysis, states that later in the treatment these interpretations-in-action could then be verbally symbolized with the patient. In brief therapy, however, we may not be able to later verbally interpret the interaction and, yet, I would suggest that the nonverbalized interaction still has profound therapeutic power.

For example, I noted that Alan, the schizoid college student and physicist described in Chapter 5, did not seem to be able to use my verbal interpretations. However, I was able to convey an understanding of him through my consistent but nondemanding interest in what he was experiencing and through my respect for his sensitivity to having his boundaries violated. This conveyed the message that his inner world was valid and important and we could relate in a different manner from what he had generally experienced with people thus far. While I did have to contain intense anxiety during the work with him, I conveyed that the issues of boundaries and control were prominent ones for him and he could relate to someone (me) without the other person either anxiously rejecting or controlling him. This mode of relating constituted interpretations-in-action and provided a shared understanding that was meaningful and affectively significant for both of us. I felt that only a small portion of this dynamic was verbally explored, but yet the interpretations-in-action had an extensive effect.

SOME SUGGESTIONS REGARDING TRANSFERENCE INTERPRETATION

Think Dynamically

The object relations brief therapist aims at operating from an empathic stance that balances attention to the symptomatic distress and to the dynamic configuration. Under the pressure of time and patient suffering and/or demands, the therapist may feel pressed to focus exclusively on presenting symptoms. At the other extreme, she may feel that she needs to focus almost exclusively on the dynamic interpretive work to see herself as doing more than "Band-Aid" therapy. Of course, both of these extremes are to be avoided. Thinking dynamically refers to an attitude or receptive capacity rather than to an overt intervention—it may or may not be acted upon.

Consider Making Interpretations on a Trial Basis

The only way to really see if a patient can benefit from verbal interpretive interventions is to try them and observe the patient's response. Done with tact, sensitivity, and restraint, this will usually not seriously harm the therapeutic alliance and usually provide the therapist with useful information on the extent to which the patient is willing or able to do this kind of work. Malan (1976) has described three potential benefits of trial interpretations: strengthening the therapeutic alliance, providing a measure of the patient's capacity to use interpretations, and providing information on the dynamics of the patient's problems. If the patient does not seem to respond well to the trial interpretations, the therapist considers the following questions:

1. Is this patient unable or unwilling to use verbal interpretations? If so, the therapy should be directed more toward interpretations-in-action, toward the contextual transference, and toward the existential and corrective elements of the therapeutic change process.
2. Have the interpretations been inaccurate? With more accurate interpretations the patient may respond well to further interpretive work. While this is an important question to consider, therapists often assume that this is the problem when it isn't and then begin a hyperactive interpretive pattern with the hope that the latest iteration of the dynamics will finally connect. This can produce the problem cycle of increased interpretive activity in the face of lack of therapeutic progress suggested by Piper and colleagues (1991a).
3. Is the timing wrong? Does this patient need more time for the alliance to develop before the therapist makes further interpretations?

As Binder and Strupp (1991) have written, skillful interpretation depends on timing, accuracy, and relevance of the content and manner in which the interpretation is made.

Make Interpretations in a Speculative Manner

Every therapist has his own style. My own is to not have my comments convey certainty. Rather, I usually express my comments in a manner that suggests that this is what I've been thinking, what does the patient think? My comments often begin with phrases such as "I'm not sure this is accurate but I was thinking that ..." or "I had a thought that maybe. ... What do you think?" Through this style I want to invite the patient to "play" with the comment with me and to modify it, challenge me on it or ultimately discard it if he wishes. Also, if I'm way off in the accuracy of the comment, the patient will usually be less resistant to it being presented in a provisional manner. This is consistent with the current object relations perspective that emphasizes the generation of meaningful experience between the therapist and patient (Mitchell 1993) rather than seeing the goal of therapy as primarily to uncover the "truth" about the past. Also, interpretation should not be considered to be the only "true" psychodynamic activity. It is one of many important types of interactions with the patient.

Emphasize the Simple Observation of the Repeated Patterns, But Also Look for Opportunities to Make T-P, T-O, and T-S Connections

The first goal of a transference interpretation is to bring into awareness for the patient the pattern of her interaction with the therapist. This may take considerable work for the patient to see that pattern. In a particular brief therapy, that may be all that can be accomplished rather than being able to go further and make T-P, T-O, and T-S linkages. See the example of Philip, below. However, even without those linkages, the patient has learned something valuable that she can take with her. She now sees a pattern that she has used with one person and the effects of such a paradigm. It is hoped her curiosity has been engaged to consider where else she may use such a pattern. Joyce and Piper (1993), among others, have emphasized the importance of keeping interpretations rather simple and not overly abstract or complicated.

If the patient seems able to examine and reflect upon the identified interaction pattern between herself and the therapist, then the therapist can consider if more can be done. The therapist then looks for moments to additionally connect the transference phenomena with parents, others, or self representations. My experience is that T-P and T-S linkages are particularly powerful interventions. Malan (1976) has pointed out the particular therapeutic strength of T-P interpretations.

The important point here is for the therapist to look for times to make T-P, T-O, and T-S interpretations and to monitor her countertransferences of impatience and need to be sufficiently "dynamic." Sometimes, pushing for these interpretations is too much within the brief therapy context and the therapeutic alliance suffers. In such instances, even the more humble goal of helping the patient to be more aware of how she interacts with the therapist in the here and now can be lost through this overly ambitious approach.

Use the Countertransference to Understand and Interpret the Transference

This is a basic point especially emphasized in object relations thinking. It speaks to the importance of the experiential quality of therapy for the therapist as well as for the patient. It refers to the merit of the therapist respecting and observing his own countertransference reactions as invaluable sources of information about the patient. Usually this does not involve directly commenting on it with the patient but rather using it to better understand the terrain of the patient's inner world. For example, the therapist's reactions may reveal some aspects of the patient's relationship to self and to others. The therapist also internally notes the pull from the patient to "be" objects from the past and resists this pull of projective identification toward repetition. For example, in seeing a new patient, I found myself feeling very (and unusually) judgmental toward him. As we continued to meet I came to understand that this was an unconscious induction on his part for me (and others in his life, especially authority figures) to reenact the behavior of his very judgmental mother.

Clinical Example: Philip

Philip, a 23-year-old single man who had graduated from college, sought therapy because he had been unsuccessful during the previous year in landing a job in his chosen field of financial analysis. He spent much of the first two sessions complaining that his chair was uncomfortable, his previous therapist had original works of art in his office and I didn't, the other therapist wore expensive Italian shoes and I wore Rockports, and on and on. He was moderately depressed and was now finding it difficult to continue the demoralizing job search process. He had seen another therapist for a few sessions but that therapist's fees had been much higher than mine and so he had to discontinue the sessions.

During these initial sessions, Philip's disparaging and condescending comments about me and my office seemed to "fill" the room. I found myself stung by some of the comments and wondered if I was not as good as the other therapist and I had competitive thoughts toward him ("More expensive shoes don't give you more soul." "Looking good isn't the same as being good."). I did not express any of those thoughts nor did I comment on his remarks. I felt that they were necessary for Philip in some way to reduce his anxiety (by reducing me). Still, I didn't like it and thought it was striking how much he was focusing on the surface issues of my office's and my appearance. I was also struck by how many of his comments were directed toward aspects of the office that I particularly liked (e.g., a favorite print).

During the next session, Philip continued his barrage of criticism and I felt both out of patience with it and, more reflectively, that we needed to address this together. Following one such comment, I said, "I think we need to understand why you're spending so much time criticizing me and my office." At first he reacted defensively and said that he was simply being honest about what he was thinking and that it *was* true that my office didn't come up to the standard of his previous therapist's. He then paused and indicated that he was very disappointed that he couldn't see the other therapist. He acknowledged that he was hurt by the therapist's unwillingness to see him for a reduced fee and that he was afraid that I wouldn't be "good enough" to really help him.

My comment was a simple transference interpretation that pointed out to him a way that he was relating to me and invited him to explore it. There was no attempt at this point to link the interaction between us to past or other present relationships. The interpretation did serve to help him be in touch with his feelings toward the other therapist and toward me so that he could directly talk about them. He was then able to explore other material and not be so obsessed with my attire or interior decorating. It should also be noted that the interpretation had an additional function in that it dealt with my own discomfort and aggression. It put it within the working therapeutic space.

Philip's father was a very successful professional, an internationally known expert in his field and Philip admired him enormously. He spoke movingly of sitting quietly as a boy at family gatherings and being enthralled by his father holding forth on some fascinating topic. On the other hand, Philip felt rejected by the father. He felt that no matter how well he did his father would always find something to criticize about it ("Nice job, Phil, but you know it could have been so much better if only you had . . ."). Philip chose to go to a state university rather than to an Ivy League school as his father had wanted, and his father and he had had several battles around that. Interestingly, he reported that his father often complained about the way he dressed, that he looked like a "peasant."

I knew very little of this history in the first few sessions with Philip (and what I did know I wasn't thinking about very effectively). It does put into perspective these early interactions with him and we were subsequently able to make some father transference connections. His relationship with the first therapist reenacted some aspects of his relationship with his father—the idealization of the father concurrent with feelings of being rejected by him. One interpretation (O-P) I offered was "I think that your experience with Dr. X felt much like the rejection you suffered from your father." In his relationship with me, he was treating me like his father had treated him—critical, rejecting, disappointed. An example of an interpretation of this material (S-T-P) was "You might carry your father around in you more than you know. When you were putting me down so much it was like the way your father put you down." Coming to see his unconscious identification with his father and that he treated other people as his father had was a difficult but important insight for him.

My countertransference to his criticisms gave me an experience through projective identification of what he had felt like in various interactions with his father—inadequate, angry, defensive. Also, I was not very aware of the significance of my response at the time. I only appreciated it a session or two later. I believe that this lack of awareness was in part due to my own denseness and defensiveness, which I continue to struggle with. However, I also think it was part of the projective identification. Philip subsequently talked about being "frozen" and unable to think in the presence of his father.

In this case we were able within ten sessions to identify the transferential interaction pattern in the here and now. We were also able to work on linking it to other relationships. In brief therapy it is not always possible to make those linkages. Therapists must respect the power of the initial steps of simply helping the patient to be aware of the pattern and its consequences. Furthermore, we need to accept that the patient may not yet be ready to deal with connecting it with other material.

In Making Interpretations, Guard against Force-Feeding

Clinical experience and recent research (Piper et al. 1991a, 1993, Hoglend 1993b) demonstrate the dangers to the therapeutic alliance and to therapeutic success of too frequent or aggressive interpretive activity. The therapist needs to carefully observe the effect of the interpretations on the patient and on the therapeutic alliance. It is, of course, less important to be "right" than to maintain an effective working alliance at the level that the patient can accept. The balance struck is with striving for the deepest level possible while maintaining the alliance and empathic attunement.

So, the object relations brief therapist looks for opportunities to bring more of the patient's inner world and external functioning into awareness through interpretative work, especially transference interpretations. While striving to accomplish this she guards against making the concentration of interpretations too high and against the patient feeling attacked, barraged, or misunderstood.

Of course, some patients will at times feel attacked, barraged, and misunderstood as part of their transference reactions, but the therapist seeks to minimize the "real" provocation of those reactions.

Accept that the Transference May Be Persistent and that You May Not Be Able to Interpret It

Depending on the patient, therapist, and time resources available, the patient may not be able to use transference interpretations or interpretations in general. The therapist does not then persist in "making the patient see it" but rather respects the strength of it and works in other ways—existential, corrective, or interpretations-in-action. For example, therapists not infrequently try to talk patients out of idealizing transferences—usually a futile and counterproductive activity.

If You Are Unable to Interpret the Transference, Use It and the Countertransference to Understand the Patient Better and to Influence the Patient

The basic point here is that understanding the transference and countertransference issues positions the therapist to be more effective and empathic. He better grasps the meaning of his and the patient's behavior and of their interactions. The therapist works more effectively not so much in this sense by *doing* anything differently but rather by *being* different.

The therapist, however, can also use the transference and countertransference in practical ways without use of interpretation. Consider the following situation that came up with two different patients. Both patients had begun to feel much better after a few sessions and said that they wanted to stop treatment. I felt that it was unlikely that the improvements were more than temporary and that a continuation of the brief therapy would help to consolidate the gains.

Henry was a 30-year-old attorney who was both embarrassed about his need for therapy and impatient to discontinue the sessions since he was so busy. A rather narcissistic man, he prided himself on getting the best of everything and striving to be the best. He responded to me with a style that suggested that he was surprised by how useful the sessions had been but that he regarded me as a gifted craftsman who was below his station in life. I told him that I was glad that the therapy had been helpful to him but that I would recommend that he continue for ten more sessions. I told him that I saw him as a complex man and that the additional sessions would do more justice to that complexity. I suggested that he owed it to himself to get more of a forum for self-enhancement. He agreed and we productively continued therapy. I believed everything I said but I was clearly appealing to his narcissism. Within the limits of our relationship, though, I felt that this was the vehicle through which I could most successfully get through to him concerning the benefits of a bit more therapy.

Ruth, 23, was a young mother who was also working full time as a secretary. Her sister had recently died and she came in to deal with her grief over this loss. She was seen as part of her employer's EAP and she was eligible for three sessions. Crying throughout most of the first session, she relived the last few months of her sister's fight with cancer. Toward the end of the session, she expressed much gratitude for the session, saying that this was the first time that she had been able to really cry for an extended time about her sister's death. She felt much better and thought that this would be enough therapy for now. While she was dealing with a rather uncomplicated mourning reaction, I thought that two more sessions in which to further process her experience would be very beneficial. I experienced Ruth as a woman who organized her self-image around being helpful to others but who was uncomfortable being in the position of receiving help. Unlike Henry, I did not think that a plea for her to continue for her own benefit would be persuasive. Instead, I suggested to Ruth that by more fully dealing with her reactions to her loss at this point she would be more emotionally available to her children. I was in effect saying, "If not for yourself, do it for them." This appeal to the positive effects on those that depended upon her was very much in keeping with her internal paradigm of being a caregiver rather than a care-receiver.

8

The Middle: II

> Any form of psychotherapy *must* be incomplete unless
> it incorporates the psychodynamic point of view. . . . But
> the converse is also true: dynamic psychotherapy itself
> is incomplete unless it incorporates the theory and tech-
> niques of other forms of therapy.
>
> David Malan, 1979

In this chapter I continue the exploration of middle-phase issues
in object relations brief therapy through discussion of the use of
nonpsychodynamic techniques and the anticipation of termination.
I then present material from the middle phase of the two therapies
detailed in Chapter 6 (Ronald and Diane).

USE OF NONPSYCHODYNAMIC TECHNIQUES

It is absolutely clear to me that nonpsychodynamic techniques can
be judiciously incorporated into brief dynamic therapy. There is

much therapeutic power in the varied techniques that have been developed by other models of change and it seems to me to border on denial to refuse to consider such interventions due to allegiance to one particular theoretical orientation. The careful selection of other interventions can very much enhance therapeutic effectiveness. There can be a synergistic effect from the blending of dynamic and nondynamic approaches. Nondynamic techniques often provide one or more of the following benefits:

1. Rapid symptom relief (this has been the major benefit in my experience)
2. Aid in building the alliance by providing the patient with prompt evidence of the usefulness of therapy
3. A quick route to unconscious material (for example, by using guided imagery or hypnosis)
4. Demonstration of material useful for the therapy (for example, by using homework assignments, role plays, and behavior rehearsal).

The dynamic approach explores the meaning of the patient's suffering and symptoms within the context of his unique personality. In so doing, it helps in solidifying the gains made. Understanding the transference, countertransference, and unconscious dynamics of the patient provides an understanding of the patient's resistances to change that may either cause noncompliance with the nondynamic exercises or cause them to be ineffective in some other ways. The criticism of an eclectic approach is that it can be a chaotic muddle of interventions based on what is needed at the moment rather than an organized strategy of treatment. Certainly, that can be the case. However, if the therapist operates from a coherent orientation, such as an object relations perspective, she can then determine whether the nondynamic intervention will support the treatment or not. On the other hand, to ignore what is known about assisting personal change from other perspectives is like being one of the proverbial five blind men who each has a partially accurate but incomplete conception of what an elephant is.

As discussed in Chapter 5, the therapist must be sensitive to the effects on the patient and on the relationship of the use of the interventions since many nonpsychodynamic interventions temporarily change the stance of the therapist to a more active, directive one. During such work, the therapy takes on more of a corrective therapy element. If the therapist finds herself inclined to use one of these more active interventions she should examine her countertransference reactions to understand the meaning of that decision. For example, I often find myself thinking about using a more active intervention, such as a cognitive restructuring exercise at a time when I am in touch with my own (and perhaps the patient's) sense of hopelessness. At such times, what is most needed may be simply to experience and endure those feelings rather than "to solve" them through some immediate activity. Later in this chapter as I discuss the middle phase of therapy with Ronald, I explore my conflict over the use of cognitive/behavioral interventions with him.

Budman and Gurman (1988) have especially highlighted the use of hypnosis as part of their I-D-E approach. As noted in Chapter 5, Strupp and Binder (1984) and Horowitz and colleagues (1984) have elements in their models that are similar to those in cognitive therapy. My own brief therapy work has included the use of the following techniques within a dynamic approach:

Relaxation training
Systematic desensitization
Contingency contracting
Role playing/behavior rehearsal
Guided imagery
Cognitive restructuring
Three-column cognitive technique
Cognitive challenging
Thought-stopping
Daily monitoring of symptom levels
Journal-keeping of various sorts
Experimental homework assignments
Stress management
Conflict resolution techniques
Sex therapy: sensate focus
Behavioral anger control techniques.

My recommendation for the consideration of nonpsycho-dynamic interventions within object relations brief therapy is based on the therapist's applying them within the context of a relationship that respects the individuality and depth of the patient. As Budman and Gurman (1988) have rather succinctly put it, "It is important to remember, however, that the therapist must always maintain a clear sense of the broader dynamics of a given situation, and should not merely apply a set of techniques in an unthinking way or in a manner that dehumanizes the patient" (p. 213).

Later in this chapter, I describe the use of nonpsychodynamic interventions with Ronald. They included homework assignments, relaxation and anxiety management training, and cognitive therapy techniques. In Chapter 11, I describe the therapy with Denise. This therapy included homework assignments, daily record-keeping of symptom levels, thought-stopping, cognitive challenging, and other cognitive techniques.

ANTICIPATING TERMINATION

The issue of termination is a crucial one and work with it should not be confined to the end phase of treatment. It should be considered as a factor affecting the therapy throughout its duration and examined with the patient from time to time. While the therapist should not coerce the patient into facing termination, he should guard against the common (universal?) resistance against dealing with endings and loss by both patient and therapist. Conditions are more conducive for facing termination when the therapy is not only brief but also time-limited and the therapist and patient know (or at least know when they are not denying it) when therapy is expected to end. Within the first few sessions of time-limited therapy the therapist should explicitly discuss with the patient the outside limit of their work together, whether it is set in terms of numbers of sessions or a particular date. Even in brief therapies in which the end point is not so clearly determined, it is important that the therapist be aware of its impact and discuss it if feasible.

In Chapter 5, I described my work with Alan. In that case there were no duration limits set but he emphasized right from the beginning that he wished the therapy to be as brief as possible. I agreed to it, although sometimes suggesting that he consider allowing the therapy to go for a longer duration (he never did). In this instance there was little direct work with him on the impact of his self-imposed brevity of treatment, although I did once or twice suggest that it caused him to feel safer (he did not agree). It was important, though, that repeatedly I internally examined the effect that it had on me. Among my reactions were heightened anxiety that he would flee treatment precipitously and concomitant hesitancy in making interventions. In my experience of his rather sudden appearances and disappearances, I believe I had a sample of what he had experienced with his frequently absent but controlling father.

While there may be times throughout the therapy contract that termination issues make their presence known, this can particularly be the case at about the midpoint of time-limited therapy. Mann (1973) and other writers have also noted this phenomenon. Just as middle age frequently brings with it consideration of one's own limits and life's end, so too does the middle time in brief therapy stimulate thoughts of the end of therapy. Just as working through a midlife crisis can help a person face the experience of loss, so too a "midtherapy crisis" can help the patient face the loss of the therapist and the therapy. If the therapist is attentive to these possibilities, she will often hear material that is related to termination.

> For example, a 25-year-old woman was seen for time-limited therapy of about twenty sessions in duration. She had suffered from multiple problems since adolescence and the therapy focused on her difficulty with separation (especially from her mother) and a recurring pattern of impulsively giving up on work/academic pursuits and on relationships. In work with her therapist (a woman), she had gained both considerable insight and greater control over her impulsivity by the middle phase of therapy. At about the midpoint of treatment, she presented in one session several pieces of material that seemed related to termination anxiety. She described fantasies of return to a psychiatric hospital she had been in as a teenager and

thoughts of the peace that suicide might bring. She requested medication for her obsessive fears about death, AIDS, and cancer. She tearfully spoke of her hatred of her father for having abandoned her and the family.

All of this material was determined by a number of factors. The fact that it came up at this point in the therapy, I believe, was related to the midpoint of treatment having been reached and it bringing up termination issues. Her hospital and suicide fantasies were in part speaking to her fears of separation from her therapist and the request for medication was partially an expression of her despair that she could not take care of herself on her own. The intensity with which she was dealing with her hatred of her father was fueled by the anger at her therapist "abandoning" her in the near future. Some confirmation for connecting this material with termination issues was provided by her question in this session: "When are we ending?" From this point on the therapist periodically would suggest that related phenomena might have to do with their impending separation and invited her to explore it.

Certainly in the middle phase of brief therapy the therapist should be thinking about the upcoming termination and how to productively work on that with the patient. In time-limited brief therapy once the midpoint has been reached I find myself looking for manifestations of termination issues and ways to bring the issues to the attention of the patient well before the end.

MIDDLE-PHASE CLINICAL EXAMPLE: RONALD

Session 1

Ronald is the 24-year-old law student described in Chapter 6 who was suffering from acute anxiety. He was feeling out of control, could not concentrate on his studies, and was having a great deal of difficulty sleeping. The initial foci were the symptomatic focus of reducing his anxiety and the dynamic focus of high all-or-nothing standards for self and others. I employed a number of nonpsychodynamic techniques in working with him. In the first session he mentioned that he had previously been very athletic in college but had not engaged in any exercise since coming to law school because he had felt he didn't have the time. I suggested that vigorous exercise is sometimes quite helpful in managing anxiety and recommended that he try some jogging (which he had previously done in college). He agreed to try it. I indicated that in the next session I wanted to obtain some background information from him and that then we would work directly on his anxiety.

I was aware in this session of wanting to help him reduce his anxiety quickly. I also was feeling pressure to rather instantly "prove" that therapy and I could be helpful to him. He had earlier in the session expressed his skepticism as to whether therapy would help at all. I thought that my plan to direct our attention immediately toward symptomatic relief was sound but I did wonder if I was also responding to his rather critical "show me but I don't think this will help" attitude.

Session 2

I came to better understand this critical attitude during this session. Ronald was the oldest of four children and was the only son. His parents divorced when he was 10 and he described great admiration for his mother who alone raised him and his three sisters. He described her as being "principled and a hard worker" but also as being "depressive and a martyr." He worried about her since she so often seemed to be unhappy.

He hated his father and was estranged from him since the divorce. Ronald seemed to feel contempt toward his father and his lack of education—he never finished high school. Also, his father was physically and emotionally abusive to his mother and to him (but not to his sisters). He described his father as being a volatile man who seemed to want to spend time with him but it had usually degenerated into arguments and fights. His father would frequently yell at him and sometimes hit him. Ronald said that his father always seemed disappointed with him.

He had had one serious romantic relationship throughout college but he and his girlfriend "just grew apart." It sounded to me as though he lost interest in her and didn't feel she was good enough for him anymore. An additional current source of stress was the end of a relationship with a woman he had been dating for three months.

Ronald did note that he was always disappointed with his performance. However, he returned the next session to correct that, saying that during his senior year in college he was "perfect"—popular, good grades, high office in student government. He noted that it has always been difficult for him to trust people and he was very ashamed about going through this present crisis. His professional goal was to run for political office—U.S. Senate or even higher.

I found, as I often do when I learn more about a patient's background, that Ronald's history evoked more empathy for him. I considered that the pressure I was feeling to prove myself was part of a concordant identification with him. This was the way his father frequently caused him to feel, and the way he was relating to me was an unconscious identification with his father. I further reflected that academic success was additionally important to his self-image because it differentiated him from his much less educated father. I wondered about unconscious identifications with his mother's depressive, martyred stance and also about whether he might expect some similar self-sacrificing devotion toward him from any woman that he would be involved with. I did not share any of these speculations with Ronald at this point. However, these insights did help me to maintain my empathy for him in the face of his critical attitude. This understanding of Ronald also helped me later in the therapy to resist the projective identification pull to be like his father—I felt it but did not act it out (at least not very intensely).

The preliminary foci that we had set in the previous session still seemed apt. He indicated that his anxiety had diminished somewhat and that the jogging had been helpful but that his sleep disturbance and inability to study were continuing. I proposed that during the next several sessions we work on his anxiety by doing some behavioral relaxation training and he readily agreed. As I stated previously, a practical focus on symptom alleviation seemed wise for several reasons: he was directly asking for that, the symptoms were quite disruptive of his functioning, a law student can easily fall hopelessly behind in a semester in a matter of only a few weeks, and he seemed to need "proof" that therapy could help him. On the other hand, I wondered if I was acting out a transference-countertransference dynamic with him being his critical father and me being the Ronald who would inevitably fail in the father's eyes and disappoint him. If that dynamic were prominent, then therapy would inevitably fail. I felt unsure of my decision but was heartened by the benefits he had reported from jogging and by his eager response to the relaxation suggestion.

Sessions 3–5

These three sessions were mostly centered around teaching Ronald deep muscle relaxation exercises and applying them to control his anxiety. By the fourth session he was able to study fairly well and his sleep had improved. He actively collaborated in this process and the rapid reduction in his anxiety through his own actions seemed to be a very positive experience for him. These behavioral interventions constituted interpretations-in-action. I believe that the perception that he could *do* something to control what he had previously felt to be uncontrollable aided him as much as the actual exercises themselves.

Therefore, I wondered if I had been too anxious to please by using these interventions. Perhaps he could more meaningfully have dealt with this issue of feeling out of control through directly talking about it and exploring it. In that way, he could have become more in touch with his own ability to regain mastery over his life. However, as I reflected on this, I basically felt it had been a good decision to take the behavioral approach initially. This was much more in keeping with what he wanted at the time and how he wished to solve his "problem." In that sense, it was less of a narcissistic injury and I thought there was a fairly good chance that we could do more dynamic work, if he persisted in treatment.

During these sessions we also examined his extraordinarily high standards for himself and what seemed to be needed for him to feel adequate. As had been the case in the first session, this intrigued him and I recommended to him that he read Burns's (1980) *Feeling Good*, a self-help book on the cognitive therapy of depression, to further look at how his recurrent patterns of thinking about himself added to his anxiety. I did not assign any readings to him but suggested that, on his own, he might find the book helpful in supporting our work together.

I found myself pleased with the progress in symptom reduction that Ronald had made and was further encouraged by his interest in working on the dynamic focus. I no longer felt that I needed to prove myself to him, but I was feeling that he might drop out of therapy soon, given that he was feeling so much better. Remember, in the first session he had indicated that he was ashamed about going through this and that he expected therapy would take a short time.

Sessions 6–7

Ronald found the book to be very useful and he brought it in to these two sessions to discuss specific passages. It gave him a framework within which to challenge his automatic all-or-nothing expectations. He had taken the self-test for depression and while he did not score high on depression himself, he said, "This is my mother!" He enthusiastically bought another copy of the book and mailed it to her (she, however, was not particularly positive toward it). He had become an ally with me in treating his internalized depressed mother.

During these sessions, there was a calm, motivated working atmosphere. Ronald was surprised and relieved that his symptoms had diminished and that he was able once again to sleep well and to study. His transference to me at this point was very positive. He was intrigued by the interpretation that he has had to be nearly perfect to feel satisfied with himself and was wanting to investigate this further. I was feeling rather relaxed during these sessions and no longer worried about an abrupt, premature termination since he now seemed to be actively engaged in psychodynamic self-study. I recall thinking, "This could hardly be going better," and felt uneasy with this self-satisfied reaction. I was feeling his idealization of me and the potential for an exciting object dynamic to become prominent. I was also feeling some discomfort with my own grandiosity being stimulated.

Sessions 8–12

These five sessions centered on examination of his inner world and I did the most interpretive work with him during this phase of the treatment. By session 8, his functioning had returned to levels prior to receiving his first semester's grades. I felt, though, that unless he was more aware of his narcissistic issues and better able to cope with them that he would likely have recurring crises of this sort. I noted that we were about halfway through our contract but he denied any reaction to that.

We continued to look at how narcissistically vulnerable he was. We specifically discussed how his grandiose standards for success intensified his disappointment and suffering when he didn't meet them and how his self-esteem was so reactive to such events. We connected his strife-ridden childhood, especially his father's influence, with his labile self-esteem (Self-Past interpretations).

A few interpretive themes were prominent during this time in treatment. We focused much work on how he had unconsciously internalized his father's abusive, critical characteristics and frequently treated himself like his father did (Self-Past link). Another theme was that he often treated other people like his father treated him and his mother (Past-Self-Other interpretation). We talked about his rather critical dismissive attitude toward me during the first session (Therapist-Self-Past interpretation). The depression and self-pity he experienced when he defined a situation as a failure was conceptualized as an unconscious identification with his depressive mother (Past-Self connection). During this period he expressed feeling that I was disappointed in him and I suggested that he felt I was responding to him like his father did (Therapist-Past Interpretation).

Ronald was an active collaborator during these sessions and was at times enthusiastic about being able to understand elements in his personality that had previously been mysterious to him. He did have difficulty acknowledging his own critical stance with other people and initially felt criticized by me for pointing it out. It was painful for him to consider that not only was he the victim of his father's attacks but also that he was unconsciously the attacker at times as well (Past-Self-Other interpretation). He had organized part of his life to demonstrate emphatically that he was *not* like his father (e.g., by getting highly educated). There were instances when Ronald would feel "put down" when I would point out something that he hadn't yet seen. We looked at this as a part of the extraordinarily high expectations he would have for himself as well as his difficulty with envy.

I was interested that in the preceding paragraph I wrote that Ronald "was an active collaborator." He was, but my experience of the sessions was that it was often a competitive collaboration. As noted earlier, he had tapped into my own narcissistic issues. I had felt a need to prove myself to him and, I think, to demonstrate that I was "good" (perhaps this is similar to what he had felt with his father). I was aware of taking some pleasure when I would point out something to him that he hadn't seemed to see yet. Therefore, his feeling of being "put down" by some of my interventions may have come not only from his own issues about envy but also because they *were* competitive attacks on my part.

During the twelfth session, he indicated that he had not yet landed a summer job. This was important not only from the standpoint of finances but also because of the role such positions often play in law students' job prospects after graduation. He was anxious about it, wanted to use the sessions to deal with this, and asked if we could spread out the last three sessions by meeting on an every other week basis. I thought this was, in part, an avoidance of termination issues but it also seemed to make sense as well. We looked at how he had expected that, of course, he would easily and smoothly be able to get a "great" summer job, but then when it proved more difficult his self-esteem plummeted. The termination phase with Ronald is discussed in the following chapter.

MIDDLE-PHASE CLINICAL EXAMPLE: DIANE

I described the focus-setting with Diane in Chapter 6. She was depressed and suicidal following her arrest for embezzling $30,000 from her employer. She had a borderline personality structure and the stealing had occurred dozens of times over the course of two years in dissociated states. The money usually went toward various family activities (e.g., vacations, birthday parties). The symptomatic focus was to help her deal with the suicidal feelings and with the anxiety and depression that came up as the legal action against her proceeded. The preliminary dynamic focus was to explore the meaning and impact of the splits in her personality and the "emotional storms" (as she called them) that were a consequence of them.

Much of Diane's difficult history has been described in Chapter 6. To briefly recap some of it, her parents divorced when she was 7 and she was frequently in the role of the substitute parent for her younger siblings. Her mother was a perfectionist who would beat Diane for small transgressions. During her childhood and adolescence she had experiences of emotional and sexual abuse. Her father and boyfriend both died when she was 19 years old. She had hated her father and felt some guilt over his death. Her boyfriend died in a motorcycle accident and, although he was "the love of my life," he had frequently beaten her.

Through some supportive work, her suicidal feelings diminished rather rapidly. She centered her thoughts on taking care of her children and felt that suicide was not an option because of her responsibility toward them. Throughout her life—starting with her younger siblings—her positive identity was centered on being a self-sacrificing nurturing figure. Diane now threw herself into being a "better than ever" mother to atone for what she had done to the family.

The dynamic focus centered around the destructive impact of having a part of her that was so consumed with being the self-sacrificing giver that she would split off and ignore her own needs. This created a deprivation, which was both self-imposed and produced by her often depriving environment. This deprivation, coupled with a denial of anger toward those close to her, made Diane vulnerable to states she called "emotional storms." These storms activated an impulsive self who would greedily act out (stealing, overeating) and/or become intensely angry at people who were not close to her (see below).

Session 14

The following are excerpts from the fourteenth session in this twenty-five-session therapy. Her lawyer was trying to work out a plea bargain that would involve some home detention and payback of the money that was stolen—but no prison time. While she was no longer suicidal, Diane at times would be overwhelmed by depression and anxiety following either setbacks in the legal proceedings when it looked as though she might have to serve some time in prison or when there would be tension with her husband.

At this point in the therapy, I was pleased with the progress and the therapeutic relationship. I was frustrated, though, with her resistance to looking at her anger, especially anger toward her husband. I generally felt very moved by her struggle against a very damaging past and a scary, uncertain future. Occasionally, I would feel mistrustful of how cooperative she seemed to be with me. Each of these feelings was connected to different parts of her inner world—her caring, courageous, responsible self and her impulsive, criminal self.

She and her husband still hoped to move to a house they owned in North Carolina once her legal problems were settled. Diane started session 14 by describing her visit over the weekend to the house and having had an altercation with a contractor doing some of the renovations on the children's bedrooms.

> D: So, I was proud of myself. He was treating me bad but I didn't yell or fight or give up or anything. I was together and said, "We can't talk anymore, you'll have to stop work until you talk to my husband." I was so cool. I started turning out the lights all over the house. He starts following me around and giving me a lot of stuff about why he can't do what we're telling him. I keep closing up (the house) and he finally says okay, that he'll do what we want.
>
> MS: You handled this very differently from the way you'd do it in the past.
>
> D: Yeah . . . I don't think I ever told you this, did I? . . . about when I got kicked out of X [a large department store]? There was bad blood between me and this salesgirl. She kept acting like I was this big bother and she should be waiting on other customers. We yelled at each other and then when she gives me the change, she doesn't give it to me. She just slaps it down on the counter. (Sighs loudly)

So, I slapped her in the face. What a bitch! Store security comes and they talk about getting the police and I'm still so mad but they decide to let me go if I promise never to shop there again. No way I'd come back there anyway. I hated losing control like that but she deserved it.

I felt uneasy with this story. Although she ended it with how she hated losing control there was a rather righteous satisfaction in having slapped the saleswoman. I thought that this was an unconscious identification with her mother and the way her mother abused her. I was identifying with the salesgirl, a complementary identification, and was feeling how threatening Diane could be.

MS: It does seem that the saleswoman treated you badly and caused you to get angry but your slapping her reminded me of the way your mother would hit you when she got mad at you [O-S-P].

  D: (Silence) . . . I guess so, I don't like to think that I act like her sometimes, . . . with her and with the family I just give in.

MS: What kept you hanging in there with the contractor but controlling yourself?

  D: Thinking about my kids' rooms and what they'd look like if we moved in without the work having been completed.

MS: Your doing this for your family kept you hanging in there. . . . It would have been harder if you were just doing it for yourself.

  D: Yes . . . I never even thought of what I needed in the past.

She then recounted tearfully how she and her husband had had a fight about her resistance to getting new tennis shoes. Her shoes had holes in the soles and her husband had repeatedly told her to get a new pair. She hadn't, feeling that she didn't deserve to get something new for herself since she had so seriously hurt the family with her stealing and arrest. The husband had reacted angrily that this was ridiculous and she should "just get them." This was one of their worst fights during the time that I saw Diane. Throughout most of this period, her husband was stoically supportive. Diane and I discussed this as another example of her self-denial and how it puts her at risk for the emotional storms.

Throughout my work with her, I attempted to bring to her attention the issue of anger. I felt it was important in two ways. First, her self-denial was often an unconscious strategy to prevent anger and rejection from others. Second, and more importantly, I thought that she had a deep well of unconscious anger toward her husband (and other men) about many things—for example, his drinking and lack of emotional availability to her, his early retirement, and largely unilateral decision to move the family. The stealing and subsequent arrest were certainly determined by many factors but it was no coincidence that these would be actions that would cause her law-and-order prosecutor husband intense humiliation.

In this session, as in most others, Diane said that she didn't think she was angry at her husband and that it didn't play a role in any of her problems. I was feeling that I had been too dedicated to getting her to "see" this point. I thought I might be feeling a bit like her frustrated husband did about the shoes. She confirmed my hypothesis about pushing this issue too hard by changing the subject and returning briefly to her handling of the interaction with the contractor.

> D: This is a good change but there's been a bad one since my arrest. . . . I'm more timid and scared. . . . I have to push myself to get out of the house. . . . I had trouble driving in the rain today to get here.
>
> MS: How did you make it?
>
> D: I thought of you . . . how you'd be wasting your time and you sitting here waiting for me.

My initial reaction was to mistrust Diane's comment that thinking of me got her to the session. What else might be making it difficult for her to come to the session? She had shifted her—our—attention to me as a way to avoid the exploration of her anger. Did she feel exposed or "caught" on this issue and feel ashamed? My next thought was to consider how so much of her behavior was controlled by how others would be affected. Throughout therapy with Diane, I often found myself with one of two reactions—either doubting her sincerity or commitment to therapy or, more frequently, being very moved by her struggles against the adversity in her past and present. As I previously noted, these responses were manifestations of my connection with two parts of her: her responsible but deprived self and her criminal but gratified self.

> MS: Not the effect on you? . . . You'd miss the session, pay for it even though you weren't here?
>
> D: No, I didn't think of that.
>
> MS: How do you feel about coming?
>
> D: Roj [her husband] thinks it helps a lot. I'm a lot calmer and I don't yell at the kids or at him as much.
>
> MS: You know, I asked how *you* feel.
>
> D: I like coming. . . . It does help but I wish it wasn't so expensive and I wish Roj would come in, too.
>
> MS: You know, your mother and father are in you. You've said before how much this helps you and Roj has too. . . . But like the shoes, it's hard to justify to yourself that you need it and ought to get it. You ignore your needs just like your parents ignored them [S-P]. Your response to me about how you felt about coming was that Roj thought it was a good idea and that it was good for him and the kids.
>
> D: (Silence) . . . I don't want to pamper myself.
>
> MS: But when you don't take care of *your* basic emotional needs you then sometimes switch to the part of you that grabs what you want and doesn't think about what happens then.

How did she experience me and therapy? She tended to be very deferential and genuinely collaborated on much of the work. However, she was rather stubbornly resistant to working on the issue of anger. Also, as seen in this session, Diane tended to resist the issue of taking care of her own needs consistently rather than sporadically and impulsively. Was therapy an unconscious replay of her arrest (exposure) and trial (judgment by me)? Was I experienced by her as the police (catching her), the judge (trying her), or the saleswoman/mother (slapping her with the issue of anger)?

The session ended with the discussion of two topics. First, we returned to her heightened fearfulness. I suggested that it was related both to the stress of the arrest and trial and to her now being more aware of consequences of her actions and that she might be experiencing a temporary overreaction. She found this explanation to be plausible and comforting and, in fact, these phobic reactions did not continue. Second, she reported needing to get away from the kids for awhile during the week and she worked that out by going for a long walk with a friend. Diane said that she only thought about doing that because I had suggested taking breaks for herself. This was one of a number of examples of some beginning internalization of a more effective caregiving function for herself.

This middle-phase session with Diane illustrates some of the work that we did following the initial crisis intervention and development of a reasonably good working alliance. Interpretive work around the dynamic focus of personality splits and self-imposed deprivation, her continuing resistance to looking at the issue of anger in her life, and some evidence of beginnings of internalization of the therapeutic process were components of this session. The termination with Diane is presented in the following chapter.

9

The End

In the final analysis, termination, separation, and death
are the bedrock of human existence, for which psychotherapy, whether it is time limited or unlimited can offer
no cure.

Hans Strupp and Jeffrey Binder, 1984

From an object relations perspective, the heart of human experience consists of relationships. Since all relationships eventually and
inevitably end, it is obvious that dealing with and working through
the experience of endings is a crucial psychological task in life as
well as in therapy. And yet, while it is a universal experience, it is
also one of the most denied and avoided. This is certainly understandable given the pain of loss and endings. Yet, much psychological development is crippled by an avoidance of the developmental task of facing endings, accepting the losses, and processing
(mourning) their effects.

The writing on brief therapy illustrates the universal human tendency to deny endings. Luborsky and colleagues (1990) point out that termination issues have received scant attention in theory and research. Budman and Gurman (1988) note avoidance of the topic of termination in the brief therapy literature. In Strupp and Binder's (1984) view, therapists in general tend to underestimate the importance of working with the termination process. The next time that you read a book or article on brief therapy note how little is said about it.

There are exceptions to this general rule, Mann being the primary one. Kupers (1988) has pointed out that Mann's therapy could be considered to be entirely termination-phase psychotherapy. No matter what specific focus is chosen in Mann's Time-Limited Psychotherapy (TLP) the therapy also centers on the meta-focus of loss and separation-individuation.

Two areas of difference are particularly striking among the brief psychodynamic models—the goals for patient progress at termination and the views on patients returning later for further treatment. The differences seem to divide along the lines of those brief therapists who look at termination from the standpoint that Freud (1937) presented in "Analysis Terminable and Interminable" and those who have taken a more contemporary, flexible view.

Freud (1937) laid out three criteria for termination of analysis. First, the patient is symptom-free or the symptoms have at least been dramatically reduced. Second, the symptom improvement seems likely to be enduring. Third, continuing analysis is unlikely to produce further meaningful improvement. In his usual insightful manner Freud did note that this theoretically ideal picture is often quite different from the one in practice. Still, these criteria have consciously and unconsciously guided generations of analysts and psychodynamic psychotherapists. Such standards for a "correct" ending of therapy serve to devalue more limited improvement and contribute to countertransference difficulties as described in earlier chapters (therapist grandiosity, therapists conveying disappointment to patients over limited improvement, etc.).

GOALS FOR PATIENT PROGRESS

While few writers would argue that brief therapy can accomplish all that psychoanalysis or intensive open-ended psychotherapy can, some have described proper termination in their models in similar terms. Malan's, Sifneos's, and Davanloo's views are comparable to the traditional psychoanalytic views of termination except in that they emphasize change in the focal area rather than more pervasive personality change. As Davanloo (1980) states,

> In terms of outcome I have pointed out that changes begin to occur between the fifth and eighth sessions and permeate the patient's entire life by the time of termination; so that at the time of termination there is definite evidence of the total resolution of the patient's core neurosis . . . everything is experienced so intensely that the neurosis is dissolved" [p. 70]

Budman and Gurman (1988) and others have taken a different stance and argued for a broad range of goals as being appropriate for successful termination depending on the patient, therapist, and other factors. Given the differences among patients and the array of factors affecting treatment, this more practical view of therapeutic goals seems to me to be necessary for most practicing psychotherapists.

PATIENTS RETURNING FOR TREATMENT

Similarly, those brief therapy writers adhering to the traditional psychoanalytic views of termination seem to suggest that if the patient returns for therapy, it indicates a deficit in the previous treatment, because, theoretically, there should be no need for further treatment. Mann and Goldman (1994) describe communicating to the patient that the termination is "unequivocal." To do otherwise would be to imply that more time may be available and that this would undermine the patient's progress in dealing with adult time.

No other area of health care holds such a standard for outcome (Cummings and VandenBos 1979). Should my internist feel guilty if I return to her with a bacterial infection a year after I was treated for a similar infection? Should my orthopedist consider his earlier treatment of my narrowed lumbar disk as a failure if I return three years later with pain in that area again? Of course not, and neither should therapists. I also discussed this issue in Chapter 5 and as I stated there, therapy, like life, is a process of becoming, not a process of arriving. Moreover, return to therapy is often a sign of the success of the therapy in that it indicates the patient's positive experience with the previous work and the hope that the therapeutic encounter can offer additional help. Also, we should simply be cognizant of *what is*, namely, that periodic return to therapy is frequently the way patients use us. I discuss these points later in this chapter in the section on serial brief therapy.

OBJECT RELATIONS CRITERIA FOR TERMINATION

Ideally, what outcomes of therapy would lead an object relations therapist to consider that termination is timely? In describing time-unlimited object relations therapy Scharff and Scharff (1992) list signs of readiness for termination (Table 9-1). Note the emphasis on relationships in this list—five of the seven pertain directly to relationships. The other two, mastering developmental stress (#1) and differentiating among and meeting the needs of the individual (#7), frequently involve other people. These signs indicate an improved symptom picture and an enhanced relational capacity. They also suggest significant change in the patient's inner world.

The object relations therapist, of course, hopes for more than symptom relief. Table 9-2 presents Scharff and Scharff's (1992) criteria for termination. They nicely illustrate the interplay between one's internal world, relationship to one's self, and relationships with people in the external world. These are ambitious criteria for any therapeutic approach. In brief therapy, it is rare for all of these improved capacities to be evidenced as termination approaches. So, the therapist and patient must accept (for the time being) more limited progress as therapy ends. And yet it is important for the therapist during the therapy to have kept in mind the greater potential that the patient has than was realized in the limited time of this now ending episode of brief therapy.

Table 9–1. Signs of Readiness for Termination in Open-Ended Object Relations Psychotherapy

Improved capacity

1. to master developmental stress
2. to work cooperatively
3. to have loving object relationships
4. to integrate hate with love and tolerate ambivalence
5. to perceive others accurately
6. to have empathy and concern for others
7. to differentiate among and meet the needs of the individual

From Scharff and Scharff 1992. Reprinted by permission of Routledge & Kegan Paul, Jason Aronson, and David and Jill Scharff.

Table 9–2. Criteria for Termination in Open-Ended Object Relations Psychotherapy

1. The therapeutic space has been internalized and a reasonably secure holding capacity has been formed.
2. Unconscious projective identifications have been recognized, owned, and taken back.
3. The capacity to work together with family members or life partners is restored.
4. Intimate and sexual relating is now gratifying and satisfying.
5. The individual can provide good holding for the self, and the couple or family can provide a vital holding environment for the individual, couple, or family.
6. The capacity to mourn the loss of the theapeutic relationship is sufficient to support a satisfactory termination and to prepare the patient, couple, or family to deal with future developmental losses and to envision their future beyond therapy.

From Scharff and Scharff 1992. Reprinted by permission of Routledge & Kegan Paul, Jason Aronson, and David and Jill Scharff.

The "good enough" mother (Winnicott 1949, 1958, 1965) takes pride in her toddler's first unsteady steps. She also holds inside her the vision of his eventual confident walking and running. She also enjoys his toddling progress and is not disappointed with him because he's not yet running. It is a similar process in therapy. The therapist, for example, holds the image of the patient's experiencing more whole object relationships with the tolerance of ambivalence and the integration of loving and hating that is involved (depressive mode). The therapist does this even though the patient is, at termination, only showing the beginning signs of whole object relating. And, like the good enough mother, the good enough therapist accepts the present limits of the progress and is not disappointed in him while she holds the vision of further growth.

The Scharffs' criteria for termination emphasize the goal of the internalization of good objects and more good object experience and coping capacities. This is intrapsychic change that goes beyond symptom relief. In object relations brief therapy, the therapist also directs her efforts toward internalization, which moves the therapy beyond a supportive function.

Strupp and Binder (1984) write of one type of internalization, "By a process which is of pivotal importance but still poorly understood, the patient learns to internalize the generally positive image of the therapist thereby freeing himself or herself from the neurotic attachment" (p. 261). They note that while this process never succeeds completely, the replacing of maladaptive identifications with new, more healthy ones is the unique achievement of psychotherapy. Mann (1973) writes that active processing of termination issues "allows" the internalization of the therapist to replace previous maladaptive objects. The disconfirmation by the therapist of the patient's transference expectations and the internalization of the "real" therapist provides a new (positive, real, healthy relationship) ending for the patient's old (transference) experiences.

GOALS OF TERMINATION

I have the following six goals in the end phase of brief object relations therapy:

1. Consolidation of gains made during the treatment
2. Exploration and some working through of the experience of loss and endings
3. "Saying good-bye" to the patient with whom I have related as intensively as possible, albeit briefly

4. Discussion of obstacles to maintaining or furthering progress and how the patient may address them
5. Strengthening of the internalization of the therapeutic process
6. At times, exploring the conditions for the patient's later return to therapy and facilitating that process.

The termination phases with Ronald and Diane are presented later in this chapter. Ronald made progress on five of these six goals. Little work was done on working through of endings and loss (#2) with him. Progress was made on all six goals with Diane, although, as you will see, she regressively reenacted an old pattern at the ending.

TRANSFERENCE AND COUNTERTRANSFERENCE ISSUES DURING TERMINATION

The ending of treatment is an event for both the therapist and the patient and it is, in one way or another, a mutual experience, although their relationship to it is different. So, as throughout therapy, the object relations perspective asks the therapist during termination to look at not only the unique meaning of it for the patient but also its unique impact on herself, the therapist. The ability of the therapist to effectively handle termination is primarily a function of her own ability to process and deal with her own feelings about it (Strupp and Binder 1984).

The process of termination and the particular transference-countertransference responses will be affected by why the therapy is ending. The best of situations is when the patient and therapist have been able to successfully address an agreed-upon goal and therapy stops because the goal has been reached.

Clinical Example: Carl

There was a quiet sadness about Carl as he first entered my office. This impeccably dressed, eloquent, 33-year-old lawyer spoke movingly about his suffering following the breakup of an eighteen-month relationship with another man, Len. He longed for him and was finding it difficult to be interested in other men. Carl was especially distressed, though, because he was feeling hopeless about eventually finding a partner. He recounted several failed love relationships and thought that maybe there was some fatal flaw in him when it came to relationships. He was functioning adequately, although he was having some trouble sleeping and concentrating on his high-pressure job. He said that he wanted a focused approach and hoped we could accomplish something in eight to ten sessions. We set as a symptomatic focus the grieving over the end of his relationship with Len. The dynamic focus was to get a better understanding of his pattern of relationships with men.

Over the course of ten weekly sessions he relived the relationship with Len and mourned its ending. The sessions frequently were very emotional and full of tears. I experienced him as having a very needy quality that paradoxically coexisted with a distancing, detached demeanor— he both drew me in and put me off. This ambivalent presentation was exemplified by his rather intensive, motivated approach to the therapy and his resolve to keep it to within ten sessions. I also found myself liking him a great deal and admiring his courage in trying to find a committed intimate relationship despite his network of friends and past lovers whose lifestyles were rather anti-commitment. Of course, this was a crucial question for us: How is it that he had been so consistently involved with men who did not seem interested in the type of relationship he wanted? We looked at his choice of partners (usually exciting object relationships). Carl rather consistently was attracted to men who were not interested in a committed, monogamous relationship.

He described recurrent dreams of being involved with a strong alien in human form who was evil and who would ultimately hurt him. In various ways the alien represented him, other men that he might be involved with, and his mother. His mother was a very inconsistent woman, at times being wonderfully attentive and loving and at other times being drunk and neglectful. He was repeating his relationship with his mother through his romantic relationships with men who were rather inconsistent.

By the eighth session he was feeling much better and felt that his heart was open to relationships again. Moreover, Carl indicated that he now saw how his pattern of object choice was a problem in terms of picking exciting but ultimately frustrating partners and how this was a replay of his relationship with his mother. He was very pleased with the therapy and said he was ready to stop. As we terminated over the last three sessions, we looked at our relationship from the standpoint that it was not a replication of past relationships in that he had rather defined, limited expectations with me and these expectations were met. On the other hand, this approach was a defense against disappointment. I, too, felt good about our work together and termination at this point seemed appropriate. I did feel a loss that I might not know how "things would turn out" for him and I did wonder what might have been accomplished if I had seen him for a longer duration (therapist narcissism?). However, we both felt we had accomplished quite a bit at termination and it was what we had set out to do.

OTHER FACTORS AFFECTING TERMINATION

I will briefly note some of the other factors affecting termination and the issues that arise. These factors can be divided into external factors, therapist factors, and patient factors.

External Factors

These factors are "outside" the patient–therapist relationship. They include limits set by the service provider organization (e.g., the EAP, the clinic) or by a third-party payer (e.g., insurance carrier, managed care company, parent, spouse). Such limits need to be clear very early in treatment; otherwise, serious problems arise such as the therapy being experienced as a pathologically exciting object. When external factors cause therapy to end there can be a tendency on the part of the patient and/or the therapist to experience this through a paranoid-schizoid mode, splitting the "good" therapist and the "bad" external entity.

I have seen a number of therapies where this has become almost the exclusive theme during termination with the patient and therapist both protesting the need to stop, hating the forces that are causing this, and fantasizing that all would be well if only they would be "allowed" to continue. Such concentration on this issue not only distracts the patient and therapist from attending to the other (often painful) material of ending but it avoids confronting the patient with the reality of the limits of time in this instance. Other common reactions are for the patient to see the therapist as being weak for not being able to stand up to the external forces or as being rejecting for not being willing to see the patient for a reduced fee or no fee. Therapist guilt and narcissistic issues can be stimulated.

Patient Factors

These include endings due to limited patient motivation for change, fear of intimacy and dependency, limited financial resources, and geographic moves. In this sense, the patient leaves rather than is left and typically it is an easier termination for the patient than those due to either external or therapist factors. Still, sometimes the patient's transference response is to feel abandoned and the therapist should be alert to this possibility. Knowledge of the patient's history can sensitize the therapist to the probability of this or other reactions. When the patient ends, in part, due to issues about intimacy and dependency (as was the case with Alan in Chapter 5) there are usually "realistic" issues that are cited. It is still often useful to at least invite the patient to consider that dynamic themes might play a role as well. Even if he consciously rejects it, it may be something that he will use after therapy ends. When patient factors cause termination, a frequent countertransference is for the therapist to be either disappointed with himself for not being able to keep the patient in therapy longer or disappointed and/or angry with the patient for not being willing (able?) to do more.

Other patient factors causing termination can, of course, be factors that have come up as specific responses to the therapy itself, such as ending because the patient is enraged at the therapist or because he is profoundly disillusioned that therapy can help. As in any therapeutic approach, the therapist needs to be vigilant to the early warning signs of such reactions and then be able to discuss them with the patient before a flight from treatment occurs.

Therapist Factors

These include termination due to the therapist's orientation or model of therapy, the completion of a training placement, therapist job change or geographic move, and, less commonly, therapist illness or death. It is best when the therapist is aware of such factors in advance and the time of stopping therapy is clear to the patient in advance. Common patient responses to therapist-caused terminations are anger and hurt, feelings of abandonment, and feelings of being inadequate to keep the therapist interested. Frequent countertransference reactions include guilt over leaving the patient, "force feeding" the patient in the last remaining sessions, grandiose fantasies of what could have been accomplished ("if only we'd had more time"), and anger at the patient for giving him such a hard time over ending. This is a rich vein of clinical material to mine if the patient and therapist can be aware of their reactions and face them together.

Strupp and Binder (1984) describe a frequent progression as patients terminated in their brief therapy model. It is a common pattern in brief therapy in general. Initially, the patient has developed a good relationship with the therapist and does not want to lose it. He, therefore, attempts to avoid separation or at least the experience of it through various controlling strategies. These may include bringing up new issues that require immediate attention (see Ronald, below), the return of old symptoms and problems, or premature termination (see Diane, below). When these defensive strategies fail, the patient reacts with frustration and/

or anger. This sequence needs to be actively addressed, and effectively working it through frees the patient to better tolerate loss and separation.

Mann (1991) eloquently describes various transference reactions at termination:

> Thus, it is to be expected in the termination phase of treatment that the man who feels unwanted, even irrelevant, will feel that the treatment comes to an end because the therapist, too, does not want him around. Or the woman who feels stupid and a phony is certain that the therapist finds her so and is pleased to send her away. Or another patient comes to feel that the therapist finds him to be second-rate and unacceptable. [p. 31]

Clearly, if the therapist and patient have been examining their relationship periodically throughout the therapy, their attention to these termination transferences can be extraordinarily productive. Often, the end phase produces a last run through of the same issues that constitute the transference. Therefore, it can be one more chance—the last one in this therapy contract—to rework them.

Interestingly, the patient may not find the termination of brief therapy to be difficult (Budman 1990, Budman and Gurman 1988, Davanloo 1980). For example, each time when Alan (Chapter 5) ended an episode of treatment he denied any difficulty with it and was pleased that he had gotten out of it what he had hoped.

How can we understand it when a patient seems to have little reaction to ending treatment? At least three hypotheses are worth considering. First, was the contact so brief and superficial that the patient did not connect sufficiently to experience a meaningful loss at termination? Second, is the patient simply denying the significance and pain of the separation and loss? Third, is the patient's lack of response to termination an example of his difficulty with intimacy and dependency? Therefore, termination after a brief episode of therapy comes as a relief rather than as a source of pain.

Clinical Example: Peter

The case is a short example of this third hypothesis. During a brief therapy contract of nine sessions this 24-year-old ski instructor worked intensely on his pattern of fearing intimate relationships and its connection with his sexual abuse as a child. We knew the therapy would be brief due to his moving out of town to return to college. He and I both felt that he had made considerable progress on this pattern and it would have been good if we'd had the opportunity to continue. We also looked at his comfort with our ending as an example of the pattern of moving on before things got too close. His reactions upon ending were a mixture of gratitude for the work we had done, satisfaction in the progress he'd made, and some mild regret that we couldn't continue, but stronger relief that he didn't have to keep looking at these issues in therapy for now.

Do these three hypotheses—superficial connection to the therapist, defense against loss and separation, and characterologically patterned response to intimacy and dependency—fully account for these patient reactions or is there something else going on?

Therapist as Transitional Object

I have been intrigued by the possibility of a connection of this lack of a reaction to termination with Winnicott's (1951) concept of transitional objects. Examples of transitional objects are children's cuddle blankets or stuffed animals that they take to bed with them. The object occupies a transitional space between reality and fantasy; it is both real and a part of the child's inner world. She exerts omnipotent control over it and uses it for comfort, soothing, and for various aggressive purposes as well. The transitional object helps the child to developmentally move from a state of fantasied omnipotent control (paranoid-schizoid mode) to more realistic perception and functioning (depressive mode). The child finds the transitional object to be crucially important, at times even more important than the mother (e.g., the child can fall asleep without the mother being present but not if the cuddle blanket is missing).

Yet, when the child develops to a point when she does not need the object she discards it without a sense of loss. Winnicott explicitly wrote that the transitional object is *not* mourned. Certainly, the therapist functions at times as a transitional object for the patient. In some terminations in which the patient does not seem to be distressed, the therapist may have been functioning as a transitional object and the patient has progressed developmentally so that the therapist can be given up without much of a sense of loss. This is because the patient now keeps the therapist alive in his mind as a new object.

I believe that brief therapy termination does put unique strains on the therapist. These strains have to do with the dynamic tension between intensely intimate relating and short-term contact. On the one hand, we ask ourselves and our patients to relate as deeply as possible and to face the most difficult human issues as can be tolerated. On the other hand, we conduct this activity within a temporal context that is brief and highlights the inevitable and near-term end of the contact. A very experienced therapist confided to me that she much prefers either the more removed contact involved with psychological evaluations or the extended connection of long-term therapy over brief therapy. With brief therapy she said she almost feels promiscuous—having intense contact but then quickly ending it and moving on.

Therapists deal with the difficulty of brief therapy termination in a variety of defensive ways. One strategy is simply not to do brief work. Another is to keep the therapy supportive and superficial ostensibly because the patient cannot tolerate more intensity, but at times the purpose is primarily to protect the therapist. A third defensive strategy can be for the therapist to deny to himself his degree of attachment to the patient.

SERIAL BRIEF THERAPY

In Chapter 5, I suggested that therapists and patients look at a particular episode of brief therapy as part of an ongoing *process* of growth and change rather than as a definitive treatment. I gave the example of Alan, who returned to therapy with me over an eight-year period for five episodes of brief therapy. From this perspective an individual piece of brief work is part of a much larger process of change that may include periodic brief episodes of therapy that occur throughout the patient's life. The brief therapist not only conducts the therapy with an eye toward dealing with the presenting issues but also attends to how the therapy may affect continued change after the therapy contract has ended. It can support and be supported by personal growth from other facilitating experiences and relationships. This continuing change process may occur without therapy or it may include periodic returns to therapy to further growth and development. Attention to the dynamic focus is very helpful in this regard in that it works on a theme or issue that usually has potency well beyond the more limited symptomatic focus of the particular brief therapy contract.

This perspective is quite different from that generally presented in traditional psychoanalytic circles and is different from that of some other brief therapists such as Malan (1976), Davanloo (1980), Sifneos (1987), and especially Mann and Goldman (1994). As I noted earlier in this chapter, Mann and Goldman tell the patient that the termination is "unequivocal." To do otherwise, they argue, would promote the illusion of always more time being available (in therapy and in life) and would undermine the patient's progress in dealing with adult time. Although Mann and Goldman plan a follow-up contact one year after termination, they do not let the patient know that it will occur. They simply contact the patient one year later.

One does need to carefully consider the impact of episodic therapy on the patient. Certainly being able to return at times of difficulty in the future can give the patient a stabilizing holding environment and may help with internalizing the therapist and therapeutic progress. However, serial brief therapy can cause the therapist and patient to collude in denying the eventual, inevitable ending of their relationship. Also, Shectman (1986) describes other potential problems with this approach: it may mask the patient's anxiety over disinterest on the part of the therapist, it can obscure the difficulty the patient has in internalizing the therapist, and it can foster pathological dependency (although not as much as long-term treatment can).

However, the potential benefits of the patient's returning from time to time for additional therapy as needed seem to me to be so great as to easily outweigh the benefits of the approach that discourages patient return. Simply knowing that the therapist is standing by can be very helpful even if the patient never returns to the therapist. The therapist's willingness to see the patient again conveys the basic human message that the therapist does care about the patient's welfare even after termination. This, in itself, may be a new ending to an old experience. Several writers have advocated conceptualizing psychotherapy as involving circumscribed treatment episodes over a person's life cycle (Bennett 1989, Budman and Gurman 1988, Cummings 1990, Shectman 1986). To quote Budman and Gurman (1988):

> We believe that patients can and should return as needed. This perspective does not preclude doing therapy efficiently and effectively, and it encourages a more flexible perspective of "not needing to do it all at once." Moreover, even relatively few visits may be viewed as sufficient if seen in the larger context of an overall primary care relationship. On the other hand, a rather large number of visits may be experienced as depriving if this is understood as *the* definitive course of therapy. [p. 290]

The notion that it is useful and even desirable for patients to periodically return for more therapy is very much in keeping with a developmental as opposed to a pathology model of therapy—development continues through the life span both in and out of therapy. I used to feel vaguely guilty when patients would return for more therapy years later. I had the classical psychoanalytic conception that it showed that my previous work was incomplete and flawed. Of course, all of my work is incomplete and flawed since psychological change and growth is a never-ending process and since I'm not perfect. What a ridiculous, narcissistic idea to think otherwise! In fact, depending on the reasons for the patient's return (see Chapter 5 for a discussion of the varied reasons patients return to treatment), it may indicate that the patient was pleased with the therapy that he had previously received and that he wishes to utilize this change-promoting process again at a time of strain and difficulty. Alternatively, patients staying away from future therapy should not be invariably seen as indicating that they don't need it. As Budman and Gurman write (1988), "There is nothing easier than getting a patient not to come back" (p. 290).

However we might conceptualize the patient returning to therapy, there is no question that this *is* the way that many patients use us and use therapy (Bennett 1989, Budman 1990, Budman and Gurman 1988, Cummings 1990): they return repeatedly at times of difficulty. Moreover, the immediate factors that bring the patient back to the therapist may enhance the patient's readiness to work on specific tough issues.

Clinical Example: Helen

Proper is the first word that comes to mind as I think of Helen. I experienced her as a very serious, subdued woman of 57 who found it very important to present herself in a proper, mature manner and to "properly" address the psychological issues she was dealing with. There was such a cool reserve about her that I wondered about her capacity for empathy. Helen was very empathic, although it was often difficult for others to see as well. She didn't like "messy" emotions.

I first saw her for eleven sessions concerning her adjustment to retirement. Helen had been an executive vice president for a national nonprofit educational organization. She had retired early to spend more time with her husband, who was fourteen years her senior. We focused on adjusting to her new lifestyle and grieving over the loss of her more "important," vibrant position at work and her self-image that was connected with it. The dynamic focus included exploring the existential meaning of her life at this point and her pattern of dealing with loss in the past. She expressed gratitude, in her formal way, as we ended and said that she felt she was on the right track now. She said that she would like to call on me in the future as different difficult issues arose. She speculated that potential issues that would cause her to consult with me again might be her husband's death, problems with her adult stepchildren, or a downturn in her health.

Helen called me again two years later and we worked together this time for four sessions. She was struggling with one of the areas that she had thought might bring her back into therapy—her adult stepdaughters. On the symptomatic level she wanted to explore how she might deal with the continuing substance abuse by one daughter, Julia, and the difficult personality style of the other, Sarah. She was also feeling guilt and self-doubt about her parenting of them when they were children. She faulted herself for being too career-oriented when they were children and for not showing her love enough to them. We explored this and the question of self-forgiveness. I felt that she had an unconscious identification with her idealized but critical, cold father but this was not really explored. On the practical side she resolved to be more open in expressing both her love for her stepdaughters and her irritation with them. She said that she now intended to set limits more strictly with Julia and not to keep rushing to her rescue whenever a crisis hit. She felt that she had been doing so to try to make up for her inadequacies as a mother years ago and it wasn't helping Julia or her. Helen decided to explicitly discuss with Sarah how she saw their relationship and was undecided as to whether a letter or phone call would be the best first step.

She once again indicated that the therapy had been beneficial to her. She added that it was a comfort to know that I was there should she need me again and predicted that she would. I might note that I believe that my awareness of my countertransference toward Helen (my experience of her being so reserved and wondering about her empathy) was instrumental in our working on her relationship with her stepdaughters. I was able to identify with her stepdaughters (complementary identification) and have a taste of what it might have been like for them to relate to Helen. One month after termination, Helen sent me a thank you letter and a copy of the letter she had sent to Sarah. She said that they subsequently had one of the longest and most frank interactions that they'd had in years.

FOLLOW-UP SESSIONS

The intentional use of follow-up sessions can enhance therapeutic effectiveness. Various other writers (Budman and Gurman 1988, Hoyt 1990, Luborsky and Mark 1991, Steenbarger 1994) have made similar recommendations. For this discussion of termination, here is a review of the three benefits of follow-up sessions that I listed and illustrated with vignettes in Chapter 5.

First, follow-up sessions can help in dealing with termination. As with spreading out the last several sessions, they can help the patient more gradually accept and cope with the ending of the therapy. This can be particularly helpful as a weaning process from therapy with patients who have intense dependency needs. However, the therapist needs to be aware of the potential for follow-up sessions to obscure termination issues or for the therapist to reactively add additional sessions that then hinder rather than enhance the therapeutic process. The therapist needs also to be aware of her own potential resistance to termination, which may be dealt with by scheduling unnecessary follow-up sessions.

Second, follow-up sessions allow for additional time for the patient to work through some therapeutic issues outside of therapy. To some extent, significant therapeutic change requires the passage of lived time (Hoyt 1990). It is interesting to consider that some of the profound benefits of long-term treatment come not only from the extended, uninterrupted contact with the therapist, but also partially from the extended experience of living one's life.

Third, the additional time between sessions permits additional life events to occur that may be usefully dealt with. As discussed below, Ronald found it helpful to spread out the last three sessions to help him deal with the impact on his self-esteem of searching for a job. Real life events that occur after regular therapy sessions have ended can very much affect whether the progress in therapy will endure or not (Steenbarger 1994). For example, the quality and presence of positive or negative external object relations can very much help or hinder the maintenance of improvement. Follow-up sessions can be used to deal with the impact of these real life influences.

ADDITIONAL SUGGESTIONS CONCERNING TERMINATION

Set the End Point of the Therapy as Soon as Possible and as Clearly as Possible

Some important work on termination occurs right at the start of treatment. Setting the end point early sets the frame for the work together, makes it more understandable to the patient why the therapy needs to be organized around the focus, and explicitly puts the issue of termination before both the therapist and patient. The end can be set in terms of a date, a number of sessions, an attitude ("let's meet for awhile and see if it is helpful"), the attainment of a goal, or the occurrence of an external event (e.g., the patient will graduate from college or will move out of town). Not all brief therapy is time-limited from the start, but it is useful to convey in some way the brevity of the contract. I favor a somewhat flexible "time-limited attitude" (Binder et al. 1987) rather than a premature or rigid setting of the end point.

I do not believe in any particular single way to convey the end point but I generally have found that setting a date, when possible, has been a useful approach. There is some evidence that setting a time limit is associated with lower dropout rates than therapy without a preset termination date (Good 1992). It would be interesting to understand which patients might respond best to a time limit. Perhaps, for instance, patients who have strong conflicts over dependency (like Jackie in Chapter 4) or who fear their boundaries being breached (like Alan in Chapter 5) would respond well to a time-limited approach.

It is important that the time limit or brevity of therapy be presented in a positive manner that emphasizes what may be accomplished within the limits of the contract. This conveys the therapist's belief to the patient that he has the capacity to change within a short period of time. Some well-intended therapists present the situation by, in effect, saying, "I'd like to work with you for much longer but since we can't you'll be getting second best." This fosters the patient experiencing the therapy as an exciting object experience and needlessly stimulates longing for the "real" good therapy. The therapist should not shrink from candidly acknowledging the limits of what can be done in the brief contract but her tone and attitude should convey realistic hope and promise rather than her own countertransference disillusionment.

Repeatedly Remind the Patient of the Impending End of Therapy

I've said it before: termination work needs to occur throughout the therapy contract, including during the middle phase of treatment. Several writers recommend this as well (e.g., Luborsky and Mark 1991, Mann 1991). Periodic reminders such as "we have three more weeks to meet together" are often useful. Similarly, the therapist may productively point out the impending end of treatment when it is connected with the clinical material being presented. For example, discussion of other separations or talking about an important event that will occur after the end of the current therapy episode would be opportunities to raise the upcoming end of therapy as well.

Be Aware of the Countertransference Power of Termination on the Therapist

I want to emphasize some points I presented in the section on transference and countertransference. The ending is an event for both therapist and patient. It is likely to touch on various aspects of separation and loss for each. The therapist (and patient, for that matter) may be less willing to accept the significance of this event in brief therapy than in longer-term work. Be aware and beware. The therapist should be aware with his receptive capacity of the impact on him of the ending and discern what this may indicate about the patient and the relationship that they have developed. The therapist should beware of such common countertransference patterns as trying to "force-feed" the patient in the last few sessions or withdrawing from the patient with the defense that "it's too late for more to be accomplished." The "more" is in the process and processing of ending.

Consider Follow-up Sessions: Use Them Intentionally

The therapist should be thoughtful in setting follow-up sessions or in spreading them out. Commonly, the therapist reacts to the patient's distress at the termination and deals with both of their anxieties by adding sessions, regular or follow-up. While sometimes extraordinary circumstances indicate adding sessions to the contract (e.g., death of a loved one near the end of treatment), I think that therapists more often add them needlessly and thereby obscure the process of ending. It is better to plan out follow-up sessions and discuss it with the patient prior to the last few sessions. If the contract is limited by a set number (say, fifteen sessions) due to financial constraints or managed care, the therapist should consider ending the weekly sessions after thirteen sessions and using the last two as follow-up sessions. So, consider the use of follow-up sessions but use them *on purpose*, not simply reactively.

Deal with the Continuation of the Process

Earlier in this chapter I described six termination goals. The fifth goal is to strengthen the internalization of the therapeutic process. I suggest that the therapist explicitly discuss with the patient not only the gains that were made but also how they were accomplished and the process by which the patient can maintain the progress and further it. The therapy aims not only at treating the problems but at promoting a *way* of addressing one's life and difficulties in living. Neilsen and Barth (1991) reported that follow-up interviews from patients who had been in a Sifneos model of brief therapy described an "internalized therapeutic dialogue" as the most important factor in change. These patients had learned the process and had, now, an internalized therapist.

Note in Ronald's and Diane's terminations the attention to particular dynamic issues that they need to keep addressing. In short, while therapy may end or is intermittent, the therapist aims at helping the patient make the therapeutic *process* portable and lifelong. And part of what we hope the patient takes with him is the internalized therapist.

Convey, Explicitly, the Option of Returning for Further Treatment

One way the patient can usefully continue the process is through periodically returning to the therapist as needed. While this serial brief therapy approach is not without its drawbacks, it can be a powerful approach to promote the maintenance of improvements and further growth. Adult development does continue throughout the life cycle and chance events can also cause the patient to benefit from another episode of brief therapy (Budman 1990). The therapist thus can consider herself to be the patient's primary care mental health consultant, not unlike a medical family physician or general practitioner (Cummings 1990).

Look at Previous Endings

The therapist can help the patient understand his experience of the ending of therapy by inquiring about his experience as other relationships ended. The extent to which the present termination is a repetition of past endings or is different is examined. I often ask the patient, "Have you thought about how you'd like to say good-bye?" to bring this discussion practically into the present and then to look at how he has said good-bye (or not said good-bye) in the past.

Accept that There Are Different Endings for Different Patients

I have been discussing common termination patterns and suggestions for dealing with the ending of therapy. Let me invite you not to take it too rigidly. In other words, I hope some of these ideas serve you well as guides but not as laws. Once again, I want to make a case for the primacy of the individual patient and particular therapeutic relationship. The therapist should be guided by training and experience, but then listen to the individual needs of the particular patient—who is he and what does he need? Different patients will end in their own idiosyncratic manner and the therapist can undermine the difficult process of terminating therapy by having rigid, preconceived notions of how it should "correctly" happen. While the following writers are not in complete agreement with the degree of flexibility I am recommending in approaching termination, Davanloo (1980), Luborsky (1991), and Malan (1976) have all written about the importance of modifying the termination process depending upon patient needs.

END-PHASE CLINICAL EXAMPLE: RONALD

Sessions 13–14

Ronald requested that we schedule our last three sessions for every other week to permit more opportunity to deal with his difficulty in getting a summer job (see Chapter 8). I agreed, although I had a conflicted reaction to the request. On the one hand, I thought it would be useful to spread out the last sessions to help him deal with the blows to his self-esteem that were part of searching for a summer job. The approach of less frequent sessions toward the end of the contract can be useful in relapse prevention and in reducing the difficulty of termination for the patient. On the other hand, it is the issue of diluting the experience of termination that gave me some concern in agreeing to meet every other week with Ronald.

He had a history of denying the importance of relationships in his life and didn't mourn their endings. His approach was hyperpractical—"It's over, time to move on." Interestingly, this was in sharp contrast with his often obsessive preoccupation with other types of losses (e.g., loss of self-esteem, loss of confidence in his academic prowess). I thought that our relationship had been very important to him and that losing a supportive, helpful connection with a trusted older man was meaningful, although difficult to be aware of. We discussed his experience of ending therapy with me, but he reacted in his usual hyper-practical mode, discounting the significance of it (see session 15, below). I did not pursue his reaction to termination very persistently and after therapy had ended I felt that I had not done enough on that important issue with him. I had been conscious of feeling that any greater exploration of termination with him would evoke strong resistance and not be productive.

My countertransference around this issue with Ronald is complex. I believe that Ronald would have strongly resisted more work on termination. However, I am also aware of my own resistance to dealing with the pain and loss of endings. Also, through projective identification, I may have come to feel that I was less significant to him than I really was and then acted that projection out. Lastly, it occurs to me that my feelings of inadequacy about the handling of his termination are, in part, a projection of how inadequate he feels at times. Where this leaves me is that I wish I had further invited him to examine his reactions to the ending of therapy.

During sessions 13 and 14, Ronald usefully examined his frustrations in his summer-job search. Landing a good summer job at this point in his career was important for possible permanent positions after graduation. His all-or-nothing way of viewing reality and how easily his self-esteem was affected by the events of the search were explored. I suggested that the nagging voice of his father ("You're not good enough") was present during the job interviews (P-O interpretation). In session 14 he said it "looked good" that he would get a job offer for a particular position that he wanted.

Session 15

Ronald did indeed get that job and he came to the last session with an air of triumph. However, there was an air of sadness in his demeanor as well. He denied that his sadness had to do with this being our last session. Rather, he said he had been thinking that perhaps he had not really changed at all and hadn't gotten that much out of therapy. I found myself feeling quite sad as he said that. I suggested that we look at his impression that he hadn't changed and asked how he saw himself now compared to when we began working together five months ago.

Like a lawyer citing evidence he listed the following: much less anxiety, eating and sleeping well, studying effectively, greater appreciation for his brittle self-esteem, recognition of the tyranny of his all-or-nothing expectations and awareness of his need to be "special." I thought to myself that this would be pretty impressive in any therapy, but especially so from someone who was disappointed with therapy. Ronald movingly said that he was surprised to note this array of improvements and was amazed that he really hadn't been in touch with them just a few minutes before. We looked at this as a dramatic example of how predisposed he was to be critical of himself and others when things weren't perfect. I acknowledged that his life wasn't perfect and that he was still struggling with some significant issues but that it was hard to hold on to good experience in the face of some things not being quite right (splitting in his self-image and in relationships with others). Also, in connecting this back to his relationship with his father, I made a number of P-S-T interpretations. What had particularly saddened me was his great difficulty in holding on to good experience unless he's feeling grandiose and "on top of the world." At another level, this dynamic we were exploring was a manifestation of an inner sense of emptiness that he would periodically experience. This a state that many patients with prominent narcissistic issues frequently feel (see Chapter 12) and would be addressed in long-term treatment.

His disappointment in therapy and me was also a way to diminish any pain over the loss of the relationship by seeing what he was ending as less valuable and valued. However, we did not explore this. I acknowledged the gains that Ronald had listed and suggested that further work in open-ended therapy on his self-esteem issues would be useful especially since he intends to eventually be in positions of power and influence. He agreed, and said that probably the government would be better run if more of our leaders had been in therapy.

END-PHASE CLINICAL EXAMPLE: DIANE

Much of the content and process of the remaining eleven sessions of Diane's therapy were similar to session 14, described in the preceding chapter. We continued to explore the split between her deprived/depriving, responsible self and her gratified/gratifying, impulsive self. We also continued the work on identifying and understanding her "emotional storms" and her frequent denial of her basic needs. Two topics did take greater prominence than they had before. First, the symptomatic focus on her anxiety and depression over the uncertainty of whether she would serve time in prison and whether the family would be able to move took more of the therapeutic space. Second, she became increasingly intolerant of her husband, Roj's, alcoholism. She had seen a television program on co-dependency and said that it dawned on her, to her dismay, that she was an "enabler." We discussed the potential benefits of going to Al-Anon meetings, although she never did. She did, on her own, resolve to never buy him alcohol again and not to drink with him, and didn't during the remainder of treatment.

Her attorney requested that I send him a summary of her therapy with me. The summary was written after twenty-two sessions and was forwarded to the court. In my report I indicated that Diane

> has approached therapy in a very motivated and cooperative manner and it has been very useful to her. Since she has begun it, she has been able to maintain successful impulse control (including suicidal feelings). We have been focusing on helping her to regulate her self-esteem more effectively so that she will not have the extreme swings toward feelings of emptiness and self-contempt that she sometimes experiences. Additionally, she and I have developed new coping strategies to reduce the frequency and intensity of emotional deprivation. Thus, she has alternatives to get her needs met other than through the problematic solutions that she has used in the past.
>
> [Diane] and her family are planning to move to Z and I believe that it is essential that she continue in psychotherapy when she does. The increased self-control and other marked gains that she has made in therapy to date are not likely to continue without additional psychotherapy. I would also recommend that marital counseling may be indicated at some point and would also help to solidify the gains she has made and prevent relapse.

By the twenty-third session, the court had resolved Diane's case. She pled guilty but did not have to serve prison time. She received six months' detention in her home but was able to serve that in their new house in North Carolina. She had to pay back the money stolen according to an agreed-upon schedule. The court also required Diane to continue psychotherapy.

As her therapy with me was coming to a close I found myself having an array of reactions. I frequently had felt overwhelmed by all of the past abuse and loss in her life and also by her present legal, marital, and personal problems. I experienced all of this as even more overwhelming due to the brief nature of my contact with her. And yet, we had been able to accomplish some meaningful work during the six months that I saw her. She had weathered this crisis. Moreover, she had developed greater self-awareness concerning her personality splits and "emotional storms" and had developed and utilized much more effective coping strategies. She seemed to be more aware of the impact that her marriage had on her, although she steadfastly denied any significant anger toward her husband. Her continuing in therapy was also a positive outcome, although I'm not sure she would have continued had it not been mandated by the court.

I was pleased that she did not have to serve any time in prison. No useful purpose would have been served and she certainly had suffered intensely over the preceding six months already. Yet, I found myself also feeling somewhat dissatisfied that she had stolen such a large sum of money and received such a light sentence. I was aware of some mild guilt for having contributed through my supportive letter to her light sentence. I do know that, in part, my dissatisfaction with her degree of punishment came from some of my own unresolved superego issues, which were distinct from my work with her. They may also have been, in part, a projection of her own guilt, with which I was projectively identifying. As noted earlier, she *consciously* seemed to be experiencing no guilt (but much shame) about the stealing.

For about one month, we had been expecting that the decision on her case would be made and that her work with me might stop. Some discussion about termination had occurred, but she had tended to deflect it. Diane's last appointment with me was scheduled for a Tuesday and she and the family were moving on the Friday of that week. Within the hour before her appointment she called to cancel the last session. Her message was, "Hello, this is Diane. I can't come today. Sorry." I felt disappointed and angered by this message—I felt *robbed* of the chance to truly say good-bye to her. I was not very surprised, however, since she had been avoiding the topic and since her history had been one of multiple losses without having or taking the opportunity to say good-bye. I wished that I had predicted to her that she might be inclined to not come to therapy as we ended, but I had not. Patients with a history of abuse, like Diane, frequently struggle with termination and often avoid it through cancellations. I debated whether to call her or not and decided that to not call was to ensure an old ending to old experience. While she may only have been willing to talk for a few minutes, at least that would be more than had been the case for her with previous relationships.

Session 25

At her appointment time, I called. The following are excerpts from this phone session.

> MS: Hello, Diane? This is Mike Stadter. I got your message, can you talk for a few minutes?
>
> D: . . . Yes. I'm sorry I couldn't come in. I've been too busy with all of the packing to do . . . and there's no way that I could make it in before Friday.
>
> MS: Okay.
>
> D: Things are really hectic but I've been feeling okay. . . . We had a going away party. . . . I guess it was okay. My brother didn't react much, the asshole! What did I expect? My mother gave us a beautiful set of comforters for the beds. She really knocked me over with that, it was *so nice*. . . . I felt so good about her. So I said, "Mom, why don't you drive down for the holiday weekend [in two weeks]. It'd be a great time for you to see our new place." She

clams up right away. She says, "Oh, no, I couldn't do *that*. It's sooo far." That's the story of my life with her. She does something nice for me and then shuts it off. . . . I'm also upset with Norma [her best friend]. She hasn't made any time to see me and I don't think she will before Friday.

She continued to discuss similar material for several more minutes. There are a number of noteworthy aspects here. First, just as Norma had made no time to see her, Diane had made no time to see me during this last week. Second, it was striking to me how quickly, with little encouragement, she began talking to me just as if it were a regular therapy session. The telephone session turned out to be a compromise way to say good-bye.

Third, she clearly was doing some work, in her own way, on termination issues. There are prominent themes in what Diane is describing of endings and people disappointing her, not wanting to deal with saying good-bye. The prime denier of endings in Diane's life has been her mother. Until the going-away party, her mother steadfastly refused to talk about Diane's moving out of town. In Diane's cancellation of our last session and in ducking the topic in previous sessions, she was unconsciously identifying with her mother and doing something herself that she has found to be infuriating when her mother does it. I also found it ironic that this highly inconsistent and frequently emotionally unavailable mother would give *comforters* as a going away gift.

MS: You know, we can have your session on the phone, if you like. This is probably the last time we'll talk before you move.

D: I'd like that. I guess leaving hasn't hit me yet. I've been looking toward it for so long and worrying that we couldn't do it . . . and there's nobody still here. . . . I guess I've felt that since Susan left [a woman who she had previously felt close to and who had moved away two years previously].

Diane talked further about feeling remarkably calm about leaving and that she didn't feel she was leaving anything behind. She was glad to get away from the Washington area and move to a place where no one knew about her arrest and conviction.

MS: How do you feel about leaving me?

   D: It's going to be weird. It keeps me calm and it's hard to think about finding someone else. (Silence) You really listen and understand and you *remember*. I can talk about what I feel and you don't intimidate me like Roj does.

I was touched by her emphasis on my remembering what she said. She'd had few experiences with people in her life who attended to what she felt, much less remembered it and referred to it. Also, her prominent use of splitting prevented her from having much of a sense of continuity or historicity in her own experience of herself—the paranoid-schizoid mode of experience. My memory of her subjective experience was an ego function often lacking for her. I have found that borderline patients frequently comment on the importance of the therapist's memory for them.

MS: What's your fear with him?

   D: That he'll think I'm silly or feel bad himself.

Diane went on at length here about her frustration with her husband and her worry about his drinking. I registered my concern about it as well and the impact it had on her, the marriage and the family. I commented on the benefits of Al-Anon and she said she would probably try it but I had my silent doubts. We discussed how isolated she may feel in their new town. She then was quiet.

   D: (Silence) I'm starting to feel it now (soft crying). (Silence)

MS: Don't block it. Just feel it.

   D: (Sobbing) I am. (Sobbing)

MS: You know, your canceling today was partly due to avoiding saying good-bye to me. You've had many losses in the past and you've rarely said good-bye [T-P interpretation]. This is hard.

   D: Yes . . . it's hard to think of not having this anymore.

MS: If you want to call me, you can. I'm interested in how things are going for you.

I was conflicted about whether to make this offer. Certainly, such an offer can dilute the experience of termination. A brief therapist of Mann's persuasion would be opposed to it and hold that it undermines one of the unique elements that can make brief therapy so powerful. I frequently would have a countertransference toward Diane of wanting to be supportive and ease her pain given all of the abuse, neglect, and loss in her life. I wondered whether my offer was a countertransference acting-out of this desire.

On the other hand, the offer that she could have further contact with me seemed to be helpful to her. It provided some greater continuity than she had had previously in her life. It also conveyed ongoing concern for her, which I think she had doubted (see below). I believe that she feared and expected that I would not think of her once therapy ended. With her tendency toward dissociative states, "out of sight, out of mind" was the way that she frequently lived and expected it of others. On this level my offer may have intensified the experience of loss since she would be losing the face-to-face contact with a person who continued to have concern for her rather than someone she might readily assume would be more indifferent to her. So, this was another aspect of how this interaction could be a "new ending to an old experience." As I write this, I think the offer was useful but that it would have been more therapeutic to delay the offer until later in the session to permit more space to explore what would develop with Diane's reactions to therapy ending.

> D: Good! I was hoping I could but I was afraid to ask.
> MS: Why?
> D: You're busy and I didn't want to ask for something I shouldn't.

Here we see her fear and expectation that I wouldn't care.

> MS: You wouldn't really lose anything by asking.
> D: I know.
> MS: So, you did feel some degree of intimidation by me as well? [T-O].
> D: Yes.
> MS: This is an example of what we've been talking about a lot. You felt that it would be helpful for you to have the op-

tion to call me but didn't ask about it. Not trying to get
your needs met makes you vulnerable to those emotional
storms of impulsivity and bad judgment [T-P-O].

D: You're right but I think I am doing better . . . but it's hard
to change.

MS: It seems to me too that you're handling these things better as well. Still, you do fall back to treating yourself the
way your parents did—ignoring your needs [S-P]. We're
almost out of time. If you only remember two things from
our time together, these are, I think, the two most important. First, what we've just been talking about. It's crucial
to pay attention to your own needs and find effective ways
to get them taken care of on an ongoing basis. It's when
you're feeling so deprived that you're so vulnerable to the
emotional storms. Second, I'm worried about the effect
that the problems with Roj have on you. If anything, they
might hit you harder with you being more isolated. Like
I've said before, it might help for you and Roj to get some
marital therapy together. I am glad that you'll be continuing in therapy and can deal further with these issues that
we've been working on together.

D: Okay.

MS: We're out of time. Take care of yourself.

D: (teary) Okay. Thank you for everything. I will call you.
Good-bye.

Despite the session being on the phone, I felt that we had been
able to end the therapeutic relationship in a way that went beyond
her past experience with endings. I was a bit uncomfortable with
my little speech at the end of the session. My intention was to highlight these important issues that we had been working on throughout therapy. I said it right at the end of the session and, as you can
see, she didn't do much with it. I was saddened by the ending and
worried about how she would fare in a new town isolated with her
husband and children. I did feel that we had been able to accomplish more than I would have expected given her personality structure and the magnitude of the external problems facing her. Diane
had an admirable toughness and resilience about her.

She called me twice over the next six months. Once, she recounted having had the biggest fight she and her husband had had since her arrest. She seemed to just want to share her distress with me and was calmer following the call. In the second call, she told me that she had begun individual therapy and that she felt it looked promising.

10

Very Brief Therapy

> Clearly, psychiatrists who undertake consultations
> should not automatically assign patients to long-term
> therapy or even to brief psychotherapy, but should be
> aware of the possibility that a single dynamic interview
> may be all that is needed.
>
> David Malan and colleagues, 1975

As she entered his office, the patient impressed the therapist with her poise and beauty. A 28-year-old artist, she
sought help for a puzzling and disturbing physical condition. She had been planning to take a trip to Europe to
visit a friend but as she was making arrangements for the
trip her tongue and lips began to swell and she had trouble
talking. Since that time, this symptom would arise whenever she talked about the trip. In fact, it happened several
times during the session as well. In obtaining some back-

ground information, the therapist learned that this young woman appeared to have difficulty with being assertive and competent. He interpreted this to her and suggested that her symptoms were symbolic signs of her difficulty in "speaking for herself." Moreover, he suggested that, for many years, she had developed only through others, not directly herself. She had been very dependent on a man for several years and had recently ended the relationship.

The patient seemed to take in what he had said and asked if she should still take her trip. The therapist said that he thought she could and that she could return to see him if the symptoms continued. She never did return for any further treatment with the therapist but, months later, he learned that she had taken the trip, had greatly enjoyed herself, and was continuing to be symptom-free.

Oremland (1976, 1991), a psychoanalyst, described this case of a single session elimination of a hysterical symptom. I noted in Chapter 4 that the therapy literature dating back to Freud has many instances of dramatic improvements being registered in one or a few sessions.

The present chapter explores the concept of very brief therapy from single-session models (Bloom 1992, Talmon 1990) to a model of up to seven sessions (Talley 1992). Most of the clinical examples come from therapies of one to four sessions.

WHY VERY BRIEF THERAPY?

Clearly, with many patients it is very difficult to do any therapeutic work of substance in only a few sessions. However, two factors persuasively argue for serious attention to very brief therapy: its prevalence and evidence of its effectiveness.

Prevalence

Much of psychotherapy actually conducted is very brief in nature. Consider the following:

1. The median number of sessions in outpatient mental health clinics and agencies is 3.7 (Pardes and Pincus 1981). It is higher in private practice (the average number of sessions is 26 for non-analysts).
2. Sizable percentages of outpatients in mental health clinics frequently come for only one session: 20 to 60 percent (Baekeland and Lundwall 1975), almost 50 percent (Phillips 1985), and 30 percent (Rosenbaum et al. 1990).

Therefore, de facto, much very brief therapy is being done and it seems sensible to consider what might be accomplished in such a limited time rather than writing off such cases as simply dropouts, treatment failures, or exclusively supportive interventions.

Effectiveness

Very brief therapy can be effective for some patients. To note:

1. Several anecdotal reports and some research studies attest to the effectiveness of one to three sessions of therapy for a significant minority of patients (Bloom 1981, 1992, Follette and Cummings 1967, Jones 1955, Malan et al. 1975, Talmon 1989, Winnicott 1971).
2. In a meta-analysis of fifteen studies of psychotherapy effectiveness involving over 2,400 patients, Howard and colleagues (1986) found that approximately 50 percent of the patients registered improvement by the eighth session. They concluded that the sessions in which the most change occurs are usually early ones. It should be added, though, that more prolonged treatment showed a higher percentage of improvement: 75 percent were improved by the twenty-sixth session and 85 percent after a year of treatment.

While more time is usually preferable (and generally yields better outcomes), very brief therapy clearly can be productive.

SINGLE-SESSION MODELS

I have already discussed Bloom's (1992) focused single-session model in Chapter 4. His single session is two hours long. He is active, very focused, and present-oriented. Bloom has two guiding dynamic principles: first, to help patients become aware of something that was previously unconscious, and, second, to initiate a process that promotes psychological health after termination. Relevant to the present discussion, I encourage the reader to review his guidelines detailed in Chapter 4 for single-session therapy.

Other writers (Hoyt et al. 1992, Rosenbaum et al. 1990, Talmon 1990) have examined what can be done in one session working within a health maintenance organization (HMO) setting. While one sometimes detects an evangelical quality about some of the descriptions of the successes in single sessions of therapy, these therapists approach therapy with a pragmatism and an effort to make the most out of limited resources. The therapist's attitude is that this session may be the only session with this patient, therefore, "What can I do *now*?"

In describing their approach, Rosenbaum and colleagues (1990) state, "In summary, the therapist asks: Where does the patient get stuck? What is needed for him or her to get unstuck? How can I as a therapist, facilitate the patient's change process? . . . therapists must acknowledge that patients can change in the moment and that change may occur through sudden discontinuous shifts of being" (p. 170). The attitude represented in this quote sounds quite similar to that of Winnicott (1962, 1971) as highlighted in Chapter 4.

Three key factors promote single-session success (Hoyt et al. 1992). First, an adequate therapist–patient relationship is important—at least a positive feeling tone between the patient and therapist. This often includes a positive contextual transference and at least a rudimentary working alliance.

Second, patients who change in single-session therapy come to see that they have the ability, themselves, to change. This is probably the case for patients in therapy of any duration. However, there needs to be an inclination in the single session for the patient to very rapidly accept the view of personal influence (*self*-control) rather than the belief that change comes predominantly from outside.

This gets to the third point of these writers—patient readiness. Hoyt and his colleagues (1992) note that the openness to change comes about through the patient's dissatisfaction with the way he had been approaching his life. He may perceive that the old patterns have "decayed" due to maturation or a lack of use or that the old patterns just are not working anymore. In single session therapy, the patient must be ready to change *now*.

While not offering a single session model, Goulding and Goulding (1979) have described starting each session with the question, "What are you willing to change today?" Hoyt (1990) has proposed that this question displays the central characteristics of brief therapy:

> *What* (specifies, focuses)
> *are* (active, present tense)
> *you* (self as agent)
> *willing* (motivation, responsibility)
> *to change* (to be different, not just "work on" or "explore")
> *today* (now, in the moment)
> ? (inquiry, therapist is receptive but not insistent).

Such a question reduces the experience of space within which to explore the material and may lessen the patient's and therapist's receptive capacity. Although I think this cost is sometimes worth it in very brief, especially single-session, therapy, I would never *start* a session with this question. Even in single-session therapy I believe it would constrict the clinical material to begin the session in that manner. The material emerges more readily when the therapist conveys a receptive attitude of mutual discovery.

CLINICAL EXAMPLE OF SINGLE-SESSION BRIEF THERAPY: KATRINA

Katrina was angry. As the manager overseeing the construction of 200 housing units, she was responsible for the work of many employees. Her anger was directed at one of her key employees, John, who seemed to have a serious alcohol problem that was affecting his job performance and their working relationship. Katrina was 32 years old and presented herself with an air of calm authority that evoked trust from most of the other employees in the organization. In some of my other work with this organization, I had heard her vice president describe her as "the most valuable player on the team." Given the unflappable professional demeanor that invariably accompanied her, it was striking in the session to see her be so angry. Even more so, I was moved when she began crying later in the session.

Katrina usually kept a professional distance from her subordinates but had not done so with John and they had become friends, confiding in each other. She learned that he had had a drinking and cocaine problem as a youth but he said he now had it under control. She believed him at the time but for at least six months Katrina had been aware of problems. John had sometimes missed meetings (usually in the morning) because of "not feeling good." He admitted to her that he was sometimes hung over in the morning after a particularly "good party." She learned that he had been selling discarded tools and materials from the job site and doing other unprofessional and perhaps unethical activities. When she confronted him on these things, he initially responded that she was overreacting but was then contrite and guaranteed that it would never happen again. She believed him.

Why did she call me now? One week before she called, she and John had been the company representatives to a builders convention in Atlanta. He missed several seminars that he was supposed to attend and she saw him obviously intoxicated at evening cocktail parties. Most disturbingly, he loudly knocked on her hotel room door twice in the middle of the night, obviously drunk, saying that he had to talk to her right at that moment. She answered through the door that it was too late and they would talk in the morning. Each time, he would apologize the next day and say he was just "cutting loose" since he was away from the pressures of the job. Katrina called her husband about this and he was appalled at John's behavior and told her that something had to be done. She now asked me what should she do (symptomatic focus).

Throughout her telling me of these experiences with John, I was feeling a strong urge to shake her and say, "Wake up. This guy's out of control. Do something, don't just stand there!" It was especially striking to see this very capable professional deny the situation so completely for so long and be so disabled. I wondered what the dynamics were that had incapacitated her. I experienced seeing the situation with great clarity and "knew" what she should do. This reaction was partially a projective identification. I was identifying with a split off part of herself—her competent ability to see and do what needed to be done.

Instead of acting on my countertransference, I held on to it. When I spoke, I empathized with her that this was a difficult situation, made much more difficult because he had become a friend of hers. Recognizing my own feeling of a need to act, I asked what she herself had considered doing. She said she had thought of only two options: ignore the behavior or fire him. This was an instance of the simple all-or-nothing thinking of the paranoid-schizoid mode within a woman who generally looked at the world with a complex and subtle vision.

I said that before we considered options, I wanted to get more a sense of her as a person and learn a bit about her background. As she began to talk about her family, tears started to flow until eventually she was sobbing. Katrina described her mother as having a "serious mental illness" including a violent temper, compulsions, and suicide threats. Her father also had an explosive temper but was rarely at home. Her older sister was frequently hospitalized for anorexia and would also fly into violent rages. She described only herself and her younger sister as being "normal." As she wrapped up her narrative of her family, she noted that she was the most easygoing of the family but she did find it hard to take criticism. Also, she felt her self-esteem was sometimes shaky.

I suggested that a question for us, in addition to the practical one, was what was it about this situation with John that disabled such a competent, successful woman (dynamic focus). She was curious about the question and we hit upon two likely factors. First, the way she got through her childhood in this very chaotic family was to "ignore the craziness." The only other option she had was to leave the family, which wasn't an option at all to her (until college when she moved out). So, she had been trying to ignore John's craziness just as she had tried to ignore the family's (Other-Past interpretation). Second, she was angry over the situation with John and she usually does not get angry. Having come from a family where there was such primitive rage, I wondered if she worried that her own anger might get out of control and so she had been avoiding it (Past-Self interpretation). Katrina readily agreed that her anger had upset her. She worried that it might become like her mother's and that some of her anger was guilt at herself for being so impotent and hurting the company through her inaction.

We then worked together on what she could do. I commented that she did have both a supervisory and friendship relationship with John. Was there some way that she could be true to herself and deal with him at both levels? In raising this question I was inviting her to experience her dilemma more from the multilayered complexity of the depressive mode of experiencing rather than from the all-or-nothing paranoid-schizoid mode ("He's either my friend or my employee.").

We discussed several options and came up with the following plan. She would meet with John and say that, as a friend, she was worried about him, detail why, and urge him to get help for what appeared to her to be a substance abuse problem. She would also give him some referrals. However, she would also tell John that she was his supervisor and had a responsibility to the company to deal with his performance, which had been inadequate and inappropriate for some time. She would document the problems so far and specify how they needed to change. She would also write up these points as a written warning that would go in his personnel file. Finally, she would indicate that, if his performance did not improve sufficiently, further disciplinary action would be taken (suspension without pay). This plan seemed sound to her but she was uneasy about carrying it out and we spent some time role-playing it and considering what problems she might run into.

I asked if she wanted another appointment. Katrina said she might but wanted to see how the meeting with John went. We agreed that if she did not call for another appointment, I would call her in three weeks for a follow-up phone contact. When I subsequently called she had had the meeting with John and she felt it had gone well. He initially accused her of being a poor friend and she felt a pang of guilt. However, she calmly remained focused on the message that she wanted to convey. He denied having a drinking problem (I had suggested that that might be his reaction) but that he agreed to the job performance requirements. It was still early but, so far, John's performance had been better and more consistent. More importantly, Katrina felt pleased with the way she had handled him and felt able to continue to confront him as needed. I encouraged her to call me in the future as needed.

The therapy was aided by Katrina's concentration on a specific issue. The symptomatic focus was her distress over what to do about John. The dynamic focus involved the family dynamics (now her internal world) that were paralyzing her in this situation: the pattern of denial and avoidance and the difficulty in dealing with her own rage. I experienced an early urge to directly advise her but, suspecting this as a projective identification between us, I waited and this delay permitted us to examine some of the dynamics that were disabling her. I did not use my countertransference awareness interpretively but it helped me to more accurately understand and empathically connect with her.

While we could not work through these issues in one session, I was hopeful that identifying them would help her to be aware of them in future situations. As I hung up after my follow-up phone call to her, I felt ambivalent about the ending (I usually do). It was good to learn that she had been able to address the situation with John and that it had gone so well (for now, at least). I was also pleased with the bit of focused intrapsychic work that we had done. I did feel somewhat disappointed that we did not have a follow-up session to further discuss her meeting with John and future dealings with him. I also wished for more time to strengthen the work on her family dynamics. I think, too, that she had wanted to stop after one session, in part, due to the shame of her difficulty and wanting to "just get on with things." However, from her standpoint the single-session therapy was very successful; she obtained what she wanted. I need to respect that (and keep my own narcissism in check).

Katrina evidenced all three of Hoyt and colleagues' (1992) key factors in single session therapy. First, we quickly established a good working alliance. Second, while she began the session feeling she could do nothing to improve the situation, she quickly became engaged in the process of looking at what she *could* do. A central benefit of the session was her perception that she could respond and do something different from the two extreme actions she had previously considered (a new ending for an old experience). Lastly, she was *ready*, having been confronted by his outrageous behavior in Atlanta and by her husband's remarks.

VERY BRIEF THERAPY: SEVEN SESSIONS OR LESS

Talley (1992) at Duke University has reported on a study of ninety-five patients in the university mental health center. The study is noteworthy for a number of reasons. First, it is one of the few research projects to explicitly investigate very short term treatment. Second, it provided therapy in a manner that is consistent with the real world of clinic practice:

1. The patients presented with anxiety and/or depression that ranged from mild to severe. The sample was limited, though, in that as a college sample they were uniformly well educated and intelligent.
2. The twelve therapists ranged widely in experience from a social work graduate student on internship to a psychiatrist with twenty-four years of experience. Similarly, there was a range of mental health disciplines represented—social work, psychology, and psychiatry.
3. The treatment was not standardized and there was significant variation in treatment. Therapy ranged from one to seven sessions. Nine of the twelve therapists operated from a psychodynamic perspective while three conducted the therapy more from a cognitive/behavioral or interpersonal perspective.

Talley (1992) found that very brief therapy was successful in significantly reducing the patients' anxiety and depression. The patients tended to be satisfied with their treatment and those who attended more sessions (four to seven) within the range of the study were more likely to be satisfied than those attending fewer sessions (one to three). He wrote that it is important to distinguish very brief therapy from brief or long-term work by setting more limited goals.

> It is proposed that these goals are to have a positive experience with the psychotherapist and at least the initiation of some change in the presenting dysphoria. This change may consist of beginning to look at self, others, or one's life circumstances at least somewhat differently. No pretense is made that the more complete work done in brief or in long-term psychotherapy is necessarily accomplished, but rather the assertion is made that a commencement on this road is, in and of itself, of value . . . thus leaving the door open for further treatment if needed in the future. However, often very brief psychotherapy is itself sufficient to result in a different perspective on the problem and alter the dysphoria or the accompanying symptoms. [Talley 1992, pp. ix-x]

In discussing the results of this study, Talley (1992) makes the following important points:

1. The therapist's careful assessment of the patient's ego strength at the beginning of treatment and *throughout* was crucial. In this way the therapist can tailor the level of the therapy most sensitively to the patient's capabilities during this very short therapeutic encounter.
2. He conceptualized the patient as a "person-at-impasse" and the very brief therapist had three tasks:
   a. to help the patient reconceptualize the problem as involving internal rather than exclusively external conflicts.
   b. to provide "support, encouragement, and problem-solving" (p. 141) while the patient works toward change and growth.
   c. to aid the patient in beginning to have greater awareness into the problem.
3. A very powerful factor in patient satisfaction was the patient's perception that the therapist "had encouraged the belief that the client could improve the situation" (p. 142), This stimulated hope in many patients and their own potential ability to improve their situation.

A THREE-SESSION EMPLOYEE ASSISTANCE PROGRAM MODEL

Over the past twelve years I have had the opportunity to offer EAP services to four organizations. Patients were eligible for a maximum of three sessions for a given problem. While I referred a sizable percentage of the patients for longer-term work, most opted to be seen only for the three sessions. The causes for this were varied: issues were resolved within that period of time, lack of motivation to seek further treatment, and lack of financial resources for additional treatment. Therefore, most patients received only three sessions of therapy, although many saw me for multiple episodes of serial brief therapy. My basic approach was the one I described in Chapter 1, "I'll think dynamically, address some underlying issues, and do what I can." My basic goals were similar to those identified by Talley (1992): for the patient to have a positive encounter with me and to have some reduction in the symptoms. Additionally, I have hoped to engage the patient in some curiosity about an aspect of his inner world. Over time, a way of conducting therapy within these constraints developed heuristically.

Session 1

I try to assess the presenting complaint and determine if it is amenable to a psychotherapeutic intervention. I look at why the patient is coming in *now* and evaluate current functioning and distress. If time permits, I usually ask for some historical material. I discuss the contract of three sessions and tentatively present my current understanding of the foci (symptomatic and dynamic) that we might work on together. I encourage a perspective of "What's here? Let's look at it together." However, I may also give some recommendations depending on the situation. I prefer this first session to be a ninety-minute one to permit more time for the two of us to connect and to allow more space for material to emerge. For purely practical reasons, it is sometimes fifty minutes in duration and that is workable.

Session 2

I spend some time thinking about the session before the current one. Based on these thoughts, I usually ask for more background information related to the foci. The patient and I then come to a clearer, more defined notion of the focus of therapy and we explore it to some extent. At the least, I try to find ways to make the work we are doing portable by verbally identifying the key issues we are investigating together. Wherever possible, I will encourage attention to in-session interpersonal reenactments of inner dynamics (transference). Frequently, in such very brief work, this is neither possible nor useful. I remind the patient that the next session is our last and suggest that she consider how she would like to use it.

Session 3

Termination issues are in the foreground. I ask the patient if there is anything that she particularly wishes to address in this last session. We usually do some additional exploration on the foci. We then review the work that we have done and discuss additional work that the patient may do on her own or subsequently in therapy. In looking at improvement we specifically consider the factors that might contribute to relapse. I encourage the patient to return to therapy in the future as needed and we often set a follow-up appointment or phone call. Or, alternatively, I may make a referral for long-term treatment. The experience of ending is discussed and interpretation of connections with other endings or themes may be offered.

CLINICAL EXAMPLE OF A
TWO-SESSION CONTRACT: ED

Session 1

I had seen Ed and his wife for a parental guidance session a few years prior to this session. He called me again and said that he wanted to see me alone to discuss recurrent depressions and a dream that he had had a few nights before. In this session, this 37-year-old sculptor described episodes of depression that went back to high school. The recent dream had great impact on him and he wanted to understand it better. He intuitively felt that it provided keys to understanding himself and his depressions.

As I write this, it sounds like a tall order for a two- or three-session contract: to analyze a dream and unearth the keys to self-understanding. However, that's not at all the way I felt at the time. I had experienced Ed as being a caring, psychologically minded person who used me well in the parent guidance consultation. He was operating predominantly in the depressive mode and, while there was some idealization of me, I experienced his expectations for our sessions as more realistic than they might appear. I also thought that he could well tolerate the limited nature of what we could do together. As it turned out we met for only two sessions.

This is the dream: "I'm looking through the rooms in my parents' house. I'm trying to find a certain room. I found it! There are beautiful mobiles hanging from the ceiling that I made and my father walks into the room. I feel great but sad. I show him one of the mobiles and it turns into one of my present sculptures. He takes it in his hands and starts to criticize it. Then things change some-how . . . it's like an out-of-body experience . . . and I'm kind of distant and observing the whole thing. My brother and mother are in the living room together. There's some sort of hole in the ceiling and there's this ethereal music. I can't explain it but I feel like I'm witnessing the death of my self. My father came out of the room and he said good-bye but I couldn't hold on to him."

He portrayed his parents as loving, conventional people who didn't understand him because he was so sen-sitive and would tease him about his sensitivity. Ed viewed his father as a perfectionist. Our initial look at the dream yielded a sad awareness of the similarities among Ed, his father, and his son ("We're 'all-or-nothing' people, things have to be just right") and the profound impact that the father's criticism had on him in the dream—it knocked him out of his body and he was feeling a death of self.

Session 2

Ed had thought more about his dream between sessions and had noted that he creates his work (stone) spontane-ously. Any sort of self-evaluative thoughts shut him down. It's an all-or-nothing experience (paranoid-schizoid mode). I suggested that his experience with his perfectionist father had heightened his already acute sensitivity to the point now where criticism paralyzed him, whether it be criticism from another or from himself (Past-Other-Self interpretation). He noted that if he thought anything was wrong with his creation, then it was no good. He was very moved by the thought that he was treating himself as his father had (Past-Self interpretation).

I noted that he had presented his father as loving but critical, and that this was a mixture of wonderful and hurtful elements. However, at times, if he felt criticism, that eliminated him being in touch with the other elements (paranoid-schizoid experiencing pushing out the depressive mode). He talked tearfully about frequently feeling different from others around him and I wondered aloud if he had ever felt a sense of belonging. He noted three instances. From age 20 to 27, he used drugs regularly (especially marijuana, and some LSD) and felt this really opened him up. However, "eventually the drugs turned on me" and caused him to feel anxious. After having a few out-of-body experiences in which he felt "dead," he stopped taking them. I noted the similarity of these experiences and what he described in the dream. I speculated that the drug use had been an attempt to deal with perfectionist feelings, but it had failed. A second positive experience was with a college art teacher who became a mentor and who "changed my life." However, this teacher subsequently broke off the relationship when he felt that Ed was too demanding. Third, he felt very comfortable and loved in his relationship with his wife of twelve years.

I commented that two of these three good experiences had ended badly and wondered if that had affected his ability to be hopeful. He said he had never thought of that but that is exactly the word he centers on when he is depressed—there's no hope—and perhaps that did contribute to his depression.

He said that he was feeling much better and was impressed by how much fear had controlled him and how much his father was "in him." Ed said he was grateful for the help and that it would be timely to stop here even though he realized that he had an additional session available to him. I acknowledged that we had done an important piece of work together and that it would be fine to stop. The depressions that he had described were incapacitating at times, with significant difficulty in sleeping and eating. On the positive side, they tended to last for episodes of only two to three weeks. I suggested that he might consider ongoing therapy at some point in the future either for self-exploration or to deal with the depressions. I also said that antidepressant medication might be helpful if he could not contain the depressions. The idea of future therapy seemed useful to him but he said he did not want to consider medication.

I heard from him ten months later. He sent me an announcement of a showing of his work at a gallery and enclosed a note saying that he had been feeling much better. While he had had some depressions he felt he "got on top" of them quicker and the insight of how much he had let fear control him was instrumental in that.

This two-session therapy with Ed had all three key elements of successful single-session therapy that Hoyt and his colleagues (1992) list: good therapist–patient relationship, Ed's view that *he* could do something about his situation, and readiness. Setting the foci was rather straightforward: helping him to deal with his depression was the symptomatic focus and understanding the dream was the dynamic focus. The dream analysis led us to the work on the relationship with his father, on the criticism and fear. I felt that his decision not to have the third session was a good one. Given the limits, we were at a good stopping point.

I was curious about some of the elements of the dream that we had not gotten to—the mother and brother in the "living" room, the ethereal music, the father not hearing him, and so on. I had a fantasy that Ed would return to see me every year or two and we would further analyze the dream (this was two years ago and it has not happened yet). Of more concern to me was my impression that there was a defensive protectiveness in him doing very brief therapy. I thought that just as drugs had turned on him and his mentor had rejected him, he was unconsciously fearful that I would eventually do that, too. Therefore, he wanted to get in and out while the experience was still good. I decided not to comment on that given the brevity of our contact and the volume of other material that we had addressed.

CLINICAL EXAMPLE OF A THREE-SESSION CONTRACT WITH FOLLOW-UP: SHARON

Session 1

When I greeted her in the waiting room, Sharon practically leapt out of the chair and hurried into my office. She anxiously and rapidly made a number of complimentary observations about my office contrasting it with how comfortable it felt to her but how uncomfortable she was. She then settled down (kind of) and said she was very glad to be here and should have come sooner, but didn't know where to begin. I said we have time and I suggested that she reflect for a moment and see where she would like to start. This 36-year-old medical clinic receptionist described how much she hated her job of four years and, more importantly, how she felt stuck in her life, especially occupationally. She had a college degree in literature and had published a short story but had never done more writing. She felt that she would like a more challenging job (e.g., gourmet cooking, managing a restaurant) but that she couldn't bring herself to make a move. Sharon would always look at both sides of a situation, think both sides made sense, and be paralyzed. She ended this part of her narrative with the comment that she had too many ideas but not enough actions. I suggested that her indecisiveness seemed to be part of a lack of awareness of who she was. She readily agreed and said she just couldn't seem to find herself. Sharon then said that the only area of her life in which she did feel "sure of herself" was that she was a good and dedicated mother to her three children.

I inquired as to why she had called me now. She was thinking so much one day at home about how she couldn't decide what to do about her work life that she literally felt paralyzed—she couldn't move her hands for a few minutes. The paralysis passed but Sharon felt shut down and numb. She told her husband and he urged her to call me. What she didn't tell her husband, which she now recounted to me, was that that incident reminded her of another time of feeling out of control. One year before, when her husband was out of town and she was alone with her children, she had a bizarre thought: that she should go into their bedroom and smother them with a pillow. The thought was not a hallucination but it was strong and vivid, although she denied any urge to act upon it. It scared and shamed her and caused her to wonder if she was a terrible parent. She had never had such thoughts before or since then with such vividness and intensity but has worried about that occurrence.

I had been experiencing Sharon as a likable, obsessive woman who sprinkled her narrative with self-deprecatory wit. Indeed, she was having trouble finding herself and had had a series of jobs that were well below her potential. She seemed to be a paradoxical mixture of spending much time considering her life but remaining out of touch with herself. Her report of the murderous thought toward her children hit me (as it had her) without warning and I became more anxious and vigilant about a possibly psychotic process. Certainly, there were indications of autistic-contiguous functioning: her attention to how comfortable my room was, the brief paralysis of her hands, the tactile nature of her description of smothering her children. Moreover, the thought I had about her being out of *touch* with herself seemed to fit this mode. As we continued to discuss it, I felt there was little risk that she might act on such a thought. I did wonder, though, about abuse in her childhood and about her being out of touch with her own anger. She denied any abuse or psychosis in the family.

She asked me what I thought of this murderous fantasy that she had reported. I said I didn't fully understand it and it would be good if we could understand it better. I did note that there was an enormous difference between thinking and action and it was appropriate that the thought made her anxious. It was also a favorable sign that she didn't feel the urge to act on the thought. I then went back to what it could mean. It had occurred at a time when the demands of being a parent had all fallen on her since her husband was out of town. I wondered if the thought was an expression of built-up anger at her children. She considered this and said she had always prided herself on being very patient with her kids and generally didn't get angry with them. She did say, though, that she was aware of how they restricted her occupational possibilities since her income was the only consistent income in the family (her husband was a free-lance photographer who had brought in little income for the past two years). Sharon denied any anger toward him concerning that.

As the session had progressed, Sharon had become calmer and more focused. She noted that she felt very relieved to have told someone about this fantasy. She considered telling her husband about it as well. This led to a brief discussion of the satisfaction that she had with her marriage and with friends but also her lack of being open with her husband and friends about her own needs.

I said that we could meet three times and that I proposed that we look further at this fantasy and at her occupational indecision (symptomatic foci) and to begin looking at the issue of "finding" herself (dynamic focus). I suggested that the later focus of self-exploration, however, really was the domain of long-term therapy and that she might consider beginning that. I suggested that she keep in mind whether any of the work that we did might illuminate the meaning of her murderous fantasy.

This case raises the difficult issue of what to focus on and what not to address in very brief therapy. Clearly, Sharon was dealing with many difficult issues, practical and dynamic, and not everything could be pursued. Certainly the material suggests that some exploration of Sharon's marriage might be useful. For example, how did she feel about having to be the primary bread-winner in a job that she hated while her husband pursued his preferred occupation? As detailed below, while this was touched upon, the therapy developed in a different direction.

Session 2

Sharon began by saying that she had told her husband about her murderous fantasy and he was very compassionate and understanding. She felt additionally relieved having discussed it with him and that it wasn't such a terrible indictment of herself. I noted that she had had the homicidal fantasy when her husband was away, leaving her with all of the childcare. I wondered if it was a disguised expression of anger toward him. She considered this and said it made sense intellectually but she didn't have a feel for it. We talked further about her recent brief paralysis and I noted that if her hands were paralyzed, she couldn't act on the fantasy (i.e., use her hands to smother the children). Since the fantasy had come to mind as we had discussed the paralysis last week, I suggested that the two might be connected. Sharon was intrigued by this idea and extended the thought to the likelihood that her "paralysis in life" might be an attempt to not hurt her family through making a bad decision.

Thirty minutes into the session she said that now she didn't know what to talk about; there were so many possibilities. As she struggled to decide what to discuss, she became more and more anxious. I was simply listening at this point, feeling comfortable with the ambiguity despite her anxiety and our limited time. I encouraged her to not pressure herself but rather to take her time and just listen to whatever came up. I was trying to facilitate her receptive capacity. She continued to struggle and there was "paralysis" in the session. I eventually said, "It looks to me like you're trying so hard to find the right thing to talk about that you can't hear what you're thinking or feeling." Sharon focused immediately and said that she doesn't pay attention to how she feels until it's intense and she gave several examples—denying that an obnoxious neighbor bothered her, denying that her job was as frustrating as it is, denying how much she would like to live in a bigger apartment or house.

We discussed this topic quite productively for about 10 minutes. She then became anxious and frustrated again saying that she didn't now know what to talk about. She noted that we could talk about her "wacky" family but she didn't want to waste our time and went on to list other possible topics. I interrupted her and remarked that her not listening to herself had occurred just a moment ago when she had said that we could talk about her family but then she moved away from it. Sharon said she didn't think that that would get us anywhere but since she didn't have anything else to talk about, she compliantly began talking about her family.

Her childhood was chaotic. Her alcoholic father left the family when Sharon was 13. His father began his career as a writer (like Sharon) but he didn't stick with it, and bounced around doing a variety of low skill, frustrating jobs. As we neared the end of the session, she passionately cried out, "I don't want to be like my father." As we ended the session, I said that this revelation was a very important one and that it wouldn't have come out if I hadn't respected her offhand comment about her "wacky" family and encouraged her to look at it. This was a part of her that she needed to develop further. I also reminded her that we had one more session in our three-session contract.

The holding and containing functions of relationships are illustrated in these two sessions. My ability to sit with her anxiety in both sessions—to contain it—permitted some transformation of her anxiety. Various comments of mine seemed to have a holding function so that she was then able to settle in and do more reflective work rather than being bombarded by her thoughts. Her symptom of paralysis had come into the therapy session as a paralysis of thought. It allowed me to see Sharon's mental paralysis and fear and then link it to her internal object world. The holding environment set the stage for this. The therapist does not have to *do* something prescriptive to promote this growth.

Comments that seemed to hold her included:

my remark about trying to find herself
my noncritical exploration of her murderous fantasy
my comment that she was trying so hard to be right
    that she doesn't hear what she feels
my noting her avoidance of talking about her family.

These interventions both calmed and focused her. Sharon and I had created the conditions to understand her paralyzed thinking and her fear of being like her father.

Regarding focus, consider how I went with the topic of not listening to herself and with the topic of family. These were not directly on track with the identified focus. This is a judgment call in conducting very brief therapy. I had an intuition that this would be related to the focus in a meaningful way. It turned out that it was connected: she feared that she was repeating her father's pattern of squandering her potential (S-P connection). My going in that direction, though, ran the risk of confusing and diffusing a very brief therapy. I also had been aware of a stronger than usual (for me) inclination to *not* direct her talking. These may have been benign and moderated unconscious identifications with her unfocused and nondirective father but they facilitated her being able to forge new links herself.

Session 3

As I anticipated the third session, I was aware of feeling strongly that Sharon could benefit much more from long-term therapy and I hoped that she would follow through on that recommendation despite very real financial problems. She was very focused in this session. She indicated that she had thought a lot since last time about her fear of turning out like her father. She felt it was part of what crippled her and made her so indecisive. Ironically, the fear itself was creating the pattern that was feared. I suggested to her that her standards for decisions approached perfection. The need to be right was keeping her from being able to choose. She therefore stayed stuck. She acknowledged that it was difficult to choose unless she was sure it was right. Since everything had its imperfections, she couldn't choose. We wondered together if this had contributed to her father's pattern as well as to his alcohol abuse.

She reported that she had been writing in a journal since the last session. This was the first time she had done so in years and she found it useful. I suggested that it was a way for her to listen to herself. She said that she realized that another factor that had "taken her away" from herself had been her role in the family after her father left. She said she became a surrogate parent to her younger sister and a surrogate husband to her mother. I remarked that it sounded like she had had to grow up too fast. We also looked at the internal pressure on her to be a good mother so as not to be like her father. Some of her distress about the murderous fantasy and her earlier denial of anger toward her children were caused by this pressure to be a perfect parent.

Sharon had investigated a clinic for ongoing psychotherapy but felt that the staff was not adequately trained, and she was not inclined to begin further treatment. We discussed this from the standpoint of her idealization of me and the pain of losing our relationship. Also, I remarked that this may be an example of her not moving on to something if it doesn't seem like a perfect choice. She reported feeling freed up about looking for other work and, surprising to her, she felt less pressured to get out of her present job immediately. The present job had some significant benefits (flexibility to spend time with her children) and she felt she could pursue a job search in a more relaxed manner.

I felt that much had occurred in these three sessions but the timing of stopping seemed premature. Sharon was

developing her focusing capacity somewhat, she was looking at how she would get locked into being indecisive, she
was beginning to listen to herself more, and she was much
more aware of her identification and counteridentification
with her father. However, these improvements felt fragile to me—more so than usual. I was also troubled by her
inclination not to follow through on more therapy. While
I was aware of all of this, I also wondered whether I was
identifying with Sharon's need for ideal conditions before
action could be taken. On balance, I felt that it would be
best to offer a follow-up session. We scheduled one for
one month later.

Session 4

Sharon began this session talking about some unusual
stresses at work that caused her to feel more isolated from
the other clinic personnel. I wondered to myself about the
isolation she might be feeling as she met with me in this
session, our last in the contract. She described the past
month as being a good one. She was feeling more comfortable with herself and with her job. She was regularly
writing in her journal and had started work on an idea she
had for a short story. She was also exerting some effort
on a job search.

Sharon said she was very grateful to me for what the
therapy had done and felt it had helped on many levels.
She was still considering calling the mental health clinic
for ongoing therapy but wondered if it might be possible
to see me privately and that she could afford monthly
sessions. I reminded her that we had already discussed that
I couldn't see her privately but that I did appreciate that
it was difficult to start over with someone new. I also said
that monthly sessions really wouldn't do justice to a serious self-exploration.

I interpreted that her reaction to ending might shed
some light on a more pervasive pattern concerning her

indecision. I suggested that it was difficult for her to directly look at the limits of what a particular situation (or relationship) might be able to provide. Could Sharon acknowledge what she can and can't get from a situation (e.g., therapy with me, her job)? If so, it would be easier to either decide to stay with it and accept its limitations (stop therapy or stay with the present job) or decide it's not enough and go for something more despite the anxiety involved (begin ongoing therapy or find another job). I further suggested that this might have been part of the pattern that kept her father from being more directed and successful. She thought that made sense and said it underlined her intense determination not to be like her father in that regard.

Sharon cognitively understood this and worked with it briefly but I wasn't confident that she was able to work with it yet at an affective level. Of course, we had no opportunity to do any working through of this interpretation. I hoped at least that with a cognitive label on the pattern she could take it with her and do further work on her own.

I was saddened by our termination and felt that I would miss her. I had felt a close connection with her despite this very brief contact. I was conflicted about this follow-up session. I had consciously offered it to her because I felt she was undecided and resistant to the idea of the therapy referral and that another session would be helpful to deal further with that as well as to further work on the foci. However, I wondered if I had unconsciously identified with her denial of limits and wasn't myself facing our ending or what we could not do. Perhaps I, then, colluded with her to ignore the limits. I also was concerned that I had contributed to the therapy being more of an exciting object experience—I set up a session one month later and she then requested (was unconsciously encouraged to request?) ongoing monthly sessions.

However, I think that we did do some additional important work in this last session (the work on acceptance of limits). But was this enough to justify that fourth session? As I write about Sharon now I am still conflicted (indecisive?) but, on balance, think it would have been better to have stopped at the third session.

SUMMARY COMMENTS ON VERY BRIEF THERAPY

Very brief therapy raises many of the same issues as does brief therapy in general but in a more highly concentrated form. I would especially emphasize the following.

A General Rule: The Briefer the Treatment, the Tighter the Focus Should Be

Since there is much less time in which to do the work, having a more narrow focus increases the chances for more adequate development of that issue.

The Patient and Therapist's Ability to Rapidly Form an Alliance Is Crucial

This is an important but rather obvious point. Since therapy can't proceed without an adequate alliance, therapy can't be very brief unless the alliance forms very quickly. The alliance need not be extensive, though. It may be simply and productively centered around the very limited focus of the very brief therapy.

The Exciting Object Relationship Potential of Very Brief Therapy Can Be Particularly Great

Very brief therapy can feel like this: Just as the patient began to feel some relief and comfort in talking to the therapist, the therapy ended and left the patient unsatisfied and longing for more. While this is an issue in brief therapy in general, it can be especially problematic in very brief therapy. Frequently there is some opportunity for the patient to have felt improvement for a while when the therapy is more on the order of twelve to twenty-five sessions. Keeping the focus more limited and explicit and clearly presenting the limits of the contact with the patient are essential in reducing this potential.

Aim to Accomplish Three Goals

1. *Provide a positive experience.* This makes it more likely that the patient will return for help in the future. Also, for some patients, having a positive experience with another person (the therapist) may run counter to their general experience with people and, in and of itself, can generate realistic hope. Once again, from an object relations perspective, therapy is fundamentally a relationship, no matter how brief.
2. *Reduce the patient's distress.* Almost all, if not all, patients enter psychotherapy to reduce their distress. The benefits of supportive psychotherapy can often come about in very brief therapy.
3. *Engage the patient's curiosity in her inner world.* As Malan (1976) reports, the patient's curiosity about the psyche was strongly connected with positive outcomes. Even if the patient and therapist cannot do more than identify certain psychological issues, when the patient is interested in these issues she can do further work on them on her own or later in future therapy.

Can the Patient Come to See Some Potential for Internal Control over the Situation?

The sense of hopelessness that brings many people into therapy frequently comes from a conviction that they have no influence over their condition. One crucial process to facilitate is for the patient to realistically examine his potential for affecting the situation. This doesn't mean that the patient would necessarily leave very brief therapy having actually changed his situation or condition, but rather that he has begun to see and respect his *potential* for affecting the situation. Even circumstances that can't be changed (e.g., a death of a loved one, a terminal disease) can be approached in a variety of ways that can lessen or intensify emotional distress, or enhance or impair functioning.

If a patient is feeling unable to have an impact on his life, I would look for ways to actively point that out to him. Moreover, in very brief therapy, I ask questions like the following:

What could you do differently?
Can you try an experiment? Try it and see what happens?
What are you willing to change today?

I also have used comments like the Chinese proverb, "If you don't change directions, you'll wind up where you're headed" (Hoyt 1990). However, I never start the sessions with these questions or comments. I want there to be some space to discover what will develop in the beginning of the session.

Less Opportunity Exists for Experiential Learning

In very brief therapy I find that I am less able to use the power of examining in-session reenactments than when I have, say, fifteen to twenty-five sessions. With many patients it takes more time to develop a holding environment that permits them to tolerate the anxiety of here-and-now observation of their interactions with the therapist. Of course, the therapist simply has fewer in-session opportunities to observe, too. Therefore, while I try to make it as experiential as possible, my very brief therapy tends to be more cognitive than longer brief therapy. This point is related to the following one as well.

There Is Little Time for Working Through, So Try to Make Learning Portable

Sometimes change and growth occur suddenly and in an instant. Rosenbaum and colleagues (1990) have referred to "decisive moments" and "pivotal moments." Other terms used to describe such experiences are *"ah ha" experiences, revelations,* and *epiphanies.* However, change in therapy is a process rather than an event. At times, the change can seem sudden but it is only the end point of an extended, gradual unfolding. Psychodynamically, we term this gradual change process working through. The experiences and insights of therapy generally take time to become integrated into the patient's personality, to take root and to grow. In very brief therapy, the therapist and patient have little or no time to work through the material. Therefore, the therapist needs to direct some attention to facilitating working through outside of therapy. I try to ask myself, What can the patient take with her? How will she be able to continue to use this? I attempt to identify particular issues that have been important in the work so the patient has a cognitive handle to use to carry on the work after therapy (e.g., Katrina's avoidance and denial of "crazy" behavior in others). Similarly, I may explicitly suggest that the patient continue to look at those issues (e.g., Sharon's indecisiveness and its connection with her father).

Be Humble but Hopeful

As Talley (1992) notes: (1) while very brief therapy cannot accomplish what can be done in brief or long-term treatment, significant aid to patients can often be provided, and (2) a high percentage of patients are satisfied with their very brief therapy experience. The three goals that I suggested above are attainable with many patients in very brief therapy. Can more usually be accomplished with more time? Absolutely.

It is important not to underestimate the impact that such quick encounters can have on patients. Therapists frequently evaluate the therapy less positively than do patients. I once saw a police officer for a single session concerning his troubled marriage. The symptomatic focus was his distress over whether to leave his wife or whether to stay. We never came up with a dynamic focus and he left the session as confused and undecided as when the session began. His subjective distress did not seem to be lessened at all by what we did, either. Yet, in the next year he sent two fellow officers to see me and each said he raved about how helpful I was. I was thoroughly surprised.

Don't Hurry

If brief therapy can incline the patient and therapist to be hurried then very brief therapy can lead them to be *very* hurried. Usually a hurried encounter is much more likely to stimulate rejecting (un-empathic) or exciting object experiencing than a more patient ap-proach that covers less territory. It is generally better to identify some material and reinforce it than to just touch on many differ-ent points. Even in very brief therapy, even in single-session therapy, the foundation of the healing power of psychotherapy is in the therapist's (and patient's) ability to *listen and truly hear.*

11

Object Relations Brief Therapy and Personality-Disordered Patients: I

> Patients with personality disorders continually demon-
> strate to mental health professionals the limits of their
> expertise.
>
> J. Christopher Perry and George E. Vaillant, 1989

The treatment of choice for personality disorders is usually long-term psycho-therapy. This is not only my own opinion but also the opinion of almost all of the contributors to the brief dynamic therapy litera-ture. I will return to this point momentarily but, first, a short story:

For several years I taught a seminar (Stadter 1993) for the American Healthcare Institute entitled Brief Therapy with Person-ality Disorders (much of the following two chapters draws on material I developed in that course and I am grateful to AHI for their permission to use this material in the present volume). As I was preparing the course, one of my colleagues said to me that this had to be the easiest course I had ever developed. He suggested that I start the course with the question and subsequent answer, "What can be done with personality disorders in brief therapy? Not a damn thing!" I could then just sit down and that would be the entirety of the course.

Fortunately, the situation is neither as simple nor as bleak as my cynical friend suggests. However, many therapists do despair concerning the possibility of providing meaningful therapeutic experiences for these patients in a short time frame. In their study on patterns of recovery in psychotherapy, Kopta and his colleagues (1994) conclude that "the characterological symptoms responded poorly to the first 52 sessions of psychotherapy, a longer time frame of individual therapy appears to be necessary" (p. 1015). Certainly, the personality structures and interaction patterns of many personality-disordered patients make it difficult to promote change and growth within the constraints of the brief therapy holding environment. It can be difficult for many of them to quickly develop a working alliance, to tolerate the exploration of their defenses and repetitive object relational patterns, and to adequately handle separation and termination. In many respects, these patients do present brief therapists with their greatest challenges and most difficult countertransferences.

However, while long-term therapy is usually the treatment of choice for serious personality disorders, significant work on a dynamic focus with these patients can sometimes be done in brief therapy. This chapter is the first of two on this topic and examines the concept of personality disorders, the distinctive contributions that an object relations perspective provides, some of the literature on brief therapy with personality disorders, and treatment considerations with dependent personalities. The following chapter considers treatment considerations in working with schizoid, narcissistic, and borderline patients.

THE CONCEPT OF PERSONALITY DISORDER

The phenomena of personality disorders have been labeled and classified in various schemas. Since many of the manifestations are troublesome to significant others and observers, there has frequently been a pejorative tone to some of these classifications and descriptions. Perry and Vaillant (1989) note that these patients have been labeled as bad or immoral (religiolegal model), as marginal or deviating from the surrounding culture (sociological model), or, in a less derogatory approach, as demonstrating extremes of normal personality traits (academic psychology).

The foundation of the concept of personality disorder is the concept of personality and herein lie some of the difficulties. Personality is a vague, multifaceted concept that refers to a configuration of persistent traits. The standard diagnostic manual, *DSM-IV*, defines personality traits as "enduring patterns of perceiving, relating to, and thinking about the environment and oneself that are exhibited in a wide range of social and personal contexts" (APA 1994, p. 630). The medical model traditionally conceptualizes personality disorders from the standpoint of the presence of a pathological condition but functionally *DSM-IV* views personality disorders, as does academic psychology, as exaggerations of normal personality. "Only when personality traits are inflexible and maladaptive and cause significant functional impairment or subjective distress do they constitute Personality Disorders. The essential feature of a Personality Disorder is an enduring pattern of inner experience and behavior that deviates markedly from the expectations of the individual's culture" (APA 1994, p. 630).

I will be using the *DSM-IV* classification system in discussing personality disorders in this chapter since it is, by far, the model most used by American mental health professionals. However, it is important to note its limitations. It comes from the objective-descriptive tradition of psychiatry rather than from the psychoanalytic tradition. As such, its emphasis is on clear, observable and measurable categorization of the domain of personality disorders. While this is a worthy enterprise, much of the unique individuality and inner experience of the patient is de-emphasized and lost. For example, we should not conclude that one borderline patient's inner world will be substantially like another's. Moreover, it is the therapist's appreciation of the patient's unique inner world that is crucially important in promoting change.

In reviewing studies on the prevalence of personality disorders, Perry and Vaillant (1989) have estimated that between 5 and 15 percent of the adults in the general population could be diagnosed as personality-disordered. Merikangas and Weissman (1986) have concluded that, "Nearly one in every 10 adults in the general population and over one-half of those in treated populations, may be expected to suffer from one of the personality disorders" (p. 274).

Perry and Vaillant (1989) list four characteristics that all personality disorders share:

1. *Inflexible and maladaptive response to stress.* This rigidity is often a manifestation of the closed system (Fairbairn 1952) of the patient's inner world, which makes it more difficult for the patient to learn from experience.

2. *Impairment in working and loving that is more severe and more pervasive than in neurosis.* I would amend this to refer to impairment in working *or* loving. For instance, many high functioning narcissistic patients are very successful at work but are severely impaired in the area of intimate relationships.

3. *Evocation of symptomatic behavior by interpersonal conflict.* While a neurotic patient may suffer in silence, the symptoms of the personality-disordered patient are typically played out in relation to other people. Even with schizoid individuals we can view their dysfunction from the standpoint of avoidance of people and intimacy and their great need for space.

4. *A "peculiar capacity"* to *"get under the skin" of others.* This characteristic is related to the strong negative countertransferences that these patients can generate and to the frequent experience of primitive projective identification dynamics in therapy with them.

CONTRIBUTIONS OF AN
OBJECT RELATIONS PERSPECTIVE

Object relations theory uniquely prepares the therapist for work with these patients. The following are some of the benefits of this perspective:

1. The therapist is cautioned not to be distracted by the symptom picture but rather to attend to what the underlying personality dynamics are for the specific patient (Fairbairn 1952). Object relations theory centers on personality and intersubjectivity rather than on symptomatology. It focuses on dynamics and meaning rather than on description and classification. The unique individuality of the patient is emphasized (Bollas 1989, Guntrip 1969, Winnicott 1965). The *person* with the psychopathology is central, not the psychopathology. The knowledge gained from the object relational study of personality disorders in psychoanalysis or in intensive psychodynamically oriented psychotherapy is invaluable in making some sense out of the very limited resources available in briefer work.

2. Since the personality-disordered patient frequently displays his disorder interpersonally, it is common for this to be rapidly and intensely reenacted with the therapist. The object relations emphasis on reenactments and projection of the inner world onto the interpersonal environment gives the therapist rich insight into what is transpiring in the, at times, chaotic and painful here-and-now exchange in the therapist's office.

3. These interactions just described can frequently evoke strongly negative countertransferences. Probably the most difficult yet crucial element for the therapist in working with many personality-disordered patients is awareness and management of countertransference. The therapist works toward understanding the patient through both her own unconscious and conscious processes. No other theory of personality or psychotherapy gives so much attention or respect to countertransference responses.

4. Object relations thinking emphasizes the mutual effects that patient and therapist have on each other. As Racker (1968) has noted, the countertransference in large measure is a response to the transference, *and* the transference is in large measure a response to the countertransference. Looking at the therapist–patient dyad as a largely unconscious, mutually influencing system helps the therapist to further under-

stand and cope with the strains of working with these patients. It is difficult for me to imagine how one could successfully work with many personality-disordered patients without some sensitivity and attention to the conscious and unconscious impact of the patient on the therapist (and, of course, of the therapist on the patient).

5. Object relations theory acknowledges the inevitability (and necessity) of becoming immersed in the patient's inner world through the processes of projective and introjective identification. This is especially the case with difficult patients like personality-disordered ones. The therapist's stance is to experientially be in that world but to be able to think about it as well. Therefore, the therapist attempts to live in and explore the patient's inner world but also then to step back and make some sense of the experience both in terms of the patient's psyche and in connection with the relationship between therapist and patient. As the Scharffs (1991) put it, understanding relating is the way the therapist relates to the patient.

6. Many personality-disordered patients experience rather primitive emotions and states of being. The language and concepts of object relations theory can often readily connect with the subjectivity of the patient. For example, the object relations therapist can frequently connect with these patients and empathically describe their states of terror, fragmentation, envy, emptiness, aching, longing, being tantalized, wordless sensory experiencing, abandonment, being smothered, isolation, and so on. Understanding and being able to put words to paranoid-schizoid and autistic-contiguous states of being can be especially powerful and holding.

SERIAL BRIEF THERAPY

While long-term, sustained treatment is preferable for most personality-disordered patients, it is probable that the treatment that most receive is short-term. This is due to a number of factors. First, as already noted, most therapy is brief. Second, the particular dynamics of many types of personality-disordered patients (e.g., schizoid, schizotypal, narcissistic, borderline, sociopathic) make it difficult for them to maintain an ongoing relationship. Third, while the brief therapist may intend to screen out personality-disordered patients from his brief therapy models, it is often not clear that a patient is personality-disordered until the brief work is well along. Diagnosis often requires a longitudinal rather than cross-sectional approach (Perry and Vaillant 1989). At that point, depending on various factors, the patient and therapist may have to do the best they can with the limited holding of the brief therapy intervention already begun (and, perhaps, almost ended!).

When personality-disordered patients receive brief therapy, it is extremely difficult to successfully modify ingrained character structure. It is, therefore, especially useful for the therapist to think of the brief therapy contract as one episode of therapy that may potentially encourage the patient to seek out future episodes of therapy and may serve as a foundation upon which the later therapy can build.

Alan (presented in Chapter 5) is an example of serial brief therapy with a schizoid patient. In the following chapter I will summarize the serial work with a borderline patient (Ann).

THE LITERATURE ON BRIEF THERAPY AND PERSONALITY DISORDERS

Consistently, studies of psychotherapy of any duration have shown that personality-disordered patients do less well in treatment than patients who do not have such disorders (Reich and Green 1991). However, as discussed below, there is evidence that brief therapy can be effective with some of these patients. (See also Steenbarger [1992] for a review of brief therapy outcomes with a variety of conditions, including personality disorders.)

At first, brief dynamic therapy models excluded these patients. In this way, the literature on brief therapy with personality disorders parallels that of psychoanalysis with personality disorders. Initially, psychoanalytic writers tended to exclude personality-disordered patients from psychoanalysis and psychoanalytic psycho-therapy but innovators (e.g., Kernberg 1975, Kohut 1971, 1977, Masterson 1978, Reich 1945) increasingly described treatment with personality disorders. Similarly, while the first two generations of brief therapists generally did not (knowingly) accept serious per-sonality disorders for their models, the third generation and prag-matic approaches have described work with them, and some have at times made the personality disorder itself a focus of therapy (Budman and Gurman 1988, Strupp and Binder 1984). See the section on selection in Chapter 4.

As noted above, one of the problems in excluding personal-ity-disordered patients from brief therapy is that this diagnosis is often difficult to make and the very nature of the disorder requires a longitudinal rather that a cross-sectional assessment. In other words, the therapist may not see the patient's underlying charac-ter pathology until the brief therapy is well under way.

Binder (1979) has presented a case study of his treatment of a man with serious narcissistic issues. Binder decided during assess-ment that long-term treatment was indicated, but since practical considerations precluded that, he decided to see him in a brief therapy contract of sixteen sessions. They identified therapeutic foci that related to parts of the patient's narcissistic personality struc-ture: they focused on understanding the patient's intense need for approval from others to regulate his self-esteem and on examining his chronic fear of not being good enough. Binder tended to ignore the deeper issues of rage and envy. They did work on trans-ference (including the devaluing of therapy and therapist), the development of higher level defenses (intellectualization and ratio-nalization), and the impact of termination on the patient.

At termination, the patient reported feeling better in all areas of his life. He was freer in expressing feelings, more self-confident, closer to his girlfriend, and more optimistic about being able to have lasting relationships. These improvements were also present at a seven-month follow-up. Binder (1979) concludes,

> Long-term psychotherapy is still the treatment of choice for these [narcissistic] patients, as their severe distortions of object relations can be resolved only within a long and intimate psycho-

therapeutic experience. The point is that few people are willing to expend the time and money for such a long treatment,
and even if a patient is willing, he may not have the resources.
[p. 266]

His case illustrates the significant but limited benefits of brief
therapy for seriously narcissistic patients.

Winston and his colleagues (1991, 1994) conducted a study of
brief therapy involving eighty-one personality-disordered patients.
The selection criteria were similar to those described by Malan (1976)
(discussed in Chapter 4). The personality disorders included compulsive, avoidant, dependent, passive-aggressive, histrionic, and
mixed personality disorders. The researchers excluded schizoid,
schizotypal, narcissistic, paranoid, and borderline disorders. Patients
were randomly assigned to three conditions: 1) Short-Term Dynamic
Psychotherapy (based on Davanloo's [1980] model), (2) Brief Adaptive Psychotherapy (Pollack et al. 1991), and (3) a waiting list. Brief
Adaptive Psychotherapy, not discussed in my historical sampling, is
also a psychodynamic model of brief therapy that is less active and
confrontational than Davanloo's approach and is more cognitively
oriented. Treatment averaged forty weekly sessions.

Winston and his colleagues found that both brief therapies
were highly and equally successful in comparison to the waiting
list condition. Significant improvements were registered in target
complaints, general psychiatric symptoms, and social functioning.
Improvement persisted 1.5 years after termination. They concluded
that Cluster C (anxious cluster) personality disorders and some
Cluster B (dramatic cluster) patients, for example, histrionic, can
be successfully treated in short-term psychodynamic psychotherapy.
It is noteworthy that they excluded from their study some of the
most difficult personality disorders, those involving acting out and
more severe object relational problems. Still, "The patient population was a difficult group because the patients had long-standing
characterological problems that have been generally considered to
be less responsive to time-limited psychotherapy" (Winston et al.
1991, p. 192).

Horowitz and his colleagues (1984) have presented the rich-
est and most articulate examination of brief therapy with person-

ality disorders (see Chapter 4). They detailed their work with hysteric, compulsive, narcissistic, and borderline patients suffering from an acute stress response. More recently, Horowitz (1991) has reported excluding borderline personality disorders from his brief therapy research studies. Attention to personality issues is important because character style plays a part in the formation of the therapeutic relationship and the patient's capacity to learn from the particular approach that the therapist takes. "Personality style is seen as an important factor in understanding symptom formation, therapeutic technique, and syndrome resolution. Our dynamic approach may also facilitate modification of some personality features" (Horowitz et al. 1984, p. 319). They did report characterological changes in some of their patients even though their approach is more problem-focused than personality-focused.

They noted that brief therapy can begin a process of change that can continue and develop further after termination.

> Indeed, the potential for character change may be found primarily in the internalization of actual transitions that began during the therapy, ones that take time to evolve into stable patterns. The brief therapy may not continue long enough for a sufficiently extensive series of trial behaviors with the therapist to take place. However, a brief therapy may instigate a start down a pathway, a start that may encourage the patient to set aside avoidant behaviors and try new life experiences in other relationships. [Horowitz et al. 1984, p. 323]

I believe they are referring to a process like the one that I have identified that makes serial brief therapy so powerful.

Horowitz and his associates have also pointed out that sometimes patients cannot maintain change without the sustaining relationship with the therapist. With those patients, long-term open-ended therapy is required.

Hoglend (1993a) conducted a fascinating study comparing the response to brief dynamic therapy of fifteen personality-disordered patients with thirty subjects who did not have a disorder. The personality-disordered patients included histrionic, borderline, narcissistic, avoidant, and dependent personalities. The approach used aspects of Malan's and Sifneos' models. Duration ranged from nine to fifty-three sessions. They found that treatment length was not correlated with outcome for the patients without personality disorders. However, there was a strong association between treatment length and positive outcome for the personality-disordered patients. Acquisition of insight and overall dynamic change measured two and four years after treatment was significantly related to treatment duration for personality-disordered patients. Hoglend (1993a) concludes, "A brief, focused dynamic treatment approach is insufficient for patients with personality disorders. But if these patients become involved in a dynamic treatment lasting 30 sessions or more, long-term dynamic outcome may be as favorable as outcome for patients without personality disorders" (p. 179). Interestingly, the Cluster B disorders (histrionic, narcissistic, and borderline) that are traditionally viewed as much more difficult to treat did just as well in treatment lasting thirty sessions or more as did the Cluster C disorders (avoidant and dependent).

Budman and Gurman (1988) have argued that most patients neither need nor want their personality issues addressed. However, these authors see their flexible model as being able to deal with these problems and they have identified personality disorders as one of their five major foci of brief therapy. Their recommendation is to address the characterological issues only if the therapist assesses that work on other foci (loss, developmental dysynchronies, specific symptoms, and interpersonal conflicts) will fail without attention to personality.

I would argue that whatever focal problem is selected, it is embedded within the person's personality. It is crucial for the therapist to attend to that part of the clinical picture in working with the patient. This is especially important with personality-disordered patients if lasting change is to occur. Therefore, the dynamic focus usually involves, implicitly or explicitly, a component of the patient's personality structure.

Budman and Gurman (1988) have made some outstanding practical contributions to organizing our thinking about working with personality-disordered patients in brief therapy. They have suggested goals, a typical intervention sequence, and some useful questions for the therapist to consider. These are presented below with my comments following.

GOALS WITH PERSONALITY-DISORDERED PATIENTS

1. To help the patient experience and realize self-defeating patterns of interaction
2. To allow the patient to feel that other modes of interaction are possible
3. To enable the patient to "test out" new, more functional patterns of relating [p. 223]

The extent to which it is possible to work on these goals will vary widely from patient to patient. The more experiential, the better. However, that may be too much for some patients and the therapist needs to accept the patient's taking with him only a cognitive understanding of the issues that he may work on later on his own or in subsequent therapy. For other patients even that may be beyond what is possible, and the therapy might be exclusively supportive.

TYPICAL INTERVENTION SEQUENCE

1. Display of the pathological behaviors and interactions in the treatment
2. Examination of the in-therapy interactions
3. Strong affective involvement
4. Therapist's description of the patient's dysfunctional pattern
5. Disconfirmation of the response the patient anticipates [Budman and Gurman 1988, p. 226]

This sequence emphasizes attention to the observable interpersonal interactions within the sessions. I would also attempt, whenever possible, to focus on the subjectivities and intersubjectivity of the patient and therapist at each of these steps to help us understand the patient's inner world as well as his interpersonal pattern. Note how this sequence, when successful, provides the patient with a new ending for old experience.

USEFUL QUESTIONS FOR THE THERAPIST TO CONSIDER

1. How am I reacting to this patient?
2. What is the patient's general way of reacting to me?
3. Is there an interactional theme developing across sessions?
4. How do my reactions to the patient and the patient's reactions to me "fit" with the patient's usual problematic scenario with people? (and/or How do these reactions "fit" with life history issues?) [Budman and Gurman 1988, p. 230]

Interestingly, it is predominantly in work with personality-disordered patients that Budman and Gurman have addressed the therapeutic relationship. This makes sense since it is of particular importance given their tendency to play out their dynamics, often provocatively, within the interpersonal domain. Of course, as I have indicated throughout this book, the strong emphasis on the patient–therapist relationship should be central in brief therapy with all patients.

BRIEF THERAPY WITH SPECIFIC DISORDERS: DEPENDENT PERSONALITY

In this chapter, I discuss brief therapy with dependent patients. In the following chapter, I examine brief therapy with schizoid, narcissistic, and borderline personalities. It is useful to consider that these are characteristics of all people and that we all have our dependent, schizoid, narcissistic, and borderline features. Their presence is not a sign of disorder but rather of humanity. When such attributes are particularly prominent and extreme they can be seen as constituting a personality disorder.

Overview

Humans are born in a state of such biological and psychological immaturity that we cannot exist without others—from birth, we have to *depend* on other people. This is a fundamental and defining fact of human existence and experience. Fairbairn (1952) wrote that the need for relationships with other people was the most basic psychological motivation, that psychic energy (libido) is "object-seeking." He further argued that adult psychopathology could be understood from the vantage point of the persistence of infantile dependency into adult life. As Greenberg and Mitchell (1983) put it, "He [Fairbairn] is suggesting that human experience and behavior derive fundamentally from the search for and maintenance of contacts with others" (p. 156). Even the pathology of a schizoid individual can be seen from this vantage point of dependency. The schizoid person deals with the issue of dependency through *withdrawal* to a world of inner objects where they are in the person's own control.

Needing others is as basic to human existence as breathing. However, when the dependent aspects of personality become particularly strong, infantile, and/or maladaptive, the person may be described as having a dependent personality disorder. For these patients, their self-esteem and self-concept are very dependent on the connection with the other person (e.g., "I'm nothing without Charles"). These are often people with patterns of anxious attachment (Bowlby 1969). They are uncertain about the reliable availability of objects and this requires them to stay overly close to the important other person.

DSM-IV

Table 11–1 presents the dependent personality from the standpoint of descriptive clinical diagnosis. As with all of the personality disorders, it is useful for us to keep in mind a dynamic understanding of these processes as we consider the descriptive criteria.

These criteria emphasize the prominence of a relationship or relationships as organizing factors in the personality as well as the intense fear of abandonment. When an important relationship is threatened, the person reacts in an anxious, submissive manner that desperately tries to appease the other. This disorder is one of the most frequently reported by mental health clinics. Depression and low self-esteem are also frequently present in the clinical picture as

Table 11–1. Diagnostic Criteria for Dependent Personality Disorder (*DSM-IV* code 301.6)

A pervasive and excessive need to be taken care of that leads to submissive and clinging behavior and fears of separation, beginning by early adulthood and present in a variety of contexts, as indicated by five (or more) of the following:

1. has difficulty making everyday decisions without an excessive amount of advice and reassurance from others
2. needs others to assume responsibility for most major areas of his or her life
3. has difficulty expressing disagreement with others because of fear of loss of support or approval (**Note:** Do not include realistic fears of retribution)
4. has difficulty initiating projects or doing things on his or her own (because of a lack of self-confidence in judgment or abilities rather than a lack of motivation or energy)
5. goes to excessive lengths to obtain nurturance and support from others, to the point of volunteering to do things that are unpleasant
6. feels uncomfortable or helpless when alone because of exaggerated fears of being unable to care for himself or herself
7. urgently seeks another relationship as a source of care and support when a close relationship ends
8. is unrealistically preoccupied with fears of being left to take care of himself or herself

From *DSM-IV: Diagnostic and Statistical Manual of Mental Disorders*, 4th ed. Copyright American Psychiatric Association, 1994. Used with permission.

well. Women are much more frequently (3:1) diagnosed as dependent personalities than men and it is most common in youngest siblings (Perry and Vaillant 1989).

Clinical Example: Denise

Denise (31 years old) was feeling depressed and overwhelmed—understandably. She was struggling with problems on almost every front: her marriage, her career, and her body. Several months before our first session, her husband, Charles, had told her that their marriage was over. He felt that there had been a "flatness" to their marriage for some time. He felt empty and that, while they liked each other, they should go their separate ways. Denise had begged him to reconsider and stay, but now she realized that it was over and she intellectually felt it was right to end it although she was terrified of living without him. She had never been alone in her life before and either her parents or Charles had directed her. She interacted with me with a markedly passive and submissive style.

Denise was a junior policy analyst for an international think tank and in four months was scheduled to go to Israel for ninety days, alone, to do research. This would be the first time she had been alone out of the country and, moreover, she expected to feel even more isolated and scared since she was of Lebanese descent (all four grandparents were born and raised in Lebanon) and would be living in Israel.

Lastly, for the past four years she had been frequently struggling with physical symptoms that were at times debilitating—headaches and stomach distress. She had had repeated medical evaluations but nothing was found. The symptoms made her feel out of control. She believed that these symptoms worsened when her depression worsened. Various physicians had prescribed different antidepressants but nothing had helped either the bodily symptoms or the depression. Prozac and Tofranil made her feel even worse. She had also tried biofeedback, but that had not helped either.

She indicated that she would like to be in long-term therapy but her health insurance would cover only twelve sessions. Moreover, she wanted help before her trip to Israel and, indeed, wanted help to enable her to be able to go. As therapy began, she was intensely afraid that she could not bring herself to take the trip and predicted that, if she did not, this would kill her career and perhaps even cause her to lose her job. She met six of the eight DSM-IV criteria for dependent personality disorder—items 2 and 4 through 8 on Table 11–1.

As I sat with Denise and heard of the depth of her suffering and the array of real-life issues facing her, the thought of having only twelve sessions with her made me feel overwhelmed, too. In the first session with her I had the strong sense that I couldn't adequately help her, and certainly not in twelve sessions. I wanted to refer her for more medical tests and for another attempt at antidepressant medication. While these reactions were, in part, reality-based, they were also a projective identification with her own feelings of being overwhelmed and of being powerless to affect these issues herself. Remember, she had already had multiple medical evaluations and medication trials. I now felt she was looking to me as her last chance. Moreover, I felt that she was passively looking to *me* to do it, not looking to *us* to work on it together. At the end of the first session, I suggested that our two symptomatic foci could be (1) reduction of the physical symptoms and (2) enabling her to go to Israel. I introduced the dynamic focus of her passivity and dependence on others in the following exchange.

> MS: You really are dealing with a lot all at once. I have the feeling that you've given up on you, yourself, having any ability to affect things.
> D: Yes! (crying) I've never been able to go it alone. And now I won't even have Charles. Dr. G. said, "If anybody can help you, it's Dr. Stadter." I'll do whatever you say.

My response to these comments was to feel additionally pressured to *do something*. This was a complementary identification with her internal objects and, I am certain, a characteristic response that people have in relationships with her. I felt that one thing I did need to do was to quickly confront her passivity and dependence on others. In long-term work I would have let this develop longer.

> MS: I appreciate your willingness to follow what I say. But, you know, I think we may have hit here on a part of your problem. In your reliance on other people and your desire to give them what they want, you don't believe in yourself. If things go well, it's due to the other person, not you.
> D: Isn't it?
> MS: I doubt it, at least always. But we should keep this as an open question. One thing I do know, though. If therapy is going to help you, it won't be just me. It won't be just you either. It'll be something we create together.
> D: Okay. If you think so.
> MS: See? You just did it again.
> D: (laughs) I didn't even notice it.

I was somewhat uncomfortable during this exchange, fearing that I was pushing too hard on the issue of passivity. I was relieved when she laughed at my last comment. I felt I had gotten the point across to her on a rather cognitive level and we had had a mild experiential sample of her dependency dynamic with people. Denise seemed to at least consider it, although she was still dealing with me within the context of me being the one with the answers and the power.

More of the Beginning

In the second and third sessions, there were three noteworthy developments. First, we discussed the likelihood that termination would be difficult, especially if therapy were helpful. She was very aware of this, although she said that she expected that it wouldn't be so bad since she would (she hoped) be leaving for Israel shortly after termination. I suggested that we both keep aware of the impact of the anticipated end of treatment and discuss it as it arose.

Second, we looked at her history and its relationship to her current problems. The youngest of five daughters, Denise described a happy childhood in which everything was done for her. As an illustrative story, she recalled how at about age 11 she had pulled a drawer off of its runners and had started to realign it. Almost immediately, one of her sisters and her mother came over and said, "You'll never be able to get it back in," took it out of her hands, and took care of it.

Her father was described as loving but very controlling ("He loves his daughters to death"). He had chronic headaches and pains in his knees. She said her mother was a "great" person, intelligent and supportive. However, her mother doubted Denise's decision to go into the field of international relations ("Do you think you can really do it?"). Her parents had a "happy marriage" with her father clearly being the dominant force in the family and her mother being submissive and dependent on him. She remembered that her parents took very good care of her when she was sick and that she was the center of attention at those times. Denise was always an accomplished student; teachers seemed to like her and she often felt that she was a teacher's preferred student. She met her husband in college and they married in graduate school.

Third, I suggested that she keep a daily record of her depression, headaches, and stomach distress. Each day Denise rated each of these symptoms on a ten-point scale. I had two goals in mind with this suggestion. First, I hoped that we could get a more precise understanding of variations in these symptoms. Second, I thought that the activity of daily monitoring would give her an experience of "doing something" herself in relationship to the symptoms and increase some sense of self-control.

The Middle

Denise's daily monitoring turned up some very useful information and it underscored how out of touch she was with some aspects of herself. Frequently, dependent patients are exquisitely in tune with the needs of others but rather uninformed about their own needs and psyche. They often describe not knowing who they are, especially who they are as separate from their role in others' lives. Denise was very surprised that there seemed to be little correlation between her depression and her physical symptoms. Sometimes they would occur at the same time. At other times, she would experience the physical distress on days when her mood was relatively good. Initially this finding was very upsetting to her because she had been counting on eliminating the physical problems if she could eliminate the depression.

The daily recording also revealed another surprise to us. She had believed that she could not be happy as long as she had the physical symptoms. However, the monitoring showed that even on the days when she physically felt very bad (7 and above on her ten-point scale), she sometimes had felt the day had been very satisfying and enjoyable. Satisfaction and enjoyment were usually associated with either achievement at work or with playing soccer and then socializing with friends. Again, much to her surprise she observed that she was able to play athletics even in the face of these physical conditions—she had not thought that to be the case.

The above insights led to a reframing of her physical symptoms. She considered that while it would, of course, be better if she no longer had these bodily complaints, her enjoyment of life need not be dependent on their elimination—her life could go on despite them. Also, the presence of the symptoms did not have to keep her from attempting some of her activities. Interestingly, there seemed to be some limited lessening of these symptoms shortly after this reframing. Over the course of treatment, she experienced a signifi-cant improvement in mood. Concerning her trip to Israel, we examined her fears on a practical level and explored strategies for handling anticipated problems there. Beyond the pragmatic effects of these discussions, Denise came to experience more of a sense of self-control over some aspects of her life (a new ending to old experience).

As we might expect, however, the prospect of changing her relationship to her physical symptoms evoked anxiety, since it might also change her relationship with other people (as well as with her-self). We examined how her role in relationships had characteristi-cally been the role of a passive, helpless, submissive person in need of someone stronger to care for her. She expressed the fear that no one would want to be with her if she were assertive and strong. In fact, some of her marital troubles had begun when she had become more professionally successful.

Interpretive connections that seemed to be important included the following: We looked at her identifications with her father's physical ailments and with her mother's submissive stance (Past-Self interpretations). We identified that she seemed to be attracted to strong, rigid men as a way of coping with her own feelings of inadequacy. I suggested that this was similar to what her mother had done with her father (Past-Other interpretation). I also raised the possibility that she was relating to herself like her parents did in undermining any efforts at independence or autonomy (Past-Self interpretation). Finally, I commented on how she had started therapy assuming that I would be the one with the answers and that periodically this continued to come up, denying her own role or power in the therapy. We looked at how this was similar to the way she had viewed her family and Charles and others (Therapist-Past-Other interpretations).

These connections seemed to be helpful to her both in giving some clarity to her relational patterns and in understanding her fears in changing them. I felt that the discussions about treating herself as her parents had and about how she was reenacting dependency patterns with me were particularly poignant for her.

The End

During the last three sessions, we focused on her fears of how could she function adequately without me or Charles, especially, in Israel. She reported feeling more optimistic about her trip and, despite her fears, she said that she had decided not to give herself the option of canceling it—she was going to go, even if she was alone and afraid. We examined again how she so often gave the responsibility for success to forces outside of herself. I interpreted that she was doing that with me and was discounting her role in the positive changes (Therapist-Past-Other interpretations).

I also wondered aloud if her decision to definitely go to Israel was an attempt to please me as much as herself. She acknowledged that, in her fantasies about returning after the trip, she frequently thought of calling me and telling me how well she had handled it. In the fantasies, I would say something like, "You're terrific." I noted that this fantasy of my joy in her success and affirmation of her was actually quite different from what she had typically experienced from family and Charles. I did acknowledge that I would be happy for her and that if she wanted to call she would be welcome to do so. I emphasized that she would be welcome to call whether or not she had taken the trip and whether or not it had gone well.

I felt rather good at termination (in part, narcissistically "pumped up"). I wondered if I felt a bit like her college teachers had—she was a good (gratifying) student. Denise's depression was dramatically reduced and she expressed considerable confidence about her trip to Israel. We had done some useful work around issues of passivity, denial of personal power, and dependency. As is usually the case in brief therapy, there was little opportunity to work through these themes. She was still suffering from her headaches and stomach pains, which were only marginally reduced. Also, we had been unable to identify the dynamic meaning of these symptoms. However, she had begun to approach them in a way that seemed to make them more tolerable and did not interfere with her life as much. I have speculated, to myself, that these symptoms have served some autistic-contiguous function of providing a sensory boundedness for her and, thus, would be difficult to give up. In the limited time we had, though, we didn't explore this.

Follow-Up

Denise called four months after termination. She had gone to Israel and was very pleased with herself that she had succeeded at completing her research and coping there for three months. Initially, it had been a nightmare. Her living arrangements fell through once she got there and she had had to scramble to find something suitable. Denise also found that getting used to a new culture was a struggle, especially since she was treated like an Arab in a Jewish state. As in her decision to take the trip, she said she wouldn't give herself the option of leaving once she was there. She was proud to have handled the adversity—alone.

Denise said that her mood was still good, although she was apprehensive about life after Charles. They were still living together but she expected him to move out imminently and she thought she could handle it but that it would be difficult. She had reconnected with friends in the area and was seeing them frequently, which was very helpful to her. She was considering beginning dating. Her bodily symptoms were still a problem but she felt they were manageable. I was glad to hear from her and to hear such good news. I did find myself wondering (silently) if things weren't quite as good as they sounded, since she might be trying to please me (like she had tried to please others, conversely, with her illnesses and neediness).

Treatment Considerations with Dependent Patients

Be Aware of Common Countertransferences

Since these patients are frequently very considerate and do not tend toward the odd or dramatic acting out of the Cluster A or B personality disorders, therapists sometimes have the countertransference that the therapy will go easily and smoothly. Rarely is this what actually happens. Once the patient realizes that the therapist "can't do it all," the work becomes more difficult and uncomfortable. The persistent work with Denise around her belief that she needed others to take care of her and her denial of her own capabilities was crucial and at times contentious. The Israel trip helped therapy in that it forcefully confronted her with the need to depend on herself.

Other common countertransferences with dependent patients are experiencing the urge to "make them independent," being burdened by the depths of their dependency, feeling anger over their resistance to self-reliance, feeling a need to give more and more, and experiencing some grandiose belief in one's ability to "save" the patient.

Accept the Dependence but Resist the Pull to Be Directive and Take Over

The time pressure of brief therapy and the interpersonal pressure of the dependent patient can cause the brief therapist to be prematurely directive. Whether the brief therapy is of one or forty sessions in duration, the key process of therapy involves the balance between meeting the patient's dependency needs to some extent but also exerting persistent, gentle pressure toward individual responsibility. Denise would frequently ask me what she should do. I sometimes would make recommendations but usually would redirect her question back to her. Furthermore, we would discuss this dynamic.

Interpret, When Present, Two Frequent Unconscious Equations: Independence and Competence = Abandonment Loss of the Other = Loss of the Self

The experience of dependent patients is often powerfully influenced by these two beliefs. First, the patient may believe that if he were truly competent and self-reliant, no one would want him. Second, he may believe that if he is no longer in a particular relationship, then he has lost not only the other but also a sense of who he is. Denise was especially troubled by the second of these two beliefs.

Sometimes Time-Limited Therapy Can Be More Powerful than Long-Term Therapy with Dependent Patients

When a dependent patient can bear its frustrations, the time constraints and focus of time-limited therapy can serve to dramatically confront him with the limits of what can be done in therapy—with the limits of dependency gratification. By contrast, long-term treatment can encourage the fantasy (in both therapist and patient) that more growth, satisfaction, and time is always available. The impending end of her treatment with me and the impending trip to Israel functioned to confront and motivate Denise to face some of her difficult clinical issues. I have recently seen several dependent patients who were referred to me specifically for brief treatment after having had some disappointing results with long-term therapy. In each case, I felt the time-limited, focused nature of our work facilitated these patients' progress. I should add, though, that I think we benefited from and were able to build upon the previous work they had done in long-term treatment.

Consistently Demonstrate Respect for the Patient's Need for Relationships

The following is a common dynamic: the therapist sees the pathology involved in a particular relationship of the patient's and tries to induce him to give it up. This is almost always counterproductive and frequently causes premature termination. The therapist must show her respect for his relationships and not cause the patient to feel that he must give up a certain relationship to stay in therapy. Rather, the therapist is trying to understand with the patient the meaning and effects of the relationship.

Termination Can Be Especially Important and Difficult

A major selection issue involves the patient's ability to deal with the ending of treatment. Brief therapy with dependent patients has a high potential for being a painfully exciting object experience. All of the issues in Chapter 9 on the importance of termination in brief therapy are even more crucial with highly dependent patients.

Therefore, termination should be discussed early and repeatedly and, where possible, patterns of previous endings should be explored. Termination of therapy brings up the key issues of loss and limits that are so central for dependent patients.

The patient may press for an extension of therapy. While this needs to be assessed on a person to person basis, I think it is generally a mistake to extend therapy for a few more sessions with these patients, since it repeats their denial of limits and/or it supports their belief that extraordinary measures *by others* need to be taken to manage loss. Basically, setting and keeping to firm limits is indicated. If, as therapy is progressing, the therapist anticipates the patient will have a terrible time with termination, she might consider spacing out the last few sessions (e.g., every two weeks or every three weeks) to more gradually end the treatment. I recommend that this be thought through in advance rather than the therapist simply responding to pressure at termination time. The therapist should also consider the meaning of her countertransference urge to modify the frame. I am always willing to see the patient in the future but I generally recommend a period away from treatment (three to six months) before any return.

12

Object Relations Brief Therapy and Personality-Disordered Patients: II

> In our view, a key factor in treatment of the patient with
> severe personality impairments is the development of
> a 'safe' environment in which the patient can risk modi-
> fying his or her rigidly maintained interactional ap-
> proach.
>
> Simon H. Budman and Alan S. Gurman, 1988

In this chapter, I continue the examination of brief therapy with
personality-disordered patients. As in Chapter 11, much of this
chapter draws on material I developed while on the faculty of the
American Healthcare Institute (Stadter 1993). I focus on the therapy
with three personality disorders with whom it can be particularly
difficult to quickly develop a therapeutic alliance: schizoid, narcissistic, and borderline. The issue of extreme or dangerous regression can also be particularly challenging.

SCHIZOID PERSONALITY

Overview

The area of schizoid phenomena is a domain that object relations theorists have richly developed. I highly recommend Fairbairn (1952), Guntrip (1969), and Ogden (1989) for additional analysis of this area of experience and psychic structure. The object relations view of schizoid phenomena is much broader than that defined in the descriptive nomenclature of schizoid personality disorder in *DSM-IV*. For example, the object relations perspective is that schizoid processes are part of every person's personality and are prominent not only in schizoid individuals but also in other personality configurations. Notably, narcissistic personalities frequently have prominent schizoid features, although that may not be readily apparent in many narcissistic individuals.

In a pioneering paper, Fairbairn (1940) described three "schizoid factors" in the personality:

1. An attitude of omnipotence
2. An attitude of isolation and detachment
3. A preoccupation with inner reality.

These factors may not be overt; rather, the surface clinical picture may look quite different while the internal functioning of the patient is characterized by these elements. Although every person's psyche includes these factors, they are particularly prominent in schizoid individuals, with the preoccupation with inner reality being especially important. Fairbairn believed that the overt lack of interest in the external, interpersonal world was misleading. Schizoid individuals are actually paralyzed by their fears of too intensely needing others and deal with their primitive and powerful dependency needs through withdrawal.

DSM-IV

Table 12–1 presents the schizoid personality from the standpoint of descriptive clinical diagnosis. As can be seen from this list of

Table 12–1. Diagnositc Criteria for Schizoid Personality Disorder (*DSM-IV* code 301.20)

A. A pervasive pattern of detachment from social relationships and a restricted range of expression of emotions in interpersonal settings, beginning by early adulthood and present in a variety of contexts, as indicated by four (or more) of the following:

1. neither desires nor enjoys close relationships, including being part of a family
2. almost always chooses solitary activities
3. has little, if any, interest in having sexual experiences with another person
4. takes pleasure in few, if any, activities
5. lacks close friends or confidants other than first-degree relatives
6. appears indifferent to the praise or criticism of others
7. shows emotional coldness, detachment, or flattened affectivity

B. Does not occur exclusively during the course of Schizophrenia, a Mood Disorder With Psychotic Features, another Psychotic Disorder, or a Pervasive Developmental Disorder and is not due to the direct physiological effects of a general medical condition.

Note: If Criteria are met prior to the onset of Schizophrenia, add "Premorbid," e.g., "Schizoid Personality Disorder (Premorbid)."

From *DSM-IV: Diagnostic and Statistical Manual of Mental Disorders*, 4th ed. Copyright American Psychiatric Association, 1994. Used with permission.

criteria, the schizoid person appears to be emotionally detached and uninterested in the interpersonal world. It is estimated that men are given this diagnosis twice as frequently as women, and that these patients often have a history of "bleak, cold, unempathic childhoods" coupled with a "shy, anxious, and introverted temperament" (Perry and Vaillant 1989, p. 1367). *DSM-IV* states that this disorder is uncommon in clinical settings. This makes sense since it is probably very difficult for a markedly schizoid individual to seek help from another person. In my own experience, the schizoid individual typically comes in for treatment either in an acute crisis or pushed into treatment by someone else.

Clinical Example: Alan

My serial brief therapy work with Alan was described in detail in Chapter 5. He was an acutely suicidal 18-year-old college student when I first met him. At the beginning of treatment, Alan met six of the seven *DSM-IV* criteria for schizoid personality disorder (Table 12–1). He did not meet criterion 1 in that he did feel he was part of his family. However, almost all of Alan's free time was spent alone, reading or working on scientific projects (criterion 2). He denied having any sexual feelings (criterion 3). He reported the only thing he really enjoyed was studying a particular area of theoretical physics (criterion 4). Alan had no close friends or confidants outside of his family. He would not even use the word *friend* to describe anyone he knew (criterion 5). Alan reacted to praise or criticism in the same emotionless manner as he did to other interactions (criterion 6). He made almost no eye contact and showed almost no emotion even when he was talking about suicide (criterion 7).

I saw Alan for five episodes of brief therapy ranging from three to twenty sessions in duration over a period of eight years. The symptomatic focus for Alan was around anxiety of various types as well as suicidal and self-mutilative feelings. The dynamic focus centered on issues of interpersonal trust and intimacy. Therapy with him did not involve a very interpretive approach and the holding and containing functions of the therapeutic relationship were particularly crucial in facilitating positive change.

Alan's initial suicidal crisis was precipitated by his rare foray into the interpersonal world (asking a fellow student to go to lunch with him). As treatment progressed he did express a desire for close and/or sexual relationships. Alan eventually married and also described several friendships. By the end of these eight years of serial brief therapy (the total number of sessions was fifty), Alan had grown and developed to a striking extent. (See Chapter 5 for an extended description of his therapy.)

Treatment Considerations

I believe that, even more than with other patients, the nature of the brief therapy relationship with the schizoid patient is the most important factor in treatment. How the therapist and patient creatively work this out forms the heart of therapy with schizoid individuals and is more crucial than any specific content that is discussed. Due to their tendency to keep interpersonally distant, termination does tend to be easier in brief therapy with these patients than it is with the other personality disorders described in these two chapters.

Be Aware of the Patient's Sensitivity to Impingement on Personal Space

The therapist tries to find a way to relate to the patient meaningfully but without making the patient feel unsafe. A sense of personal space and safety is a key issue. Alan had experienced another therapist whom he had seen as being too intrusive and causing him to feel very unsafe. It precipitated a crisis and caused him to contact me for a second episode of brief therapy. My efforts to be responsive to his needs for space and safety and acceptance of the controlling manner that he used to protect himself were, I believe, the single most important aspect of the treatment.

The Brevity of Brief Therapy May Help the Patient Feel Safer

Setting a limited number of sessions can help the patient with fears of intimacy or of being engulfed. While Alan and I never set a specific number of sessions, he raised the idea in most sessions that he did not want to continue for a long time and wanted the treatment to be as brief as possible. I think my willingness to accept that with only minimal comments and interpretations about it contributed to his sense of safety. The other therapist he had seen required that he commit to twice weekly therapy for at least six months. This was one of the factors that had caused him to flee that treatment.

Serial Brief Therapy May Be Helpful with the
Patient's Discomfort with Intimacy

While the idea of open-ended therapy may feel unendurably frightening to the schizoid individual, he may be able to tolerate episodic returns for brief treatment. As noted in my general discussion of serial brief therapy, each of these episodes can build upon the work of the previous ones.

Be Aware of the Common Countertransferences
with Schizoid Patients

Frequently, therapists feel frustrated with the patient's lack of affect and with the degree of connection that they feel with schizoid patients. Therapists often feel bored and uninvolved and underestimate the impact that they have on the patient. I rarely felt bored by Alan but I did frequently underestimate the effect I was having and the importance I had in his life. It is important to understand the significance of these reactions. What these concordant and complementary identifications indicate about the patient's inner world and other people's reactions to him is crucial in both understanding the patient and "being with" him.

Examine the Consequences of Interpersonal Involvement
versus Noninvolvement

Schizoid patients often function effectively within the realm of intellect. Alan's superior intelligence was helpful. He examined cognitively what he might have to gain and/or lose in the area of relationships. In a given brief therapy episode, this may be all that the therapist and patient can do but it can start or facilitate work the patient then does on his own. Alan clearly showed much evidence of developing the clinical material between the episodes of therapy. Schizoid patients tend to be more comfortable doing therapeutic work alone than in the presence of the therapist.

Adjust Sessions According to Individual Patient
Needs and Tolerance

A particular schizoid patient may not be able to tolerate the intensity or intimacy of weekly, fifty-minute sessions. If the therapist sees evidence of this, she should then consider less frequent or shorter sessions to promote more a sense of safety for the schizoid person.

Consider Encouraging Involvement in
Structured Interactions

The idea of just being with people individually or in groups may be overwhelming for the patient. My experience, though, has been that the schizoid person can frequently feel fairly comfortable with and benefit from interactions that have a structured process. For example, interest groups (e.g., exercise or environmental groups) or community meetings (e.g., condominium associations) may serve as a controlled way to become more involved with the interpersonal world. When Alan began therapy with me, his primary human contacts (outside of his family) were via E-mail and a computer bulletin board on physics topics. Later, he became a member of a local group that met monthly on issues in the physical sciences.

Consider Periodic Follow-up Sessions for
Relapse Prevention

This was not a part of Alan's treatment but I have found it helpful for other schizoid individuals. Depending on the person, we have scheduled a follow-up appointment two, three, or six months later to maintain some interpersonal connection.

NARCISSISTIC PERSONALITY

Overview

The ability to regulate self-esteem and self-concept is a core dimension of personality. Defects and deficits in this domain (narcissistic pathology) have been a central area of study for the self theorists (e.g., Kohut 1971, 1977). Object relations theorists have been increasingly emphasizing this concept as well (e.g., Ogden 1994). Schizoid phenomena as described by Fairbairn (omnipotence, detachment, and preoccupation with one's inner world) are often prominent in narcissistic personalities. Narcissistic personalities may function more effectively in the interpersonal arena than schizoids due to the development of a narcissistic defensive structure that has been variously described as a type of false self (Winnicott 1960) or a pathological grandiose self (Kernberg 1975).

DSM-IV

Table 12–2 lists the *DSM-IV* criteria for the diagnosis of narcissistic personality disorder. These diagnostic criteria highlight the grandiose elements of the narcissist's personality as well as the intense need for affirmation and difficulties with intimacy. It is crucially important to remember, however, that the narcissistically vulnerable person has a part of her personality that is also prone to terrible states of self-contempt and inadequacy. Therapy breaks down when the therapist only attends to the manifest clinical picture of grandiosity.

The narcissistic individual tends be overly affected by success or failure. Success or praise produces a grandiose overvaluation of one's assets; failure or criticism causes an intensely negative response (self-denigration, depression, anxiety). Two etiological factors have been proposed for narcissistic personality disorder (Kernberg 1975, Kohut 1971, 1977, Perry and Vaillant 1989): Emotional deprivation and neglect on the part of the person's parents (rejecting object relationship) have been cited. Also, parents idealizing and overvaluing the patient (exciting object relationship) has also been suggested as causing this disorder. Probably either pattern or, perhaps especially, a combination of the two contributes to a personality structure with difficulties in self-esteem regulation.

DSM-IV reports that this disorder is diagnosed more commonly in males (50 to 75 percent are men). Adolescence is a time when many narcissistic traits are prominent and these traits do not necessarily predict the development of an adult narcissistic personal-

Table 12–2. Diagnostic Criteria for Narcissistic Personality Disorder (*DSM-IV* code 301.81)

A pervasive pattern of grandiosity (in fantasy or behavior), need for admiration, and lack of empathy, beginning by early adulthood and present in a variety of contexts, as indicated by five (or more) of the following:

1. has a grandiose sense of self-importance (e.g., exaggerates achievements and talents, expects to be recognized as superior without commensurate achievements)
2. is preoccupied with fantasies of unlimited success, power, brilliance, beauty, or ideal love
3. believes that he or she is "special" and unique and can only be understood by, or should associate with, other special or high-status people (or institutions)
4. requires excessive admiration
5. has a sense of entitlement (i.e., unreasonable expectations of especially favorable treatment or automatic compliance with his or her expectations)
6. is interpersonally exploitative (i.e., takes advantage of others to achieve his or her own ends)
7. lacks empathy: is unwilling to recognize or identify with the feelings and needs of others
8. is often envious of others or believes that others are envious of him or her
9. shows arrogant, haughty behaviors or attitudes

From *DSM-IV: Diagnostic and Statistical Manual of Mental Disorders*, 4th ed. Copyright American Psychiatric Association, 1994. Used with permission.

ity disorder. A number of sources have reported that this is a diagnosis that has low interrater reliability (e.g., APA 1994, Perry and Vaillant 1989).

Clinical Example: Ronald

I have detailed in Chapters 6, 8, and 9 the fifteen-session therapy with Ronald, a 24-year-old law student. He had sought treatment due to the crisis caused by his first semester's grades. He had scored in the middle of his class but had felt he was much better than that. He reacted with an acute stress response: high anxiety, and great difficulty sleeping, eating, and concentrating. His self-esteem had plummeted and he was very self-critical, although he was also at times furious with the "unfair and arbitrary" faculty.

Ronald met seven of the nine criteria (Table 12–2) for narcissistic personality disorder. He said that he had believed he was one of the "best" students in his law school and often stood out at whatever he did (criterion 1). He frequently would dream about the future in which he would have a high government position—U.S. senator or even higher (criterion 2).

Ronald felt misunderstood by the "ordinary" other students and faculty at his law school. He also wondered whether I would be sufficiently intelligent and insightful to be able to help him. He was depressed about feeling the need for therapy because it made him feel ordinary (criterion 3). He did not feel that the law school students or faculty appreciated him enough—the average grades confirmed this (criterion 4). He asked if I would handle payment differently with him than I did with other patients, since his situation was special (criterion 5).

Ronald hated that the students who were at the top of the class were "basking in that glory." He also wondered if some professors had given him lower grades because they were intimidated by him in class (criterion 8). He spoke dimissively about many people—other students, faculty, his ex-girlfriend, and the patient who had come out of my office before him (criterion 9).

Ronald was not generally interpersonally exploitative (criterion 6) and he did evidence a capacity for empathy (criterion 7), although both of these characteristics dramatically changed during times of inflated self-esteem. During treatment, however, Ronald also showed the other side of his personality—his insecurity and his own difficulty in being "good enough"—which is part of the narcissistic personality, although it may not be overt.

The symptomatic focus was to diminish his acute stress response and the dynamic focus was the exploration of his grandiose expectations of himself. I utilized some cognitive-behavioral interventions early in treatment with him and his acute stress reaction had subsided. We spent the middle part of his treatment looking at his internal object world and his way of relating to himself and others. Ronald significantly benefited from the therapy (see Chapters 6, 8, and 9).

Treatment Considerations

Expect Narcissistic Countertransferences

Intimately connecting with a narcissistically vulnerable patient will almost inevitably evoke countertransferences in the therapist that have an impact on his own self-esteem and self-concept. Such countertransferences have diagnostic significance. As concordant or complementary identifications they experientially convey the patient's inner world to the therapist.

The following is an incomplete listing of common narcissistic countertransferences:

Difficulty with the patient's lack of empathy and impersonal use of the therapist (unsatisfied need of therapist for mirroring)
Feeling pressure to prove oneself
Anger at demands and attitude of entitlement by the patient
Feeling inadequate
Feeling exploited (especially after feeling charmed by the patient)
Grandiose feelings being stimulated in the therapist
Discomfort with the patient's idealization of the therapist.

These countertransferences do not exclusively occur with narcissistic personality disorders but they do indicate that the therapist's system of self-concept regulation has been affected. In my work with Ronald, I initially felt much pressure to prove myself to him and periodically felt inadequate. During termination, I also felt discounted. For a more in-depth look at narcissistic countertransferences, see Kohut (1968) and Wolf (1988).

Use the Dynamic Focus to Prevent Premature Termination

Even in brief therapy premature termination by narcissistic patients is a serious issue. To seek help is, in itself, humiliating and narcissistically injuring for many patients. Often, the patient begins treatment in acute distress (like Ronald) and her acute symptoms diminish after a few sessions (also like Ronald). At this point, the combination of feeling better and being embarrassed about coming for treatment can combine to cause the narcissistic patient to quit therapy. If the therapist has been able to engage the patient's curiosity in her inner world and (if possible) link the dynamic focus to the symptoms, this can often motivate the patient to continue. This is what happened with Ronald, who was intrigued by the identification of the very high standards and expectations he had for himself and how they "supercharged" his suffering.

Be Especially Aware of Tact and Timing and the Maintenance of Empathy

While this is obviously crucial with all patients, the narcissistic patient's heightened sensitivity to criticism and the intense need for affirmation makes the therapist's awareness of this especially important. Even then there will inevitably be empathic ruptures at times because (1) no therapist is perfect, (2) these patients are so hypersensitive, and (3) the transference-countertransference dynamic frequently evokes a lack of empathic attunement on the part of the therapist.

Some therapists will try to compensate for the difficulty in staying empathically connected with the patient by being overly supportive. This is usually not helpful. I have found that typically supportive interventions (e.g., direct acknowledgment of strengths, direct expressions of concern for the patient, etc.) frequently backfire. The narcissistic patient feels she is being seen as pathetic or judged or is being insufficiently affirmed. Interventions and interpretations that address both parts of the patient's narcissistic vulnerability (grandiosity and inadequacy) are usually more successful in causing the patient to feel understood. I was very impressed in my work with Ronald that if I commented solely on either his "specialness" or on his sense of inadequacy, he felt misunderstood. Empathically responding to one part or one side of a split in the narcissistic patient is experienced as unempathic and/or disorganizing (Kohut 1971,1977).

Examine Consequences of Actions

Narcissistic patients often run into difficulty with others because of their lack of empathy. At a cognitive level, the brief therapist can help to increase awareness in this area by exploring the possible consequences of various actions of the patient (e.g., "What happened then?" "I wonder how that [a patient's action] affected him?" "That's interesting. I wonder if we can consider why a person would respond that way to you."). Done with care and timing, these interventions can introduce the patient to examination of areas that she has heretofore been blind to without intensely activating her defenses.

Work on Limits Is Important But Can Be Injuring

The impact of the limits of the therapy is a promising but delicate area for examination. The limits of number and spacing of sessions, the ending of each session, the therapist's unwillingness to modify the frame for this "special" patient, and the limited foci and goals all frequently evoke discomfort and reactions such as "This isn't enough," "Why can't I have more?" "You're putting me down." When patient and therapist can explore these issues together, they can powerfully, directly, and experientially work with a part of the patient's difficulties with self-concept and with interpersonal relationships. With Ronald, our dealing with my unwillingness to handle his insurance claim differently than I did with other patients and his disappointment at termination were important therapeutic moments that helped both of us more fully appreciate his narcissistic vulnerability.

The Patient May Not be Ready for Persistent Interpretation of the Idealizing Transference

The idealizing transference is an excessively and unrealistically positive view of the therapist. It is the goal of most therapy to help the patient to see the world, self, and others as realistically as possible. In keeping with that goal, therapists interpret the idealizing transference a narcissistic patient might form. In brief therapy, though, the patient may not be able to face it or work it through. Therapy can be seriously impaired by the therapist's lack of respect for this and subsequent "pushing" of such interpretive work despite the patient's strong resistance to it. Often such interpretive vigor is stimulated by a countertransference of discomfort with the idealization. In many brief contracts, the therapist will have to accept that he was still idealized at termination. While this is an issue that frequently arises, it was not so problematic in my example of Ronald. He tended to idealize me throughout the treatment until termination, when he was flooded with feelings of disappointment with me and the therapy. As noted above, our work on this disappointment was an important therapeutic event.

BORDERLINE PERSONALITY

Overview

If personality disorders head the list of most challenging patients to treat in brief therapy, then borderline patients are near the top of the list of most difficult personality disorders. As previously discussed, dynamic brief therapy models tend to exclude borderline patients from their model. This makes sense theoretically and in research studies. Yet, in practice, I believe that most borderline patients are being treated in brief therapy. This is due to the following reasons:

1. Most therapy is brief.
2. These patients frequently have unstable relationships, making long-term treatment difficult (although clearly the treatment of choice).

3. Their degree of pathology may not be apparent until well into treatment.

Stone (1990b) has reported that borderline patients who are in a stable life situation (e.g., stable marriage) and who enter treatment due to a life crisis can benefit from brief therapy. Budman and Gurman (1988) have stated that borderline patients can effectively use intermittent (serial) brief therapy throughout their lives. (See also Leibovich [1981] and Pollack et al. [1991].)

Chaotic, primitive elements of personality are prominent in borderline individuals. Splitting is a predominant mode of experiencing self and others and borderline patients characteristically show a mixture of profound dependence coupled with a tendency to experience intense rage. Paranoid-schizoid and autistic-contiguous modes dominate the clinical picture. It is the most studied of all personality disorders and is the most common. Gunderson (1989) has estimated that 15 to 25 percent of patients in treatment (inpatient and outpatient) are borderline. I recommend the following for further readings on borderline pathology: Gunderson (1989), Kernberg (1975; Kernberg et al. 1989), and Stone (1990a, b).

DSM-IV

Table 12–3 lists the *DSM-IV* criteria for the diagnosis of borderline personality disorder.

It can be tempting for the clinician to see the borderline patient as being quite different from himself. However, it is more useful and accurate, I believe, to see the borderline's style as dramatically showing a primitive, chaotic personality segment that is universal. The manifest picture of borderline personality disorder is extremely variable and varied. Indeed, this disorder has been called the personality disorder that never specialized. Instability in relationships, instability in the sense of self and mood, impulsivity, intense dependence, and rage and self-mutilative or suicidal ideation or behavior are characteristic. It is diagnosed most frequently in women (2:1) (Gunderson 1989) and in individuals in late adolescence and early adulthood (Stone 1990a). There is a high rate

Table 12–3. Diagnostic Criteria for Borderline Personality Disorder (*DSM-IV* code 301.83)

A pervasive pattern of instability of interpersonal relationships, self-image, and affects, and marked impulsivity beginning by early adulthood and present in a variety of contexts, as indicated by five (or more) of the following:

1. frantic efforts to avoid real or imagined abandonment (**Note:** Do not include suicidal or self-mutilating behavior covered in criterion 5)
2. a pattern of unstable and intense interpersonal relationships characterized by alternating between extremes of idealization and devaluation
3. identity disturbance: markedly and persistently unstable self-image or sense of self
4. impulsivity in at least two areas that are potentially self-damaging (e.g., spending, sex, substance abuse, reckless driving, binge eating) (**Note:** Do not include suicidal or self-mutilating behavior covered in criterion 5)
5. recurrent suicidal behavior, gestures, or threats, or self-mutilating behavior
6. affective instability due to a marked reactivity of mood (e.g., intense episodic dysphoria, irritability, or anxiety usually lasting a few hours and only rarely more than a few days)
7. chronic feelings of emptiness
8. inappropriate, intense anger or difficulty controlling anger (e.g., frequent displays of temper, constant anger, recurrent physical fights)
9. transient, stress-related paranoid ideation or severe dissociative symptoms

From *DSM-IV: Diagnostic and Statistical Manual of Mental Disorders*, 4th ed. Copyright American Psychiatric Association, 1994. Used with permission.

of negative therapeutic response among borderline patients, and about 40 percent drop out of treatment. However, somewhat surprisingly, about 67 percent of borderline patients have been reported to be functioning rather well once they reach their thirties (Stone 1990a).

Clinical Example I: Diane

I provided an extended description of the twenty-five-session therapy with this 32-year-old, married mother in Chapters 6, 8, and 9. She was in a suicidal crisis following her arrest for stealing thousands of dollars from her employer. Therapy focused, symptomatically, on her suicidal tendencies and on the anxiety and depression she felt in the wake of her arrest and as her case made its way through the legal process. Dynamically, we focused on the splits and discontinuities in her personality that could cause her to be, at times, a responsible mother and wife, and at other times, impulse-ridden and destructive to herself and her family.

Diane met six of the nine *DSM-IV* diagnostic criteria (Table 12–3). She had unstable and intense interpersonal relationships, notably with her mother, husband, and friends in the present and with her father and boyfriend in the past (criterion 2). She demonstrated impulsivity with her stealing, spending, and eating disorder (criterion 4). She demonstrated affective instability. Her mood could swing within a matter of minutes or hours from happiness to depression to fear. These changes could also be triggered by relatively minor incidents (criterion 6). Diane had chronic feelings of emptiness. During the few moments when she was not racing around to take care of her responsibilities, she would be aware of a painful inner void (criterion 7). Diane demonstrated intense, uncontrolled anger, such as when she slapped a sales clerk (criterion 8). She had dissociative symptoms. The stealing occurred in dissociated states (criterion 9).

While she sometimes had made frantic efforts to avoid abandonment (criterion 1), Diane did not seem to characteristically approach rejection in this manner. Similarly, I felt that she did not meet criterion 3 for identity disturbance because she had a definite self-image in her role as mother and wife, although it was shaky and disrupted by the splits within her personality. Also, while she was suicidal when I first met her, she had reported feeling suicidal at only one other time in her life and these feelings did not seem to be recurrent (criterion 5).

Within a few weeks after beginning treatment, Diane was no longer suicidal. During therapy, she experienced a significant reduction in her anxiety and depression and also seemed to gain insights into her acting out and the discontinuities within her personality. Therapy ended with her moving out of state following a plea-bargained conviction. As recommended by me and required by the court, she subsequently began long-term treatment. (See Chapters 6, 8, and 9 for further discussion of her therapy.)

Clinical Example II: Susan

This case illustrates the limits of very brief serial therapy with a borderline patient. I saw Susan for three encounters of brief therapy over a 2½-year period. I saw her each time for three sessions, the maximum that her employer's EAP permitted. She met all of the *DSM-IV* criteria for borderline personality disorder.

Susan was 23 years old when I first met her. She was a divorced mother who coordinated a customer service program for a financial institution. Her manager, Kate, had been concerned with her irritability on the phone with some customers. In a meeting with Susan about this, Susan tearfully told her that she had become obsessed with her weight (her weight was normal), was inducing vomiting, was feeling overwhelmed with her life, and wanted to die. Kate referred her to me following this meeting.

Susan told me that she had always been obsessed with her weight and had been very overweight as an adolescent. Her mother was very thin and her father had been critical of Susan's appearance, nicknaming her "Butterball." She acknowledged feeling overwhelmed by a variety of recent events: her divorce, the death of her beloved grandmother, the pressures at work, and the demands of being a single parent with an 8 month old child. We identified a pattern of heightened obsession with her weight when she felt either overwhelmed or alone. While this seemed to be a useful insight, the therapy was almost exclusively supportive and I was unable to engage her curiosity in her dynamics. Still, the supportive and practical tenor of the sessions helped in reducing her distress and improving her functioning. I strongly recommended long-term treatment and/or an eating disorders program to her but she said she felt better now and was no longer vomiting, and a referral would definitely not be necessary.

During this very brief therapy I found myself having several reactions. First, I was initially very touched by her struggle in the face of many pressures and obstacles. Second, as I had felt with Diane, I was overwhelmed by the array of issues and symptoms. Third, I was irritated with her persistent projection of problems onto others (it was the fault of the customers, Kate, her ex-husband, and so on) and by her rather emphatic dismissal of my recommendations. I wondered if she came to therapy only to placate her manager. Several months later Kate told me that Susan was doing very well on the job and Kate was amazed that therapy had been so effective (I was too—and thought that it probably wasn't).

Fifteen months after I had last seen Susan she was back in my office, having again been referred by Kate. She was now on probation at work following an incident in the company's parking lot. She had gotten into an argument with another driver over right-of-way, had screamed obscenities at him, and pounded on his window with her

fist, shouting, "I'm going to punch your goddamn face in."
Once again the three-session therapy followed the previous supportive course. Despite this more extreme incident with lack of control of her rage and her job now being in jeopardy, she still refused my recommendations for further treatment. Yet, she felt considerably better and more under control than when she had begun this episode of therapy. This time when she left, my countertransference alternated between feeling inadequate for being unable to have Susan face the seriousness of her situation and feeling hopeless ("Why bother? She's going to do what she's going to do.").

Susan called in crisis four months later. Work had been fine but her personal life was not. She had referred herself this time following a nasty verbal fight with her fiancé, Joe. In a state of intense rage, she did the following: destroyed several possessions of his that had sentimental value, let his dog run away, and poisoned the fish in his aquarium. Finally, she acknowledged that while Joe was largely to blame, that she, indeed, had a terrible problem with her own anger. Susan was terrified that her fiancé would leave her. I suggested that the two of them have a cooling off period. She took a referral from me and began open-ended treatment. She was motivated most strongly by her fear of abandonment and by her fear that, if she could lose control so badly with her fiancé, then perhaps she could do it with her son.

Primarily, I believe it was the escalating nature of her crises, in general, and the fear of losing her fiancé, specifically, that eventually activated her to follow through on therapy. Additionally, my role as a stable, good object may have helped as well. Specifically, the positive experience with me, my calm with her, and my persistence in recommending ongoing treatment were possibly meaningful to Susan. It was, though, probably frustrating to only be able to see me for short episodes of therapy (although she denied this).

This story does not have a happy ending. Susan

began seeing a very experienced therapist who recommended twice weekly therapy, which she refused. She saw the therapist weekly and was prescribed lithium, which she discontinued after one month. Susan terminated therapy after three months. Six months after our last session I learned that she had been frequently missing work and her manager, Kate, had run out of patience and fired her. Within that period of time Susan did marry Joe (I was not optimistic about their future together).

I have described this case to illustrate the strains and frustrations that can be part of working with a borderline patient. I evaluate this case as a failure. I would acknowledge that the therapy with me was possibly helpful in temporarily reducing her distress and improving functioning. It was also successful in getting her into ongoing therapy. However, her crises continued to escalate and she did not stay in treatment. I never felt that she really connected with me and the alliance she formed with me seemed to be exclusively around immediate reduction in painful affect and getting others off of her back (Kate and Joe).

Perhaps, Susan will be ready at some later point to use some of what we began. Frequently, resistant borderline patients only come to really be involved with therapy after several crises and false starts. I find myself left with a hopelessness about her. While there is much to be pessimistic about, some of my hopelessness is a concordant identification with some of her own hopelessness and emptiness. She is a young woman with considerable strengths in addition to her chaotic, needy parts.

Treatment Considerations

Management of Countertransference and Steadiness of the Therapist's Approach Can Be the Most Therapeutic Elements of the Treatment

Even more than narcissistic patients, borderline individuals seem to have the capacity to "get under the skin" of the therapist and evoke or provoke countertransferences that affect the therapist's self-concept. Certainly any of the examples of narcissistic counter-transferences described in the previous section may occur in working with a borderline patient. The internal chaos, intense dependency needs, and primitive rage that are part of the borderline structure can make the relationship difficult and troubling for both therapist and patient. Gunderson (1989) describes the frequent experience of therapists "whose efforts to develop a helping relationship were countered by hostility and manipulation that led them to feel alternately helpless and enraged" (p. 1387).

The therapist cannot hope to change borderline personality structure in brief therapy. One hopes, at best, to make some progress within the limited symptomatic and dynamic foci. Even when this is not accomplished, something therapeutic may occur—the experience of a different type of relationship (a new ending for old experience). Through powerful and primitive projective identifications, people in relationships with borderline individuals often feel compelled to rescue, abuse, withdraw, or allow themselves to be abused. The therapist often feels the pull to respond in these ways as well, and the clinical literature has many examples of how therapists have fallen into these unconscious reenactments of primitive components of the patient's inner world (e.g., Kernberg 1975, Kernberg et al. 1989). Strupp and Binder's (1984) finding of the crucial importance of the management of hostility in brief therapy is particularly applicable with these patients.

The therapist needs to creatively and flexibly find ways to stay as intimately and as consistently connected as possible to the borderline patient during the treatment. If nothing else occurred in the treatment other than that the patient had the experience of a relationship with someone who stayed with him but did not allow herself to rescue, abuse, withdraw, or be abused, then much was accomplished. The patient would have experienced a new type of relationship, perhaps for the first time ever. Lastly, it is inevitable that the therapist will find herself caught in some pathological reenactments—it comes with the territory. Having been immersed in it and now seeing it, she must work her way out of it (Strupp and Binder 1984).

Manage Regression through the Brevity,
the Focus, and Clarity

The holding and containing capacities of brief therapy are quite limited. Brief therapists need to carefully help borderline patients to keep regressive tendencies within the boundaries of the limited treatment. As I discussed in Chapter 2, the focus helps to limit regression and it is important with borderline patients to repeatedly remind them of the limits of what can and what cannot be accomplished. Similarly, reminders of the time constraints help to hold the patient and to encourage functioning more in reality-based time (Mann's categorical, as opposed to existential, time).

The brief therapist working with a borderline patient should also be sensitive to the regressive and disorganizing impact of ambiguity. She should adopt a strategy of prompt and repeated reality testing instead of allowing a progressive deepening of transference-based feelings. Because the potential for uncontrolled rage is so great for many borderline patients, the therapist should take particular care to notice early signs of irritation and to clarify, interpret, confront, or otherwise intervene to keep the hostility bounded. She should be aware of her own potential for rage, too.

All of these measures reduce the risks of uncontrollable, malignant regressions and make it possible to treat borderline patients in brief therapy. In my own practice, borderline patients tend to regress and act out less in brief therapy than in long-term work with me. The creative balance is to adequately manage the frame of the brief therapy to minimize malignant regressions and yet to facilitate some expression and exploration of unconscious material (see Chapter 4 for a discussion of the role of time in brief therapy).

Firmly but Compassionately Maintain the
Therapeutic Boundaries and Convey the
Necessity of Pain Tolerance

Borderline patients frequently attempt to extend or manipulate the boundaries (e.g., extra or extended sessions, emergency contacts, "special" arrangements, etc.). The calm but firm stance of the therapist around these boundaries is crucial. The patient can genuinely feel much pain and frustration in response to them. It has been impressive to me how often borderline patients (and others) have a fantasy (frequently conscious) that they should never be in pain. One borderline patient was furious at a friend for recommending a book to him, Peck's *The Road Less Traveled* (1978). He said, "I couldn't even get past the first sentence, 'Life is difficult.' What bullshit! Life shouldn't be difficult!"

The therapist tries to help the patient see the inevitability of pain as a part of the human condition and it does not necessarily indicate that the patient is bad or his relationship is bad or that his life and future are doomed. One of Susan's frustrations was the belief that she should not be suffering and that it should immediately stop.

Manage the Focus Despite the "Crisis of the Week"

One of the major challenges in brief therapy with borderline patients is to maintain the focal work in the face of the chaotic nature of the patient's life. A new problem or crisis may arise almost weekly. The following are some strategies to consider.

First, look for an underlying dynamic theme that may link the apparently disparate problem areas. For example, with Diane, a pattern of self-imposed deprivation evoked by her low sense of self-worth was a common theme in her various problems with impulsivity (anger, eating, spending, and stealing). Another patient of mine came to three consecutive sessions with very strong affect. First, she was intensely anxious about an evaluation by her supervisor. The next week, she was furious at me for an insensitive remark I had made in the preceding session. In the third session, she was depressed and sobbing over a fight she and her boyfriend had had. During all three of these sessions we worked on the theme of rejection and her sensitivity to it that was embedded in all three of these "crises."

Second, explicitly discuss the pros and cons of maintaining the focus versus discussing the more current crisis issue.

Third, set aside a portion of the session to deal with the ongoing focus, and another portion to address the current crisis.

Fourth, consider that the focus should be changed or modified. While the focus should be seen as a guide that likely will change and develop as therapy progresses, the therapist facing the sense of urgency from a borderline patient to change the direction of the therapy should carefully reflect upon the meaning of this development. For example, is this an example of the patient's pattern that keeps him from being able to complete activities? Is it part of his difficulty in dealing with the limitations of the therapy? Can I help him in some other way with the experience of being flooded by the current event?

Deal Directly and Immediately with Noncompliance

Lack of compliance in both psychotherapy and pharmacotherapy is a common problem with borderline patients (Stone 1990a, b). Note Susan's resistance to my recommendations concerning further treatment and to the ongoing treatment that she eventually began. In brief therapy it is usually important to address noncompliance immediately. Consider the following: First, avoid counterproductive power struggles by clearly acknowledging the patient's ability to say no. Second, examine the consequences of noncompliance. Third, explore the possibility that the noncompliance is an automatic transference-based pattern. Consider interpreting it and highlight the importance of choice versus being driven to act.

Sensitivity to Termination Is as Important as It Is with Dependent Patients

All of the points I noted in the discussion of termination with dependent patients are applicable here. Additionally, there is more potential for manipulative behavior (e.g., suicide threats and other regressive behavior) by borderline patients to deny or prevent termination. In brief therapy the work on termination with these patients needs to be part of treatment throughout. I believe this is the best way to help the patient prepare for and manage the strain of ending and to minimize the potential for a pathological exciting object experience. Managing this limit is very important. With Diane, she had never really said good-bye to anyone and attempted to repeat that pattern with me by her last-minute cancellation of our last session. My calling her and having the session on the phone achieved a modification of her old pattern. Susan did not seem to have difficulty leaving me (although she did keep coming back). Perhaps frustration with the acute time limitations with me prevented her from making an intimate connection.

13

Reflections on Object Relations Brief Therapy and Managed Care: Brevity and Integrity

> Brief therapy, as a legitimate field of theory and techniques, was never intended to be a universal mode of treatment.
>
> Steven Stern, 1993

> The simplest answer to the question "How much therapy is enough?" is—as much as the patient needs.
>
> Glen O. Gabbard, 1995

Brief therapy is not managed care. While managed care organizations do promote brief and very brief therapy, both of these modalities preceded the managed care movement. However, I have included a chapter on managed care and brief therapy for two reasons. First, managed care has a significant impact on the actual practice of brief therapy. Second, it has an impact on the way brief therapy is viewed by clinicians and by the general public. There are few topics in the mental health field today that raise as strong emotions as the managed care movement in the United States. It has been both demonized and idealized. In this chapter, I will define managed care, list some of its beneficial and detrimental effects on brief therapy, and then present some cautionary tales (true stories) to illustrate some of the issues.

MANAGED CARE DEFINED

Managed care is not a unitary entity but an array of strategies developed for health insurance programs. These strategies continue to evolve. Advocates state that managed care models are designed to contain treatment costs and improve or maintain quality of care. There are currently three major strategies (Stern 1993):

1. Health maintenance organizations (HMOs) or the staff model, where the therapists providing psychotherapy are employees of the HMO.
2. An annual dollar or session limit (e.g., $1,000 or twenty-five sessions). While the clinical work may not be "managed," the limit of financial outlay for this health benefit is managed.
3. Utilization reviews that pre-certify and then monitor the therapy offered. Some plans restrict services covered to those offered by members of their panels, which are called preferred provider organizations (PPOs). Others permit treatment by other professionals who are "out of network" but often at a reduced amount of reimbursement.

The greatest controversy seems to occur with strategy # 3, utilization reviews. I will emphasize that model in this chapter. While I believe there are some benefits to utilization review, my opinion is that most of the present systems are seriously flawed.

BENEFICIAL EFFECTS OF MANAGED CARE ON THE PRACTICE OF PSYCHOTHERAPY

Innovation

This is the most significant benefit. An effect of managed care is to induce therapists to attempt to accomplish therapeutic goals quicker. If results can be obtained more quickly, then the patient and the third-party payer benefit from less cost and the patient benefits from improved psychological health sooner. The current explosion in interest, research, and training in brief therapy is in part due to managed care.

A Check on Collusive Long-Term Therapy

Certainly, some psychotherapies go on and on without benefit to the patient and may even harm him. The therapist and patient have developed an unconscious, comfortable antitherapeutic contract that maintains the status quo. In a private practice setting, it is up to the integrity and awareness of the therapist and to the awareness of the patient to "regulate" this. This is one reason that continued consultation and peer supervision throughout a therapist's career is essential. From the therapists I know and supervise, this self-regulation works rather effectively. However, I have observed instances where an "as if" therapy goes on year after year fueled by the infantile dependency needs of the patient and by the financial and caretaking needs of the therapist. Third-party payers are frequently mistrustful of therapists who primarily provide long-term therapy, and they worry that the integrity of many therapists is compromised by their financial and/or other self-interests. Careful utilization review has the potential to intervene in such cases and to at least get or give a second opinion on these cases.

Accountability

This is a related issue. In a private practice setting, the therapist may be professionally accountable only to himself (and, of course, to the patient). Utilization review asks valid questions concerning the need for the treatment, its effectiveness, and its benefits. These questions need to be answered *primarily* by the therapist and patient. However, if they are answered *exclusively* by the therapist and patient, without independent input, there is potential for pathological and maladaptive unconscious processes to distort the answers.

Reduced Costs

In general, when a patient ends therapy having had fewer sessions, costs of treatment for both the patient and the third-party payer are reduced. Managed care, in all probability, has had the effect of reducing fees and overall expenditures for psychotherapy. However, much of this cost reduction may be offset by the expense of maintaining the administrative system to pre-certify and review cases (Stern 1993).

Understandably, health insurance companies want to cover only psychotherapy services that have an impact on the patient's health and/or use of health services. This line can be a difficult one to draw for at least two reasons. First, much research has accumulated to indicate that brief psychotherapy actually reduces the utilization of other medical services (e.g., Cummings and VandenBos 1981). Second, psychological stress plays a very important role in health, and psychotherapy is frequently used successfully to treat it (e.g., VandenBos and DeLeon 1988).

Sometimes, carriers try to draw the line very tightly by covering only psychotherapy that is a "medical necessity." It is the case, though, that patients come to psychotherapy for reasons other than for symptom relief or to restore adequate functioning. Patients also seek therapy for personal growth, for self-knowledge and actualization, and for training and educational reasons. Managed care seeks to eliminate coverage for these therapies. If such therapy is no longer "subsidized" by insurance companies, fees for such services will often decrease (although what the patient pays out of pocket would frequently increase).

DETRIMENTAL EFFECTS OF MANAGED CARE ON THE PRACTICE OF PSYCHOTHERAPY

Managed Costs, not Care

Unfortunately in practice, managed care is primarily managed cost rather than managed quality. There is certainly a financial incentive for third-party payers to keep mental health payments as low as possible just as it is in the financial interests of therapists to have as much therapy as possible subsidized by third parties. Moreover, it is much easier to measure costs (dollars) than it is to measure quality of care (e.g., quality of the therapeutic relationship, degree and nature of symptom improvement, quality of life, etc.). A central point here is the conflict between costs and care: "Any system in which the provider stands to gain by a reduction in service will *unavoidably provide substandard care*" (Berman 1992, p. 41, italics added). Of course, there is a parallel conflict when there is financial gain if more services are provided. This encourages overtreatment.

Stern (1993) has argued that the majority of mental health costs are registered by inpatient and other residential treatment and that it is sensible for managed care to direct its efforts there. He has also questioned the wisdom and motives of managed care's attention to outpatient psychotherapy. "In light of the fact that the vast majority (75% to 90%) of all psychotherapy is short term (less than 25 sessions) and most of that very short term (less than 10 sessions), one begins to wonder whether the primary issue for third-party payers with respect to outpatient mental health is containment of unreasonable costs or simply minimization of costs" (p. 170).

Intrusion

The demand for detailed and frequently requested confidential information and the control over the frame of therapy constitute intrusions that strain and deform the therapeutic relationship and often decrease its effectiveness.

Rationing Makes the Therapy Unstable

When sessions are rationed two, four, or six at a time, it makes the holding environment of the therapy unstable and often causes the patient to feel unsafe. The patient and therapist do not know how much longer therapy may last—another four or eight or what? This tends to make therapy more superficial and less likely to get to the painful material troubling the patient. See the cautionary tale, "Just a Little Bit More Should Do it," below.

Hurried Rather than Efficient Therapy

In Chapter 2 I described how brief therapy can cause the therapy process to be more superficial and hurried. This constrains the receptive capacities of both patient and therapist and inhibits unconscious material from surfacing. Managed care can exacerbate this problem. Early identification of the focus (documented in the utilization review report) can influence therapist and patient to exclusively stay with that focus and not be open to how it may change or evolve. Such pressure for early closure and commitment to a particular treatment plan undermines the process of discovery that is central to dynamic therapy.

Stern (1993) notes that patients can be made to feel defective if they have not progressed as fast as their insurance carrier says they should have. He also argues that it is in the area of termination that managed care most interferes with the therapeutic process by pushing the therapist to terminate due to managed care pressures rather than due to what the patient needs. This directly raises the issue of the therapist's integrity. As Karon (1992) states, "For competent and ethical psychotherapists the well-being of their patients is the prime consideration. This is an entirely different criterion from cost effectiveness" (p. 58).

Dilution of and "De-professionalization" of Psychotherapy

What is being described as psychotherapy in many plans is very brief therapy or crisis intervention. When the crisis has passed or when the patient's symptoms diminish, there is pressure on the therapist to end treatment without regard for the lasting effects of the treatment. I have no problem with very brief therapy being offered or encouraged. It is often useful to patients in rapidly reducing their suffering. My problem is in the message (implicit or explicit) that this is the extent of psychotherapy and all that it has to offer (see the cautionary tale "Is That All There Is?"). This dilutes the public's perception of psychotherapy and ultimately causes it to be seen as a much weaker intervention than it, in fact, is and can be.

With the pressure to minimize costs, my experience is that some plans have reviewers making decisions about care who are minimally or even inadequately trained. Similarly, some plans have services offered *exclusively* by bachelor's-level and master's-level therapists rather than by doctorate-level providers. Because it is not assessed as cost-effective, some plans will not cover psychotherapy of any duration offered by psychiatrists.

Westermeyer (1991) has written an alarming article documenting this problem in the pharmocotherapy and psychotherapy of seven patients who were at major psychiatric risk. Five of the patients committed suicide, one progressed to psychosis, and one became permanently disabled. Westermeyer concludes that these tragic outcomes were preventable. Inadequate care was offered to these patients and the treatment was monitored by insufficiently trained case managers. "The deaths of five patients demonstrate the failure of the concept of medical care as a public utility, in which any one psychiatrist can substitute for any other, irrespective of preexisting doctor-patient relationships" (Westermeyer 1991, p. 1223).

Brief therapy that has the potential that I have described in this book actually requires *more skill* than long-term therapy, not less. These trends toward dilution and de-professionalization constitute a vicious cycle. If the "commodity" of psychotherapy is so weakened as to simply involve crisis intervention and supportive therapy of a few sessions in duration or is a watered-down version offered by poorly trained practitioners, then it *can* be offered by much less sophisticated providers.

"Industrialization" of Psychotherapy Runs Counter to an Object Relations Approach

Several observers (e.g., Shore 1995) have stated that American health care is becoming "industrialized." An industrial approach values cost effectiveness, standard operating procedures and protocols, identical services and products, and the interchangeability of service and product providers. These standards rather aptly describe the managed care approach. There is certainly much to admire in some of these standards but contrast them with the object relations approach described in this book: respect for the individuality of the patient, core emphasis on the therapeutic relationship and its uniqueness, appreciation for the process of discovery and the state of not knowing. Clearly these are two disparate traditions. I believe that managed care professionals and object relations–oriented therapists do frequently work successfully together. It does, however, require mutual respect for each other. The lack of respect this conflict sometimes engenders is illustrated by the language used in the debates. Managed care staff have been described as members of a "totalitarian regime" (Shore 1995), while therapists who resist the industrial model are "dinosaurs" (as reported in Haas and Cummings 1991).

CAUTIONARY TALES

The following are true stories that illustrate some of the dilemmas and problems faced by brief therapists in working with managed care.

Who Are You?

> I had seen Karla in weekly psychotherapy for 18 months. At this point she was profoundly depressed, had made a serious suicide attempt, and was still suicidal. In my opinion, this 17-year-old high school student needed short-term hospitalization—at least time in a day hospital but preferably a full inpatient experience. Karla had seen her physician and was medically stable but she, her family, and I were awaiting pre-certification from her insurance company for more intensive treatment. Karla's mother, Lenore, received the call from the Service Utilization Reviewer. He told Lenore that he wanted to talk to her to determine if more treatment would be indicated. Lenore asked, "Don't you want to talk to Dr. Stadter who has been seeing Karla for a year and a half?" Lenore was astonished when the reviewer said no, he would make the decision based on what she told him. After 10 minutes, he authorized one week of day hospitalization but not full hospitalization.

Comment

The outcome in this case was minimally adequate for the immediate situation. While I believe that short-term full hospitalization would have been more beneficial in the long run, Karla's eventual two weeks at the day hospital were adequate to get past the suicidal crisis. Unfortunately, Karla's parents had to pay fully for the last several days since the reviewer would not approve the full two weeks, despite what I deemed to be the clear "medical necessity" (suicide and drug abuse prevention).

The thought that a telephone interviewer who has never met the patient would make a treatment decision of this magnitude on the basis of a 10-minute structured interview with the patient's mother without consulting with the therapist is incredible. Fortunately, I had a good working relationship with Karla and her parents. Imagine the effect that the reviewer's discounting of my role could have had on our alliance. It exemplifies the lack of appreciation for the patient–therapist relationship and the unique information that could be provided because of that relationship. Rather it was an industrial decision (standard operating procedure–based) without attention to the unique elements of the situation or individuality of the patient or competence of the therapist (a crucial element in sustaining an at-risk patient outside of the hospital). This time it worked out but this is the type of approach that can lead to the tragic consequences identified in Westermeyer's (1991) article.

Just a Little Bit More Should Do It

I had seen Frank (married, 47 years old) for about one year. Several years later, he called to return to therapy for some focused work concerning his marriage. As he requested, I called his insurance carrier to obtain precertification. The carrier authorized two sessions for assessment. I thought that we could do some meaningful work on his issues in ten sessions. Therefore, I requested ten sessions. The reviewer said that what I recommended made sense but that I should try to do it in four sessions. He only authorized four more after the two assessment

sessions and suggested that I submit more documentation
in the future for a possible four more sessions.

Comment

As discussed throughout this book, the holding environment in
brief therapy is a key element of the context of therapy and its limits are some of the major constraints that challenge the brief therapist and patient. Consider how ten sessions of therapy is experienced when it is clear that the patient and therapist will have the
ten within which to work. Alternatively, consider how the ten sessions would be experienced when it is unclear if ten sessions would
be available and the sessions are doled out in groups of four, four,
and two sessions to total the ten. It makes the holding environment
of therapy shaky and decreases the ability of the patient to feel safe
enough to face his issues or to feel the space is available to explore
them. Even from a strictly cost-effectiveness standpoint, I question
whether it really saves money to go through the expense of a utilization review for four sessions.

Frank decided that he did not want the uncertainty of having
his therapy ended prematurely (as he put it, "yanked out from under
me"). Therefore, even if his carrier did not approve the full ten
sessions, he was committed to it and would pay for the sessions on
his own. In this way he secured the stable holding environment
necessary for his treatment. In both this and the preceding example,
the patients were able to receive adequate care but, to do so, they
(or in Karla's case, her family) had to be willing to pay for more
treatment than the managed care reviewer was willing to approve.
But, what about those patients who cannot afford to do that?

Anyone Will Do

A therapist at an HMO met with a new patient and they
set up a brief therapy contract of twelve weekly sessions.
Therapists at this HMO did not manage their own sched-
ules, and appointments were centralized in the mental
health services department. When the patient went to the
scheduling secretary, she asked to set an appointment with

her therapist for the next week. She was told that the therapist did not have an opening during the next week but she
could schedule the patient for an appointment with
another therapist. The HMO's policy was to schedule
patients with a different therapist if there was a scheduling problem with the current therapist. Somewhat confused, the patient hesitated, then asked when "her" therapist would be available. She got an appointment with him
two weeks later.

Comment

There is a profoundly disturbing philosophy underlying this simple
scheduling interaction: that therapy is a procedure that can be
offered by interchangeable providers. This is an instance of
the industrialization or depersonalization of psychotherapy. I
would argue that even in physical medicine, consistent contact with
the same physician provides a context for greater comfort, safety,
and higher quality care than contact with multiple physicians. However, the issues of comfort, safety, and trust are even more crucial
in a psychotherapy encounter. Perhaps not much is lost by different providers giving a patient her allergy shots (but even there, she
should have the same allergist monitoring the treatment plan).
There is an enormous loss if sequential therapists try to give the
patient her marital problem or self-esteem "treatments." *Therapy
is not possible.*

Thus, on grounds of fundamental principle, I am opposed to
this denial of the importance of the individual relationship in psychotherapy. Denial of the relationship is denial of the treatment
known as psychotherapy. Dynamically, this scheduling policy is a
schizoid policy. Moreover, there are practical problems in this
example. What if the patient had had some ambivalence about continuing to see the therapist? For example, she could have felt
ambivalent about treatment, in general, or she may not have felt
comfortable talking to a man about her issues, or he may have
brought up transference reactions that she had had with her father
or boyfriend. Such issues should be examined, in session. The
offer of an appointment with another therapist will most often func-

tion in the service of resistance and avoidance and make it less likely that she would deal with these issues in therapy. Perhaps, it would even make it less likely that she would continue—of course, in that eventuality, the HMO would save money (in the short run).

Least Is Best

At a seminar, the director of a national EAP described his program to me. After a telephone assessment, employees (or their families) of client companies are referred to a local therapist from the EAP's list of providers for very brief therapy (maximum six sessions). The EAP has developed a Provider Profile System that tracks the therapy offered by their therapists. The director told me that therapists who are "preferred" and who subsequently receive the most referrals are the ones with the lowest average sessions per client and who make the fewest referrals for long-term treatment.

Comment

I have two serious concerns. First, it may be that this EAP is making the most referrals to, and is "preferring," its worst therapists. Remember with a maximum of six sessions, the EAP is comparing therapists with average contracts of, say, 2.5 sessions with therapists who have a 4.5 average. I would not be surprised if many therapists with low averages are having difficulty sufficiently connecting with their patients to have them return to treatment. It takes no great skill to get a patient to *not* return for psychotherapy (Budman and Gurman 1988). Moreover, if the therapists know about these profiles and how they are evaluated, this has the potential of compromising their clinical judgment on what the patient needs so that the therapist will offer less to become more "preferred."

Similarly, the question of whether further treatment is indicated beyond the very brief therapy contract should be an open one. However, if therapists realize that they may get fewer referrals because they are recommending long-term treatment when it seems indicated, then this creates a conflict between the therapist's integrity and economic self-interest. One of the selling points of an EAP contract to a business is that its presence will reduce the company's health insurance costs. Therefore, the EAP would likely hope that its providers would not make recommendations that would cause usage of the company's health benefits.

I recognize that, on the other hand, there can be a conflict between the therapist's integrity and self-interest, since the therapist would derive more income by recommending that the patient stay in treatment with her for long-term therapy. I do not know if that was possible with this EAP; however, the conflict of interest problem is solved in this situation by not permitting the EAP provider to see the patient in extended treatment, but, rather, requiring the provider to refer the patient to another therapist.

Is That All There Is?

A highly ethical and competent therapist in private practice was also a member of a group that provided services for a managed care insurance plan. The plan referred a patient to him whom he saw for a brief contract of twelve sessions. The patient's acute depressive symptoms significantly diminished during the therapy but the therapist was aware of the patient's narcissistic personality structure and how it contributed to his distress and interpersonal problems. He assessed that the therapy had been helpful but had been exclusively supportive and that the personality issues would cause these problems to recur.

The therapist chose not to comment on the patient's personality structure and interpersonal style, partly because it would broaden the focus beyond what they could accomplish within the time limits. However, the therapist also did not identify the issue and suggest further treatment because he was concerned that to do so would possibly jeopardize his group's contract with the insurance carrier. In their negotiations, it had become clear to him that the carrier not only wanted the therapy to be as brief as possible. The carrier also wanted the patients to have the impression that the mental health coverage

provided to them was all that they would need. To make
a referral for additional treatment that was not covered
might cause the patient to be less satisfied with the carrier. So, the patient ended therapy feeling grateful for the
reduction of his symptoms but the issues of personality
style and what additional treatment could offer him were
not discussed.

Comment

The issues raised here include a discussion of some of the ways such
arrangements with insurance carriers challenge the therapist's
integrity and can lead to a diminished public perception of what
therapy can do. In this case, the therapist felt inhibited from even
saying something like, "I'm pleased that you are feeling better than
when I first saw you. As we've discussed, there are some additional
issues related to your approach to yourself and others that could
be helpful to address in further therapy. Your insurance coverage
is for short-term therapy for acute problems so it will not cover that
type of additional therapy. If you like, though, I can give you some
referral possibilities."

Karon (1992) has written about the multiple ways that the needs
and benefits of additional therapy (even additional brief therapy)
are concealed. For instance in some HMO settings, "Medication is
often relied upon to obviate the need to provide more than six
sessions; psychologists as well as psychiatrists act as if meaningful
psychotherapy were not an alternative, ignoring the real cost-
effectiveness data, as well as the even stronger argument of quality
of life" (Karon 1992, p. 61).

In describing the effect of increased managed care on private
practice in Michigan, Karon (1992) reports that there was an initial decrease in private practice referrals but that referrals returned
to normal levels within a year "as patients learned that six sessions
for everything is not psychotherapy, that therapists who are willing to pretend that six sessions for everything is reasonable do not
even do those sessions well, and that if they want help, they must
escape managed care" (p. 61).

THE THERAPEUTIC RELATIONSHIP IN
THE AGE OF INDUSTRIALIZATION

Therapists do not have to "escape" managed care. Rather, we have to deal with it in a way that preserves our integrity and the healing and developmental power of psychotherapy. Therapists should not ignore issues of cost-containment or financial self-interest. I did not ignore these issues when I administered clinics and I do not ignore these issues in the business of my own private practice. So, I do not expect to ignore them in working with managed care plans. While it is legitimate and necessary to consider these issues, the patient's well-being must be the *prime*—although not exclusive—consideration when determining the appropriate treatment.

For our part, therapists need to accept the realities of the costs of psychotherapy and the understandable, limited willingness of third-party payers to subsidize those costs. We also need to continue to speak out about the crucial importance of the therapeutic relationship and its key elements of stable holding and containment. We need repeatedly and clearly to articulate what therapy can do, including additional therapy. We must not let it become a weakened, pale shadow of what psychotherapy can be.

On the managed care side, there is a need to realize that the rules of industrialization and the concept that "one size fits all" do not work with psychotherapy. As Stern (1993) states, "There is no disputing the efficacy and widespread utility of brief therapy (Butcher and Koss 1978); however, when it is mandated for an entire clinical population, significant problems arise that have not been adequately addressed by managed-care psychologists" (p. 163). Additionally, managed care needs to become more interested in the quality, not just the cost, of treatment. Moreover, quality needs to be defined not simply as the reduction of acute symptoms. Interestingly, the research on the effects of psychotherapy on stress and on utilization of other medical services indicates that attention to what I am suggesting will actually decrease costs in the long run (Karon 1992, Stern 1993).

14

A Brief Epilogue

In my writing of this book and your reading of (at least part of) it, we have had a human, if somewhat schizoid, encounter. I hope it has been meaningful to you. In your reading of my writing you have done *something* with it and we have created an intersubjective space. I have imagined you at different times and in different ways as I have struggled to first say what I intend and then to convey it to you. I imagine that you, too, have sometimes had an internal representation of me as you have read my words. So, where does this experience leave me? Where does it leave you? Us?

The writing of this book has reinforced my own conviction of the crucial importance and the profound power of the therapeutic relationship in brief therapy. In the first and last analysis, psychotherapy is a human relationship whether it lasts for one or twenty-five or fifty or a thousand sessions. I believe the greatest potential danger to brief therapy in the current managed care models of treatment is damage to the relationship. There are already plenty of cultural factors that inhibit relationships in our society.

I have found the issue of interpretation in brief therapy to be especially intriguing. It is no surprise that it is a controversial area. For some brief therapy patients, the power of interpretation to promote lasting change cannot be exaggerated—especially transference-based and self-oriented interpretations. As with any powerful intervention, interpretation also has great potential to impair the therapy as well (as we saw in Chapter 7). This is a domain where the high skill and comprehensive training of the therapist is especially crucial. We need to further study the issue of interpretation in brief therapy.

I have become increasingly impressed (and distressed) by how difficult it is for many therapists to thoughtfully consider the effectiveness and appropriateness of brief therapy *and* long-term therapy. The issues have become so politicized as to frequently lead to predominantly paranoid-schizoid thinking rather than to depressive mode reflection. Some of the champions of brief therapy argue that brief therapy is all that anyone needs and long-term work is a waste of time. Some proponents of long-term therapy arrogantly dismiss brief therapy as superficial and trivial. Both of these positions are delusional. I have tried to convey how the richness of a perspective that comes from long-term psychotherapy can inform the brief therapist and can be applied to enhance a short-term approach. Similarly, I hope that therapists can take some of what I have discussed in these chapters to, at times, focus their long-term work and accelerate it.

Finally, I have become more acutely aware of the therapist's influence (positive and negative) on the nature and development of the working alliance in brief therapy. The therapist's contribution to this is rarely considered (Binder et al. 1987) and I have tried to convey my own struggles and impact on the alliance in some of the case material. I agree with Guntrip's (1969) statement, "Only when the therapist finds the person behind the patient's defenses, and perhaps the patient finds the person behind the therapist's defenses, does true psychotherapy happen" (p. 352). There are differing degrees to this but I see it as being just as relevant for brief therapy as it is for long-term work.

This does not mean, of course, that the therapist is invariably nice or supportive or can just "do her own thing." But it does mean that the therapist should not delude herself into thinking that she is a neutral, impersonal dispenser of wise and skillful techniques. If the therapist interacts with the patient in an impersonal way, that has a particular impact and is a specific type of object relationship. In 1977 I attended a seminar at the Washington School of Psychiatry conducted by the late J. D. Sutherland of the Tavistock Clinic in London on object relations therapy. He remarked that an object relations therapist tries to steer a course between "mushy sentimentality" and "technological routinization." What more can I say?

At a given point in time, when a particular therapist and an individual patient can rather quickly form a strong working alliance, it can be truly remarkable what they can create and accomplish—in brief therapy.

References

Alexander, F. (1956). Two forms of regression and their therapeutic implications. *Psychoanalytic Quarterly* 25:178–198.

Alexander, F., and French, T. M. (1946). *Psychoanalytic Therapy*. New York: Ronald.

American Psychiatric Association (1994). *Diagnostic and Statistical Manual of Mental Disorders*, 4th ed. Washington, DC: American Psychiatric Association.

Anderson, W. T. (1990). *Reality Isn't What It Used to Be*. San Francisco: Harper and Row.

Baekeland, F., and Lundwall, L. (1975). Dropping out of treatment: a critical review. *Psychological Bulletin* 82:738–783.

Balint, M. (1957). *The Doctor, the Patient and His Illness*. New York: International Universities Press.

———(1968). *The Basic Fault*. London: Tavistock.

Balint, M., and Norell, J. S., eds. (1973). *Six Minutes for the Patient: Interactions in General Practice Consultation*. London: Tavistock.

Balint, M., Ornstein, P. H., and Balint, E. (1972). *Focal Psychotherapy*. London: Tavistock.

Barber, J. P., and Crits-Christoph, P. (1991). Comparison of the brief dynamic therapies. In *Handbook of Short-Term Dynamic Psychotherapy*, pp. 323–355. New York: Basic Books.

Bennett, M. J. (1989). The catalytic function in psychotherapy. *Psychiatry* 52: 351–364.

Berman, W. H. (1992). The practice of psychotherapy in managed health care. *Psychotherapy in Private Practice* 11(2):39–45.

Bick, E. (1986). Further considerations on the function of the skin in early object relations. *British Journal of Psychotherapy* 2:292–299.

Binder, J. L. (1977). Modes of focusing in psychoanalytic short-term therapy. *Psychotherapy: Theory, Research, and Practice* 14(3): 232–241.

——(1979). Treatment of narcissistic problems in time-limited psychotherapy. *Psychiatric Quarterly* 51:257–280.

Binder, J. L., Henry, W. P., and Strupp, H. H. (1987). An appraisal of selection criteria for dynamic psychotherapies and implications for setting time limits. *Psychiatry* 50:154–166.

Binder, J. L., and Strupp, H. H. (1991). The Vanderbilt approach to time-limited dynamic psychotherapy. In *Handbook of Short-Term Dynamic Psychotherapy*, ed. P. Crits-Christoph and J. P. Barber, pp. 137–165. New York: Basic Books.

Bion, W. R. (1961). *Experiences in Groups*. New York: Basic Books.

——(1967). *Second Thoughts*. London: Heinemann.

Bloom, B. L. (1981). Focused single-session therapy: initial development and evaluation. In *Forms of Brief Therapy*, ed. S. Budman, pp. 167–216. New York: Guilford.

——(1992). *Planned Short-Term Psychotherapy: A Clinical Handbook*. Needham Hts., MA.: Allyn & Bacon.

Bollas, C. (1987). *The Shadow of the Object*. New York: Columbia University Press.

——(1989). *Forces of Destiny: Psychoanalysis and Human Idiom*. London: Free Association Books.

Bowlby, J. (1969). *Attachment and Loss. Volume 1: Attachment*. New York: Basic Books.

Breuer, J., and Freud, S. (1895). Studies on hysteria. *Standard Edition* 2:125–134.

Budman, S. H. (1990). The myth of termination in brief therapy: or it ain't over till it's over. In *Brief Therapy: Myths, Methods, and Metaphors*, ed. J. K. Zeig and S. G. Gilligan, pp. 206–218. New York: Brunner/Mazel.

Budman, S. H., and Gurman, A. S. (1988). *Theory and Practice of Brief Therapy*. New York: Guilford.

——(1992). A time-sensitive model of brief therapy: the I-D-E approach. In *The First Session in Brief Therapy*, ed. S. H. Budman, M. F. Hoyt, and S. Friedman, pp. 111–134. New York: Guilford.

Budman, S. H., and Stone, J. (1983). Advances in brief psychotherapy: a review of recent literature. *Hospital and Community Psychiatry* 34:939–946.

Burke, J. D., White, H. S., and Havens, L. L. (1979). Which short-term therapy? *Archives of General Psychiatry* 36:177–186.

Burns, D. (1980). *Feeling Good*. New York: Morrow.

Butcher, J. N., and Koss, M. P. (1978). Research on brief and crisis-oriented therapies. In *Handbook of Psychotherapy and Behavior Change*, ed. S. Garfield and A. E. Bergin, 2nd ed., pp. 725–768. New York: Wiley.

Butler, S. F., Strupp, H. H., and Binder, J. L. (1992). Time-limited dynamic psychotherapy. In *The First Session in Brief Therapy*, ed. S. H. Budman, M. F. Hoyt, and S. Friedman, pp. 87–110. New York: Guilford.

Crits-Christoph, P. (1992). The efficacy of brief dynamic psychotherapy: a meta-analysis. *American Journal of Psychiatry* 149(2):151–158.

Crits-Christoph, P., & Barber, J. P., eds. (1991). *Handbook of Short-Term Dynamic Psychotherapy*. New York: Basic Books.

Cummings, N. A. (1990). Brief intermittent psychotherapy throughout the life cycle. In *Brief Therapy: Myths, Methods, and Metaphors*, ed. J. K. Zeig and S. G. Gilligan, pp. 169–184. New York: Brunner/Mazel.

Cummings, N. A., and VandenBos, G. R. (1979). The general practice of psychology. *Professional Psychology* 10:430–440.

——(1981). The twenty year Kaiser Permanente experience with psychotherapy and medical utilization: implications for national health policy and national health insurance. *Health Policy Quarterly* 1(2):159–179.

Davanloo, H., ed. (1978). *Basic Principles and Techniques in Short-term Dynamic Psychotherapy.* New York: Spectrum.

——(1980). *Short-term Dynamic Psychotherapy.* New York: Jason Aronson.

——(1991). *Unlocking the Unconscious.* New York: Wiley.

Eisenstein, S. (1980). The contributions of Franz Alexander. In *Short-term Dynamic Psychotherapy,* ed. H. Davanloo, pp. 25–41. New York: Jason Aronson.

Engelman, T. C., Day, M., and Durant, S. (1992). The nature of time and psychotherapeutic experience: when treatment duration shifts from time-limited to long-term. In *Psychotherapy for the 1990s,* ed. J. S. Rutan, pp. 119–137. New York: Guilford.

Fairbairn, W. R. D. (1940). Schizoid factors in the personality. In *An Object Relations Theory of the Personality,* pp. 3–27. New York: Basic Books, 1952.

——(1952). *An Object Relations Theory of the Personality.* New York: Basic Books.

——(1958). On the nature and aims of psycho-analytic treatment. *International Journal of Psycho-Analysis* 39:374–385.

——(1963). Synopsis of an object-relations theory of the personality. *International Journal of Psycho-Analysis* 44:224–225.

Ferenczi, S. (1926). The further development of an active therapy in psychoanalysis. In *Further Contributions to the Theory and Technique of Psycho-analysis,* ed. E. Jones, pp. 198–217. London: Hogarth, 1950.

Flegenheimer, W. V. (1982). *Techniques of Brief Psychotherapy.* New York: Jason Aronson.

Follette, W., and Cummings, N. A. (1967). Psychiatric services and medical utilization in a prepaid health plan setting. *Medical Care* 5:25–35.

Frances, A., and Clarkin, J. F. (1981). No treatment as the prescription of choice. *Archives of General Psychiatry* 38:542–545.

Freud, S. (1917). Mourning and melancholia. *Standard Edition* 14: 243–258.

——(1918). From the history of an infantile neurosis. *Standard Edition* 17:7–122.

——(1920). Beyond the pleasure principle. *Standard Edition* 18: 7–64.

——(1923). The ego and id. *Standard Edition* 19:12–66.

——(1937). Analysis terminable and interminable. *Standard Edition* 23:209–253.

Fromm-Reichmann, F. (1950). *Principles of Intensive Psychotherapy.* Chicago: University of Chicago Press.

Gabbard, G. O. (1995). How much therapy is enough? *Menninger Letter* 3(2):7.

Garfield, S. L. (1978). Research on client variables in psychotherapy. In *Handbook of Psychotherapy and Behavior Change*, ed. A. E. Bergin and S. Garfield, 2nd ed., pp. 191–232. New York: Wiley.

Goldsmith, S. (1986). *Psychotherapy of People with Physical Symptoms: Brief Strategic Approaches.* Lanham, MD: University Press of America.

Good, M. I. (1992). Factors affecting patient dropout rates. *American Journal of Psychiatry* 149:275–276.

Goulding, M., and Goulding, R. (1979). *Changing Lives through Redecision Therapy.* New York: Grove.

Greenberg, J. R., and Mitchell, S. A. (1983). *Object Relations in Psychoanalytic Theory.* Cambridge, MA: Harvard University Press.

Grotstein, J. (1981). *Splitting and Projective Identification.* New York: Jason Aronson.

Groves, J. E. (1992). The short-term dynamic psychotherapies: an overview. In *Psychotherapy for the 1990s*, ed. J. S. Rutan, pp. 35–59. New York: Guilford.

Gunderson, J. G. (1989). Borderline personality disorder. In *Comprehensive Textbook of Psychiatry/V*, ed. H. I. Kaplan and B. J. Sadock, pp. 1387–1395. Baltimore: Williams & Wilkins.

Guntrip, H. (1961). *Personality Structure and Human Interaction: The Developing Synthesis of Psychodynamic Theory.* New York: International Universities Press.

——(1969). *Schizoid Phenomena, Object Relations and the Self.* New York: International Universities Press.

Gustafson, J. P. (1981). The complex secret of brief psychotherapy in the works of Malan and Balint. In *Forms of Brief Therapy*, ed. S. H. Budman, pp. 83–128. New York: Guilford.

——(1986). *The Complex Secret of Brief Psychotherapy.* New York: Norton.

Haas, L. J., and Cummings, N. A. (1991). Managed outpatient mental health plans: clinical, ethical, and practical guidelines for participation. *Professional Psychology: Research and Practice* 22:45–51.

Hartlaub, G. H., Martin, G. L., and Rhine, M. W. (1986). Recontact with the analyst following termination: a survey of seventy-one cases. *Journal of the American Psychoanalytic Association* 34:895–910.

Hildebrand, H. P. (1986). Brief psychotherapy. *Psychoanalytic Psychology* 3:1–12.

Hoglend, P. (1993a). Personality disorders and long-term outcome after brief dynamic psychotherapy. *Journal of Personality Disorders* 7(2):168–181.

——(1993b). Transference interpretations and long-term change after dynamic psychotherapy of brief to moderate length. *American Journal of Psychotherapy* 47(4):494–507.

Horowitz, M. J. (1986). *Stress Response Syndromes*, 2nd ed. Northvale, NJ: Jason Aronson.

——(1988). *Introduction to Psychodynamics: A New Synthesis.* New York: Basic Books.

——(1991). Short-term dynamic therapy of stress response syndromes. In *Handbook of Short-Term Dynamic Psychotherapy*, ed. P. Crits-Christoph and J. P. Barber, pp. 166–198. New York: Basic Books.

Horowitz, M. J., Marmar, C., Krupnick, J., et al. (1984). *Personality Styles and Brief Psychotherapy.* New York: Basic Books.

Howard, K. I., Kopta, S. M., Krause M. S., and Orlinsky, D. (1986). The dose-effect relationship in psychotherapy. *American Psychologist* 41:159–164.

Hoyt, M. F. (1990). On time in brief therapy. In *Handbook of the Brief Psychotherapies*, ed. R. A. Wells and V. J. Giannetti, pp. 115–143. New York: Plenum.

Hoyt, M. F., Rosenbaum, R., and Talmon, M. (1992). Planned single session therapy. In *The First Session in Brief Therapy*, ed. S. H. Budman, M. F. Hoyt, and S. Friedman, pp. 59–86. New York: Guilford.

Jones, E. (1955). *The Life and Work of Sigmund Freud.* New York: Basic Books.

Joyce, A. S., and Piper, W. E. (1993). The immediate impact of transference interpretation in short-term individual psychotherapy. *American Journal of Psychotherapy* 47(4):508–525.

Karon, B. P. (1992). Problems of psychotherapy under managed health care. *Psychotherapy in Private Practice* 11(2):55–63.

Kernberg, O. (1975). *Borderline Conditions and Pathological Narcissism*. New York: Jason Aronson.

Kernberg, O., Selzer, M., Koenigsberg, H., et al. (1989). *Psychodynamic Psychotherapy of Borderline Patients*. New York: Basic Books.

Klein, M. (1948). On the theory of anxiety and guilt. In *Envy and Gratitude and Other Works, 1946–1963*, pp. 25–42. New York: Delacorte, 1975.

——(1958). On the development of mental functioning. In *Envy and Gratitude and Other Works, 1946–1963*, pp. 236–246. New York: Delacorte, 1975.

——(1964). *Contributions to Psychoanalysis, 1921–1945*. New York: McGraw-Hill.

——(1975). *Envy and Gratitude and Other Works, 1946–1963*. New York: Delacorte.

Kohut, H. (1968). The psychoanalytic treatment of narcissistic personality disorders: outline of a systematic approach. *Psychoanalytic Study of the Child* 23:86–113. New York: International Universities Press.

——(1971). *The Analysis of the Self*. New York: International Universities Press.

——(1977). *The Restoration of the Self*. New York: International Universities Press.

Kopta, S. M., Howard, K. I., Lowry, J. L., and Beutler, L. E. (1994). Patterns of symptomatic recovery in psychotherapy. *Journal of Consulting and Clinical Psychology* 62:1009–1016.

Koss , M. P., and Butcher, J. N. (1986). Research on brief therapy. In *Handbook of Psychotherapy and Behavior Change: An Empirical Analysis*, ed. A. E. Bergin and S. Garfield, 3rd ed., pp. 627–670. New York: Wiley.

Kupers, T. A. (1986). The dual potential of brief psychotherapy. *Free Associations* 6:80–99.

——(1988). *Ending Therapy: The Meaning of Termination*. New York: New York University Press.

Laikin, M., Winston, A., and McCullough, L. (1991). Intensive short-term dynamic psychotherapy. In *Handbook of Short-Term Dynamic Psychotherapy*, ed. P. Crits-Christoph and J. P. Barber, pp. 80–109. New York: Basic Books.

Langs, R. (1973). *The Technique of Psychoanalytic Psychotherapy*, vol. 1. New York: Jason Aronson.

Leibovich, M. (1981). Short-term psychotherapy for the borderline personality disorder. *Psychotherapy and Psychosomatics* 35:257–264.

Luborsky, L. (1984). *Principles of Psychoanalytic Psychotherapy: A Manual for Supportive-Expressive Treatment*. New York: Basic Books.

Luborsky, L., Barber, J. P., and Crits-Christoph, P. (1990). Theory-based research for understanding the process of psychotherapy. *Journal of Consulting and Clinical Psychology* 58:281–287.

Luborsky, L., and Crits-Christoph, P. (1990). *Understanding Transference: The CCRT Method*. New York: Basic Books.

Luborsky, L., and Mark, D. (1991). Short-term supportive-expressive psychoanalytic psychotherapy. In *Handbook of Short-Term Dynamic Psychotherapy*, ed. P. Crits-Christoph and J. P. Barber, pp. 110–136. New York: Basic Books.

Malan, D. H. (1963). *A Study of Brief Psychotherapy*. London: Tavistock.

——(1976). *The Frontier of Brief Psychotherapy*. New York: Plenum.

——(1979). *Individual Psychotherapy and the Science of Psychodynamics*. London: Butterworth.

——(1980). The most important development since the discovery of the unconscious. In *Short-term Dynamic Psychotherapy*, ed. H. Davanloo, pp. 17–23. New York: Jason Aronson.

Malan, D., Heath, E., Bacal, H., and Balfour, F. (1975). Psychodynamic changes in untreated neurotic patients. II: Apparently genuine improvements. *Archives of General Psychiatry* 32:110–126.

Mann, J. (1973). *Time-Limited Psychotherapy*. Cambridge, MA: Harvard University Press.

——(1981). The core of time-limited psychotherapy: time and the central issue. In *Forms of Brief Therapy*, ed. S. Budman, pp. 25–43. New York: Guilford.

——(1991). Time-limited psychotherapy. In *Handbook of Short-Term Dynamic Psychotherapy*, ed. P. Crits-Christoph and J. P. Barber, pp. 17–43. New York: Basic Books.

Mann, J., and Goldman, R. (1994). *A Casebook in Time-Limited Psychotherapy*. Northvale, NJ: Jason Aronson. Originally published, New York: McGraw-Hill, 1982.

Marziali, E. A. (1984). Prediction of outcome of brief psychotherapy from therapist interpretive interventions. *Archives of General Psychiatry* 41:301–304.

Marziali, E. A., and Sullivan, J. M. (1980). Methodological issues in the content analysis of brief psychotherapy. *British Journal of Medical Psychology* 53:19–27.

Masterson, J. F. (1978). *New Perspectives on Psychotherapy of the Borderline Adult.* New York: Brunner/Mazel.

Meltzer, D. (1975). Adhesive identification. *Contemporary Psychoanalysis* 11:289–310.

Merikangas, K. R., and Weissman, N. M. (1986). Epidemiology of *DSM-III* Axis II personality disorders. In *Psychiatry Update: American Psychiatric Association Annual Review,* vol. 4, ed. A. J. Frances and R. E. Hales, pp. 258–278. Washington, DC: American Psychiatric Association.

Mitchell, S. A. (1988). *Relational Concepts in Psychoanalysis: An Integration.* Cambridge, MA: Harvard University Press.

——(1993). *Hope and Dread in Psychoanalysis.* New York: Basic Books.

Neilsen, G., and Barth, K. (1991). Short-term anxiety-provoking psychotherapy. In *Handbook of Short-Term Dynamic Psychotherapy,* ed. P. Crits-Christoph and J. P. Barber, pp. 45–79. New York: Basic Books.

Nuland, S. B. (1994). *How We Die.* New York: Knopf.

Ogden, T. H. (1982). *Projective Identification and Psychotherapeutic Technique.* New York: Jason Aronson.

——(1986). *The Matrix of the Mind.* Northvale, NJ: Jason Aronson.

——(1989). *The Primitive Edge of Experience.* Northvale, NJ: Jason Aronson.

——(1994). *Subjects of Analysis.* Northvale, NJ: Jason Aronson.

Oremland, J. D. (1976). A curious resolution of a hysterical symptom. *International Review of Psycho-Analysis* 3:473–477.

——(1991). *Interpretation and Interaction: Psychoanalysis or Psychotherapy?* Hillsdale, NJ: Analytic Press.

Pardes, H., and Pincus, H. A. (1981). Brief therapy in the context of national mental health. In *Forms of Brief Therapy,* ed. S. H. Budman. New York: Guilford.

Peck, M. S. (1978). *The Road Less Traveled.* New York: Simon and Schuster.

Perry, J. C., and Vaillant, G. E. (1989). Personality disorders. In *Comprehensive Textbook of Psychiatry/V*, ed. H. I. Kaplan and B. J. Sadock, pp. 1352–1387. Baltimore: Williams & Wilkins.

Phillips, E. L. (1985). *A Guide for Therapists and Patients to Short-term Psychotherapy*. Springfield, IL: Charles C Thomas.

Pine, F. (1990). *Drive, Ego, Object, & Self: A Synthesis for Clinical Work*. New York: Basic Books.

Piper, W. E., Azim, H. F. A., Joyce, A. S., and McCallum, M. (1991a). Transference interpretations, therapeutic alliance, and outcome in short-term individual psychotherapy. *Archives of General Psychiatry* 48:946–953.

Piper, W. E., Azim, H. F. A., Joyce, A. S., et al. (1991b). Quality of object relations versus interpersonal functioning as predictors of therapeutic alliance and psychotherapy outcome. *Journal of Nervous and Mental Disease* 179(7):432–438.

Piper, W. E., Azim, H. F. A., McCallum, M., and Joyce, A. S. (1990). Patient suitability and outcome in short-term individual psychotherapy. *Journal of Consulting and Clinical Psychology* 58(4):475–481.

Piper, W. E., de Carufel F. L., and Szkrumelak, N. (1985). Patient predictors of process and outcome in short-term individual psychotherapy. *Journal of Nervous and Mental Disease* 173:726–733.

Piper, W. E., Joyce, A. S., McCallum, M., and Azim, H. F. A. (1993). Concentration and correspondence of transference interpretations in short-term psychotherapy. *Journal of Consulting and Clinical Psychology* 61(4):586–595.

Pollack, J., Flegenheimer, W., and Winston, A. (1991). Brief adaptive psychotherapy. In *Handbook of Short-Term Dynamic Psychotherapy*, ed. P. Crits-Christoph and J. P. Barber, pp. 199–219. New York: Basic Books.

Racker, H. (1968). *Transference and Countertransference*. New York: International Universities Press.

Rank, O. (1929). *Will Therapy*. New York: Knopf, 1936.

Reich, J. H., and Green, A. J. (1991). Effect of personality disorders on outcome of treatment. *Journal of Nervous and Mental Disease* 179:74–82.

Reich, W. (1945). *Character Analysis*, 3rd ed. New York: Simon and Schuster.

Rosenbaum, R., Hoyt, M. F., and Talmon, M. (1990). The challenge of single-session therapies: creating pivotal moments. In *Handbook of the Brief Psychotherapies*, ed. R. A. Wells and V. J. Giannetti, pp. 165–189. New York: Plenum.

Rubenstein, E. A., and Lorr, M. (1956). A comparison of terminators and remainers in outpatient psychotherapy. *Journal of Clinical Psychology* 12:345–349.

Schacht, T. E., Binder, J. L., and Strupp, H. H. (1984). The dynamic focus. In *Psychotherapy in a New Key: A Guide to Time-Limited Dynamic Psychotherapy*, ed. H. H. Strupp and J. L. Binder, pp. 65–109. New York: Basic Books.

Schacht, T. E., and Strupp, H. H. (1989). Recent methods of psychotherapy. In *Comprehensive Textbook of Psychiatry/V*, ed. H. I. Kaplan and B. J. Sadock, pp. 1556–1562. Baltimore: Williams & Wilkins.

Scharff, D. E. (1982). *The Sexual Relationship: An Object Relations View of Sex and the Family*. London: Routledge and Kegan Paul.

——(1992). *Refinding the Object and Reclaiming the Self*. Northvale, NJ: Jason Aronson.

Scharff, D. E., and Scharff, J. S. (1991). *Object Relations Couple Therapy*. Northvale, NJ: Jason Aronson.

Scharff, J. S, (1992). *Projective and Introjective Identification and the Use of the Therapist's Self*. Northvale, NJ: Jason Aronson.

——, ed. (1994). *The Autonomous Self: The Work of J. D. Sutherland*. Northvale, NJ: Jason Aronson.

Scharff, J. S., and Scharff, D. E. (1992). *Scharff Notes: A Primer of Object Relations Therapy*. Northvale, NJ: Jason Aronson.

Shectman, F. (1986). Time and the practice of psychotherapy. *Psychotherapy* 23:521–525.

Shore, K. (1995). Managed care as a totalitarian regime. *The Independent Practitioner* 15:73–77.

Sifneos, P. E. (1972). *Short-term Psychotherapy and Emotional Crisis*. Cambridge, MA: Harvard University Press.

——(1987). *Short-term Dynamic Psychotherapy: Evaluation and Technique*, 2nd ed. New York: Plenum.

——(1989). Brief dynamic and crisis therapy. In *Comprehensive Textbook of Psychiatry/V*, ed. H. I. Kaplan and B. J. Sadock, pp. 1562–1567. Baltimore: Williams & Wilkins.

Smith, M. L., Glass, G. V., and Miller, T. I. (1980). *The Benefits of Psychotherapy*. Baltimore: Johns Hopkins.

Stadter, M. (1993). Brief therapy with personality disorders. *Audio Library Presentations*. Silver Spring, MD: American Healthcare Institute.

Steenbarger, B. N. (1992). Toward science-practice integration in brief counseling and therapy. *The Counseling Psychologist* 20:403–450.

——(1994). Duration and outcome in psychotherapy: an integrative review. *Professional Psychology: Research and Practice* 25:111–119.

Stern, S. (1993). Managed care, brief therapy, and therapeutic integrity. *Psychotherapy* 30(1):162–175.

Stewart, H. (1993a). *Discussion comments on "Brief therapy from an object relations perspective" by M. Stadter*. Presented at the Washington School of Psychiatry Object Relations Theory Training Program Conference, April 17.

——(1993b). *The work of Michael Balint*. Presented at the Washington School of Psychiatry Object Relations Theory Training Program Conference, April 17.

Stolorow, R. D., and Atwood, G. E. (1992). *Contexts of Being: The Intersubjective Foundations of Psychological Life*. Hillsdale, NJ: Analytic Press.

Stone, M. H. (1990a). *The Fate of Borderline Patients*. New York: Guilford.

——(1990b). Treatment of borderline patients: a pragmatic approach. *Psychiatric Clinics of North America* 13(2):265–285.

Strupp, H. H. (1993). The Vanderbilt psychotherapy studies: synopsis. *Journal of Consulting and Clinical Psychology* 61:431–433.

Strupp, H. H., and Binder, J. L. (1984). *Psychotherapy in a New Key: A Guide to Time-Limited Dynamic Psychotherapy*. New York: Basic Books.

——(1992). Current developments in psychotherapy. *The Independent Practitioner* 12:119–124.

Sullivan, H. S. (1953). *The Interpersonal Theory of Psychiatry.* New York: Norton.

——(1954). *The Psychiatric Interview.* New York: Norton.

Talley, J. E. (1992). *The Predictors of Successful Very Brief Psychotherapy.* Springfield, IL: Charles C Thomas.

Talmon, M. (1990). *Single-session Therapy: Maximizing the Effect of the First (and Often Only) Therapeutic Encounter.* San Francisco: Jossey-Bass.

Tustin, F. (1986). *Autistic Barriers in Neurotic Patients.* New Haven: Yale University Press.

VandenBos, G. R., and DeLeon, P. (1988). The use of psychotherapy to improve physical health. *Psychotherapy* 25:335–343.

Westermeyer, J. (1991). Problems with managed psychiatric care without a psychiatrist-manager. *Hospital and Community Psychiatry* 42(12):1221–1224.

Winnicott, D. W. (1945). Primitive emotional development. In *Through Paediatrics to Psycho-Analysis*, pp. 145–156. New York: Basic Books, 1958.

——(1949). Mind and its relation to the psyche-soma. In *Through Paediatrics to Psycho-Analysis*, pp. 243–254. New York: Basic Books, 1958.

——(1951). Transitional objects and transitional phenomena. In *Through Paediatrics to Psycho-Analysis*, pp. 229–242. New York: Basic Books, 1958.

——(1958). *Through Paediatrics to Psycho-Analysis.* New York: Basic Books.

——(1960). Ego distortion in terms of true and false self. In *The Maturational Processes and the Facilitating Environment*, pp. 140–152. New York: International Universities Press, 1965.

——(1962). The aims of psycho-analytical treatment. In *The Maturational Processes and the Facilitating Environment*, pp. 166–170. New York: International Universities Press, 1965.

——(1963). The development of the capacity for concern. In *The Maturational Processes and the Facilitating Environment*, pp. 73–81. New York: International Universities Press, 1965.

——(1965). *The Maturational Processes and the Facilitating Environment.* New York: International Universities Press.

——(1971). *Therapeutic Consultations in Child Psychiatry.* New York: Basic Books.

——(1977). *The Piggle: An Account of the Psychoanalytic Treatment of a Little Girl.* Madison, CT: International Universities Press.

Winston, A., Laikin, M., Pollack, J., et al. (1994). Short-term psychotherapy of personality disorders. *American Journal of Psychiatry* 151(2):190–194.

Winston, A., Pollack, J., McCullough, L., et al. (1991). Brief psychotherapy of personality disorders. *Journal of Nervous and Mental Disease* 179(4): 188–193.

Wolberg, L. R. (1965). *Short-term Psychotherapy.* New York: Grune & Stratton.

Wolf, E. (1988). *Treating the Self.* New York: Guilford.

Index